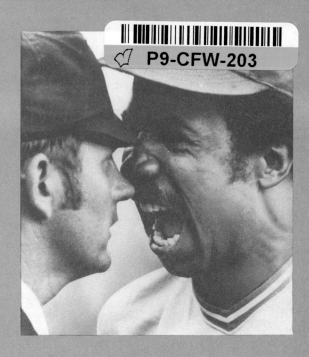

Field of Screams

Richard Scheinin

W.W. NORTON & COMPANY ◆ NEW YORK ◆ LONDON

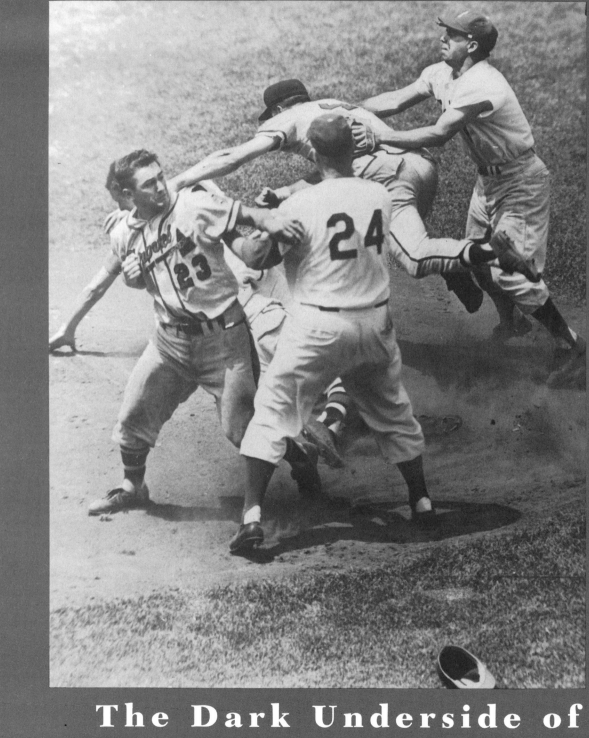

The Dark Underside of

Field of Screams

America's National Pastime

First Edition

The text of this book is composed in New Caledonia,
with the display set in New Caledonia Black and Morgan.
Composition and manufacturing by the Haddon Craftsmen, Inc.
Book design by Beth Tondreau Design.

LIBRARY OF CONGRESS CATALOGING-IN-PUBLICATION DATA
Scheinin, Richard.
Field of screams : the dark side of America's national pastime /
by Richard Scheinin.
p.   cm.
1. Baseball—United States—Corrupt practices. 2. Baseball—
United States—History. I. Title.
GV863.A1S32   1994
796.357′0973—dc20   93-32448

ISBN 0-393-31138-4 (pa)

W. W. Norton & Company, Inc., 500 Fifth Avenue, New York, N.Y. 10110
W. W. Norton & Company Ltd., 10 Coptic Street, London WC1A 1PU

1 2 3 4 5 6 7 8 9 0

For my father, Hyman Scheinin

Contents

1900 to 1910　　　　　　　　　　　　　　　　93

The Darkest Hours: 1910–20　　　　　　　131

The Roaring Twenties　　　　　　　　　　161

Acknowledgments

This book began with a conversation with two friends in the cafeteria at the newspaper office where I work. It was August 22, 1990, the twenty-fifth anniversary of Juan Marichal's beaning of Johnny Roseboro with a baseball bat, and we joked crassly, "Wouldn't it be a riot to write a book about the hundred most gruesome incidents in the history of baseball?" I started to poke around, looking for odd facts about violence and deviant behavior in the national pastime. I phoned the baseball historian Lloyd Johnson in St. Louis and he left this message on my answering machine: "Of *course*, there is a rich vein of violence in baseball. It's sitting there, waiting to be tapped, and I'd be happy to help you find it." I was surprised by this encouraging reply and started thinking that this subject might be worthy of more than a trivia book. I subsequently spent many hours on the phone with Lloyd who painstakingly set the game in its historical context. After interviewing scores of historians, journalists, and players, I became convinced of what now seems rather obvious: that the All-American game reflects all the worst aspects of our society, as well as the best.

Lloyd was the first of three people who were indispensable to the preparation of this book. The second was Gabe Schechter, whom I stumbled upon, over the telephone, at the National Baseball Library in Cooperstown where he was doing research into his own projects. From the beginning, I was amazed by Gabe's knowledge, enthusiasm, and constant willingness to scour hundreds of files for information about this odd subject. How many totally competent people do you meet in life? Gabe is one of the few. So is my wife, Sara, the third indispensable one. Sara, at the outset, forced me to develop my thesis for this book. When it was time to write, she talked me through the subject matter, decade by decade, and edited all my words, forcing the book into coherent shape. This was a time-consuming business; our children spent many months wondering when their father's immersion in this strange topic might finally end.

There are others whom I want to thank: John Hubner and John Krim, my two friends at work who first got me thinking about violence in baseball; Amy Linn, who thought of the book's title; David Peterkin, who pushed me to begin my research and introduced me to Kris Dahl, my agent. Kris shepherded this book through all its phases; her attentiveness and friendship are a comfort. My editor at W. W. Norton, Gerry Howard, painstakingly supervised the book's assemblage. His assistant, Madeline McIntosh, attended to about a million details as production schedules ran down to the wire. The list doesn't end there: Patricia Kelly and Milo Stewart of the National Baseball Library were always patient and flexible in dealing with my photo demands; researcher John Beckham unearthed all sorts of nuggets about violence in the nineteenth century; and author Mike Sowell not only taught me about the early-twentieth-century game, but offered kind advice about the pitfalls of publishing.

These good friends offered no end of spiritual support as I verged on physical collapse under looming deadlines: Ben Rice, David Early, Syma Solovitch, Ellen Baker, Manfred Warmuth, Gary Scheinin, and Mike Oricchio. Probably the nicest part of writing this book was talking to my father about it; he loved the stories, offered all sorts of cogent advice about its writing, and stunned me with the information that he turned stiles at Yankee Stadium when it first opened in 1923. It was my father who took me to my first ball game, a double-header at the Stadium against the Tigers in 1963. As a lifelong baseball fan, I was thrilled, in writing this book, to have the chance to interview the likes of Bobby Bonds, Orlando Cepeda, Eddie Joost, and Andy Messersmith, all of whom were open, thoughtful, and kind.

R.S.
Santa Cruz, California
January 1994

11

Acknowledgments

Field of Screams

Introduction

Wake up the echoes at the Hall of Fame and you will find that
baseball's immortals were a rowdy and raucous group of men who
would climb down off their plaques and go rampaging through
Cooperstown, taking spoils, like the Third Army busting through
Germany.
   —*Bill Veeck*

Aren't you tired of it? It's been foisted on us for years now, decades
even. All this literary bilge about how baseball is some sort of
gentle art form, the game for poets. You know the titles: *The Boys of
Summer. The Glory of Their Times. Baseball and the American Dream.*
On and on it goes, the perpetration of the Big Baseball Myth: *The
Image of Their Greatness. Baseball the Beautiful.* And worst of all: *Take
Time for Paradise,* written by Bart Giamatti, the late commissioner of
Major League Baseball. I mean, come on. You want to learn something
real about baseball? Just talk to one of the hundreds of sportswriters
who have been crushed to learn that their heroes are, by and large, a
bunch of wealthy arrogant men whose interests are limited to golf,
clothes, and stereo equipment.

The Big Baseball Myth casts the game and its heroes in a golden
haze, as if that were some sort of ballet they've been performing out
there all these years. Well, it's time for a reality check. I appreciate a
well-executed squeeze play as much as the next guy, but everything
that happens between the foul lines is not pretty. It's time to put some
perspective on the myth: that's no ballet and that's no Field of
Dreams.

This book, *Field of Screams: The Dark Side of America's National
Pastime,* is going to take the shine off the myth. It's going to subvert
some of those cherished ideas you've held about the game all these
years.

Sorry.

The glory of their times?

It's 1894. Future Hall of Famer John McGraw waits at third base for a hell-bent base runner named Tommy Tucker who plays for the Boston Beaneaters. Tucker slides hard and McGraw, who's been feuding with Tucker (he feuds with everyone), kicks Tucker in the head as he lays on the tag. Tucker jumps to his feet and the two start punching it out. The crowd rises to egg the pair on, eating up the action. Midway through the fight, someone notices that the right-field stands are on fire. McGraw and Tucker keep fighting as the fire spreads through Boston's old South End Grounds and destroys the grandstand behind home plate.

Now it's 1965. Future Hall of Famer Juan Marichal slams his bat over the head of Johnny Roseboro in the closest thing to on-field attempted murder in the game's history. Close-up photographs of Roseboro, veteran catcher for the Los Angeles Dodgers, with the blood pouring down his face, were published in pretty much every newspaper and magazine in the country.

Baseball the beautiful?

It's 1987. Joe Cowley, a pitcher on the Philadelphia Phillies, suffers a streak of wildness. The beer-guzzling Phillies fans, among the meanest and unruliest in the game, heckle him every time he takes the mound—"Cow-LEE! Cow-LEE!"—and Cowley starts to lose his confidence. Pretty soon, he can't get anyone out. He starts to see a psychiatrist. He's sent to the minors, where he walks eleven batters in less than three innings in one game, and then he retires, the empty shell of a former major leaguer, mentally broken, hounded out of baseball by those fabulous Phillies fans.

I saw it happen. I was in the stands with my six-year-old son, who asked me, "Daddy, why are they being mean to the pitcher?"

Some field of dreams. Some paradise.

A gentle game?

"I have observed," Ty Cobb once said, "that baseball is not unlike a war."

Eighty years later, Andy Messersmith concurs: "It's a war! It's a war out there," says Messersmith, who pitched for the Los Angeles Dodgers and California Angels in the 1960s and '70s. "This guy wants to knock your head in, and you want to knock his head in. I mean, you wanna get this guy *out*. It's not like, 'Hope you make that putt, pal.'"

A poets' game?

I made the suggestion to Orlando Cepeda, ex-slugger for the San Francisco Giants and St. Louis Cardinals, who stared at me, stone-faced and incredulous. "Are you trying to say that baseball is some kind of sophisticated game?" he asked after a moment's silence. He floundered for the right words. "No, I don't think so," Cepeda said. He paused again, flustered, then shouted, "Baseball is . . . Go! It is Go!"

I think Cepeda was saying that baseball is a hard-bitten game of instinct. In a near-monotone, slumped on his living-room sofa, Cepeda recited a litany of pitchers who knocked him down in the batter's box, their attempt to put fear in the Baby Bull: "When I was in Triple A, Tommy LaSorda threw at my head, knocked me down, hit me in the back." In the majors there was Don Drysdale ("my first game, the second pitch"), Don Cardwell, Fergie Jenkins, Jim Bunning, Don Newcombe, Roger Craig, even his pals Juan Marichal and Bob Gibson. "Everybody knocked you down. I remember one time Jack Sanford hit Ernie Banks in the middle of the back. It sounded like a bomb. Ernie didn't say a word. He just walked to first base."

The knockdown pitch has been a part of baseball for a hundred years. Sometimes a knockdown pitch slips or is thrown intentionally at a player's head, in which case it is known as a beanball. In 1920, a surly character named Carl Mays, a pitcher for the New York Yankees, killed Cleveland Indians shortstop Ray Chapman with a beanball. This is the only on-field fatality in the 118-year history of the major leagues, although half a dozen minor leaguers have been fatally beaned and scores of professional players have been severely injured. These include Colorado Rockies coach Don Zimmer, who has steel plugs inside his head, reminders of one of the numerous beanings he received during his ill-starred career with the Dodgers.

The vocabulary that is used to describe the knockdown pitch is chilling. The man who throws the pitch is the "intimidator." If he throws it at someone on your team, then your pitcher will throw it right back at the opposition: this is called "protection" or "retaliation." A pitcher who is brought into the game specifically to knock down opposing batters is known as an "enforcer." In the 1940s and '50s, perhaps the heyday of knockdown pitching, almost every National League team had an "enforcer" on its pitching staff.

Mafia talk in the great American game.

There's an old adage that if you want to understand America, you must first understand baseball. But sports reflect our culture; they don't lead it. So I would turn the adage around: if you understand America, *then* you understand baseball.

This is a country with noble aspirations, but rooted in violence. There was a musket in every colonial household, and the nation was built on the backs of slaves. Two hundred years later, we proclaim democratic ideals for the world, but our streets are ruled by violence and the country remains racially torn. We can't escape our past.

Neither can baseball. The game was born in the big Northern cities of early nineteenth-century America, and was played predominantly by middle-class athletes who saw it as a rather civilized activity, not unlike cricket. But with time, as baseball grew in popularity, ball games came to provoke anxiety among local authorities. The very idea of a crowd of people attending a sporting event was something new. Going back to Roman times, a crowd was viewed as a threat to municipal government. Throughout the 1860s and into the '70s, thugs circulated through crowds at ball games—and the authorities were alarmed.

The thugs were big, beefy men, usually hired by gamblers to incite spectators against umpires, physically intimidate and bribe the players, and otherwise influence the outcome of the competition. This was one way in which the "swirling street life and boisterous amusements" of the teeming cities, as historian Warren Goldstein puts it, came to influence baseball. The New York Mutuals, a well-known club into the 1870s, was founded by Manhattan's Mutual Hook and Ladder Company No. 1. This was a volunteer fire company—a fact of symbolic interest in that rival companies had terrorized urban neighborhoods earlier in the century. These gangs—for that's what they were—set fires, fought with one another to put them out, extorted money from citizens, and provoked race riots and drunken brawls. The Mutuals, founded in 1857, never engaged in such activities. But one can imagine the macho cachet enjoyed by a ball team with ties to such a violent heritage. Other clubs went ahead and named themselves after volunteer fire companies and wore uniforms that were exact copies of uniforms worn by volunteer firemen. Can you imagine if the major league expansion clubs of the twenty-first century were to be named the "Crips" and "Bloods" and dress in gang colors?

No, the athletes of baseball's early decades were wannabes, only a little violent. But that's the point: ever since the organized game began, it has swung between exhibitions of macho violence and efforts at respectability. It's as if the volunteer firemen lay a symbolic curse on the national game. Baseball, like America, has never quite escaped its thug roots.

Let's look at the game at the turn of the century.

Ban Johnson, an ex-newsman who was appalled by the violence surrounding the National League game as epitomized by McGraw, founded the American League in 1901. He did this specifically to clean up baseball. He was convinced that the fans wanted to see a good, clean brand of ball and that women and families would attend games if the parks could be rid of the rowdies, gamblers, and assorted low-lifes who congregated there, on and off the field.

Well, Johnson had some success with his plan—and then who arrived to disrupt things for nearly a quarter of a century? None other than Ty Cobb, the ultimate baseball thug. One day, this man will be played by Robert De Niro in the movies. The Georgia Peach was *that* pathological, a twisted character out of a Flannery O'Connor novel.

On the field, Cobb was "a holy terror," as one contemporary put it. He liked nothing more than to lay down a drag bunt along the first base line and skin the back of the pitcher's leg with his spikes as they converged at the bag. Opponents hated him and paid him back aplenty—Cobb's legs and thighs were grotesquely scarred and covered with oozing sores inflicted by spikes. His own teammates hated him—Cobb knew this and slept with a loaded Luger in his train berth. He liked to relax by listening to classical recordings by the violinist Fritz Kreisler. Then Ty would hit the streets to beat up a black man or two, or gore a mugger with his gun. Here he describes the punishment he inflicted on a knife-wielding street assailant he chased into a dark dead-end alley in Detroit in 1912: "I used that gunsight to rip and slash and tear him for about ten minutes until he had no face left. Left him there, not breathing, in his own rotten blood."

Cobb suffered a five-inch gash in his back in the attack. The next day, he arrived on schedule at the Tigers clubhouse and taped up the wound. No stitches. Just tape. Then he went out onto the field and played. He doubled and tripled. By the end of the game, his uniform was soaked with blood.

Cobb was an extreme version of the many tough nuts who played the game at the turn of the century. There was a rougher sense of justice in this country then and that was reflected on the diamond—and Cobb embodied this connection between violence in baseball and violence in society.

Skip a generation and the connection is even clearer. In 1946, scores of players returned to the major leagues from military service in World War II. The hormones were flowing. That year, ballplayers were responsible for superhuman accomplishments on the field. In one doubleheader, Stan Musial had eight hits in nine at bats. Bob Feller struck out 348 batters in 1946, a new record. Bill Kennedy, a minor league pitcher in the Coastal Plain League, struck out 456 batters—more than anyone else in baseball history.

More to the point: the players, tightly wired from the war effort, were looking to kick butt. In the minor leagues, there were far more assaults on umpires than in any other year before or since.

The civil rights movement was budding. In 1947, Jackie Robinson integrated the majors. But 1949 was the first year of widespread integration in the game. Not counting pitchers, there were twelve black players in Triple A minor league ball that year, and four of them were carried off the field on stretchers that season, the victims of beanballs. In 1950 in the American League, the two hitters who led the league in being hit by pitched balls were Luke Easter and Al Rosen—a black and a Jew.

From the beginning, baseball has struggled to define its values: big league club owners in the late nineteenth century gave free passes to ball games to local clergymen. Hallelujah! The same owners gave free tickets to professional gamblers. This is called confusion.

Oh, Judge Kenesaw Mountain Landis tried to get rid of the

gamblers in the '20s. And Commissioner Peter Ueberroth tried to clean up the druggies in the '80s. And no one wants the players to fight in front of the television cameras anymore, because that's not the image the game is selling these days.

But you still get Jose Canseco jumping into the stands after fans who taunt him about his midnight visit to Madonna's apartment in New York. You still get Albert Belle firing a ball at the chest of a fan who heckles him about his alcoholism. And you still get Rob Dibble throwing a fastball at a schoolteacher in the stands for no reason other than that Dibble was in a pissed-off mood.

The party line these days is that baseball is less violent than in the old days. Bobby Bonds, star outfielder with the Giants, Yankees, Angels, and Cleveland Indians in the 1960s and '70s, calls today's game "country club baseball." It's one fat cat versus another, he says. Pitchers, with a few exceptions, don't throw at batters. Runners don't slide too hard. No one wants to endanger his own extended, multimillion-dollar contract—or that of another player. The rise of the players' union has made everyone a member of the same well-paid fraternity. Its credo is "You don't hurt me, I don't hurt you," says Ron Fairly, the former Dodgers and Expos first baseman. "I'll let you make your $3.4 million and I'll make my $3.4 million. Used to be in baseball it was survival."

I'm not sure this analysis is correct.

First of all, there is the phenomenon of charging the mound.

This goes back eons: a pitcher throws a ball at a hitter, the hitter charges toward the pitcher, angry words are exchanged or a fight breaks out.

In the old days, this was not the preferred form of retaliation. It was better to let your own pitcher retaliate or to bide your time until the opportunity arose to "cut the legs off" an infielder on a double play ball or close play at one of the bases. Better yet, lay down a drag bunt, like Cobb.

Today the batters charge the mound often, almost reflexively. Bonds, Fairly, and other observers say this is because today's players are thin-skinned. The media treat them like movie stars. If a pitcher throws one high and tight, it's a blow to the modern player's bloated ego. "You can't throw at me!"

It's hubris in a macho era; they charge the mound.

The paradox is that the thin-skinned players are responsible for the most blatant rowdyism on the field in years. Maybe, when the baseball history books are written, we'll see that the mode of retaliation simply changed in the last decade.

Violence in the game has been a constant through the years. The decades pass, the dust settles, and we're left with a residue that tells us something about the underlying flavor of the game. You flip through old newspaper clippings and you'll find the story of a fight between Dodgers outfielder Reggie Smith, whom I nominate as the leading brawler of his time, and Pittsburgh Pirates pitcher Pasqual Perez. This was in Los Angeles in 1981. Smith beckoned to Perez and they left the field, followed by their teammates. The crowd, left to stare at an empty diamond, didn't know what was going on.

Dozens of Dodgers, Pirates, and news reporters flocked to watch the fight under the stands. Smith faced off against Perez, who had a "crazed expression on his face," one reporter wrote, taunting and threatening Smith with his bat as the crowd circled around them.

When the annals of baseball are updated, that encounter will stand beside the fight between Cobb and umpire Billy Evans under the stands in Washington, D.C., after an exhibition game in 1921. What's the difference?

Well, actually, there is a slight difference: Cobb beat Evans to a pulp, smashing the ump's head repeatedly into the cement floor. (No one was hurt in the Smith-Perez bout.) But my point here is that the looming threat of violence continues to surround the game.

You still get middle-class kids driving in from New Jersey to sit in the stands at Yankee Stadium and throw batteries at the heads of the Boston Red Sox. Which is pretty much what happened in Louisville a hundred years ago when the owners of the club there sponsored "suburban days" to draw a "respectable" crowd and wound up with rioters in the box seats.

Incidentally, these are some of the other objects that "fans" have thrown at their favorite players over the years: darts, pen knives, butcher knives, beer steins, soda pop and whiskey bottles, golf balls, billiard balls, ball bearings, bullets, bolts, rocks, phonograph records, metal tape measures, Frisbees, slats torn from the backs of ballpark seats, folding chairs, bags of ice, snowballs, pennies, articles of clothing, hot dogs, hair brushes, wet newspapers, smoke bombs, candy bars, cushions, cabbages, and more common vegetables and fruits.

Not to forget exploding iguanas. In Nicaragua, fans have been known to tie a firecracker to a lizard's tail, light the fuse, and heave the animal onto the field.

Look out!

I'm not going to be completely ungenerous. I'm not going to deny that walking into a ballpark in April and seeing the grass for the first time in a new season isn't a thrill. Because it is one of the greatest thrills imaginable.

I'm not going to deny baseball its heroes—Gehrig, Musial, Clemente, Aaron, men of upstanding character.

I'm not saying that baseball and its players are seedier than society, only *as* seedy. In baseball, you can see the whole panorama of the lower end of the human experience: alcohol, drugs, wife-beating, horrible murders, suicide by carbolic acid (popular around the turn of the century). The vices have grown more expensive as salaries have risen—cocaine costs more than booze. But the vices are still essentially the same. They are myriad. They are all in the game. And they are all in this book.

Baseball's official mythology has no room for the dirt. It pretends that the Hall of Fame in Cooperstown, New York, is something akin to a temple to the Greek gods. But ballplayers are men, not gods.

In true mythology, there is tragedy. Not just the tragic misfortune of a man like Lou Gehrig, struck down in his prime by disease. But real tragedy in which people are brought down not *only* by the fates, but by their own vanity, greed, and myriad other flaws.

In real mythology, there are heroes and antiheroes.

I propose to concentrate on the antiheroes.

The villains of the game.

I will show you Cobb and McGraw, together in a Dallas hotel lobby in 1917, cursing at one another, spoiling for a fight. "If you were a younger man," Cobb sneered, "I would kill you." McGraw answered, "I'm young enough, you yellow-livered coward."

I will introduce you to Andrew Freedman, the cheap, obnoxious, meddling owner of the New York Giants, who out-Steinbrennered

Steinbrenner, eighty years before George arrived in New York; to Hal Chase, the single most amoral, corrupt player in the history of baseball; to Willie Wells, known as "the Devil" in the Negro Leagues of the 1920s and '30s, who packed pebbles into the fingers of his mitt so that he could leave a welt on opposing base runners every time he made a tag.

You will meet brawling umpires, managers who beat up umps, players who beat up managers, fans who beat up players, news reporters who harassed players until they left town. You will see your heroes in a new light, as when Yogi Berra, trapped in a crowd of friendly fans at the airport in Kansas City, told them, "Go home, you little cocksuckers."

You will see how McGraw trained the scrappy, battling Frankie Frisch, who trained the vile, braying Leo Durocher. And how McGraw also trained Casey Stengel, who trained the brawling, alcoholic Billy Martin.

You will see how Dolf Luque, a knockdown pitcher who won twenty-seven games for the Cincinnati Reds in 1923, became a mentor to Sal "the Barber" Maglie, probably the most celebrated knockdown artist of the modern era. And how Maglie, in turn, became mentor to the young Don Drysdale.

Entire lineages of brawlers and headhunters!

A panoply of villainy!

A new way to look at baseball.

The game's marketers won't like it, but who cares?

They say Pete Rose isn't fit to be in the Hall of Fame. Pete consorted with gamblers and bet on baseball, maybe even on the team he managed, the Cincinnati Reds.

Well, let's take a stroll through the Hall of Fame.

Cobb was caught up in a gambling scandal in 1926. So was Tris Speaker.

McGraw invested in a Manhattan pool hall frequented by hustlers. One of his partners was Arnold Rothstein, the mobster who was reputedly behind the 1919 Black Sox scandal.

I won't say that the corruption of one era precisely equals that of the next, because, sure, the game has changed. More and more ballplayers are suburban kids, and maybe they're less confrontational than the old-timers. Maybe. After all, where are the Eddie Stankys of today?

Maybe television has tamed the game. You can't scratch your crotch on TV, and you sure don't want Carl Mays killing Ray Chapman on the tube. How many times would that be shown on instant replay?

Not good for baseball.

Still, something makes me suspicious. Old-timers always say the new generation of players is soft and overpaid. They've been saying this since the 1880s. But I don't see how Dizzy Dean knocking down seven Giants in a row in the 1930s is really different from Dock Ellis throwing at five Reds in a row in 1974. Both wanted to instill fear in the hitters. Both were born of the same breed: macho warriors, a little bit crazy.

Baseball is an odd game. There's no justice in it. Hitting a ball is incredibly difficult. Bloop singles win games all the time. So ballplayers look for every advantage. They cheat. They play dirty. They intimidate.

One guy throws a ball at ninety-five miles per hour at another guy who tries to bash it with a stick. Big guys run into each other on the base paths. Outfielders crash into fences. And fans pour beer on the outfielders as they lie immobile on the warning track. It's true—it happened to Houston Astros outfielder Bob Watson in 1974. He crashed into the center field wall at Riverfront Stadium in Cincinnati and as he lay dazed on the ground, the fans poured beer on his head.

Some field of dreams. Some paradise.

You remember how Pete Rose wiped out catcher Ray Fosse at home plate to score the winning run in the twelfth inning of the 1970 All-Star game? Rose's take-out was one of the most celebrated, brutal plays on record. He was vilified for blasting through Fosse who never quite recovered from the injuries he suffered that day.

"Ray was in Pete's way," shrugs Bobby Bonds. The charging base runner, in Bond's world, has no choice but to take out a catcher who blocks the way to the plate. Bonds compares Rose's situation to that of a man or woman who's stuck in a room without an exit: "You get locked in there and they don't have no doors and the only way you can get out is that window—I bet you'd break it," Bonds says. "That's the way Pete played the game. That's the way a lot of guys played."

We began by discussing book titles. Maybe you remember a book called *How Life Imitates the World Series.* It was written by Thomas Boswell, who covers baseball for the *Washington Post.* Apparently the book's title was intended to conjure up the many cosmic ways in which baseball—the symmetry of the ball field, the perfect beauty of the game itself—is resonant of physics, the laws of the universe, and how human life gently unfolds outside the stadium gates.

I say, this is how life imitates the World Series:

It's 1939 and Cincinnati Reds catcher Ernie "the Schnozz" Lombardi is lying unconscious in the dirt next to home plate, knocked out by the errant knee of Yankees base runner Charlie Keller. The ball is ensconced tightly in the glove of the inert Lombardi as one, two, and then three Yankee runners race past him with two outs to score the winning runs in the final inning of the final game of the World Series.

Now that's how life imitates the World Series: you knock down your competitor and go for the gold.

That's Baseball and the American Dream.

And just another episode from the Field of Screams.

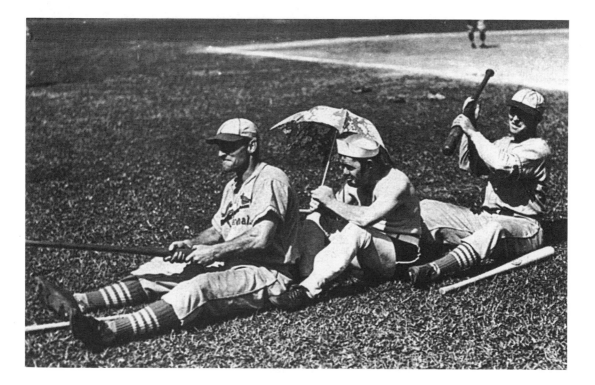

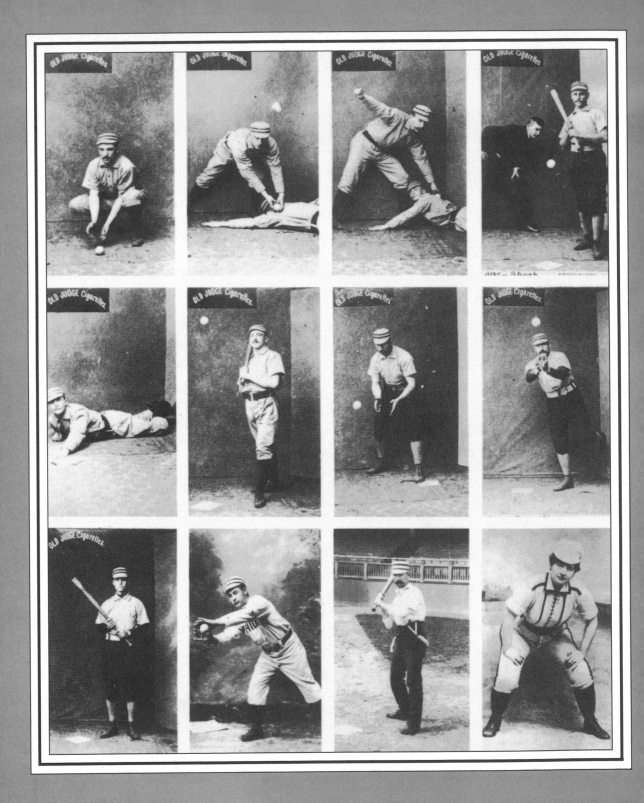

The Early Game

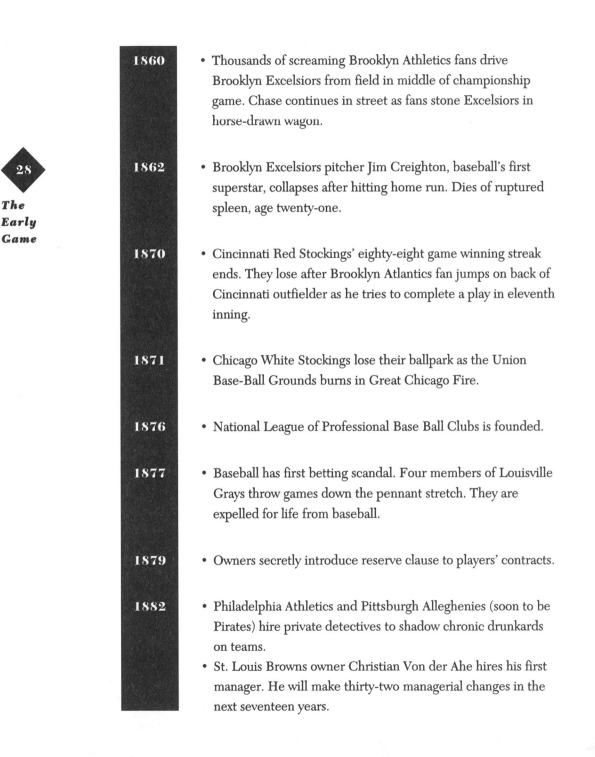

28

*The
Early
Game*

1860 • Thousands of screaming Brooklyn Athletics fans drive Brooklyn Excelsiors from field in middle of championship game. Chase continues in street as fans stone Excelsiors in horse-drawn wagon.

1862 • Brooklyn Excelsiors pitcher Jim Creighton, baseball's first superstar, collapses after hitting home run. Dies of ruptured spleen, age twenty-one.

1870 • Cincinnati Red Stockings' eighty-eight game winning streak ends. They lose after Brooklyn Atlantics fan jumps on back of Cincinnati outfielder as he tries to complete a play in eleventh inning.

1871 • Chicago White Stockings lose their ballpark as the Union Base-Ball Grounds burns in Great Chicago Fire.

1876 • National League of Professional Base Ball Clubs is founded.

1877 • Baseball has first betting scandal. Four members of Louisville Grays throw games down the pennant stretch. They are expelled for life from baseball.

1879 • Owners secretly introduce reserve clause to players' contracts.

1882 • Philadelphia Athletics and Pittsburgh Alleghenies (soon to be Pirates) hire private detectives to shadow chronic drunkards on teams.
• St. Louis Browns owner Christian Von der Ahe hires his first manager. He will make thirty-two managerial changes in the next seventeen years.

1883
- Former Chicago White Stockings pitcher Terry Larkin shoots his wife and cuts his own throat in first of series of violent acts. Both live.

1885
- Pitching star Tony Mullane is suspended for season for failure to honor contracts of the previous year.
- Charles Comiskey of St. Louis Browns incites crowd against umpire in second game of World Series against Chicago. Mob chases umpire Dave Sullivan across field. Umpire scales outfield fence and disappears.

1887
- Chicago White Stockings manager Cap Anson forces Newark club to bench its black pitcher and catcher in exhibition game.
- International League owners draw color line.
- Ohio State League draws color line.
- St. Louis Browns refuse to play exhibition game against Cuban Giants, a black team.
- Louisville slugger Pete Browning is too drunk to make first part of road trip to Cincinnati. Arrives for second game. Doubles, takes lead off second, and falls asleep.
- Ella Latham, wife of St. Louis Browns third baseman Arlie Latham, files for divorce. Accuses husband of repeated beatings.

1889
- Browns owner Von der Ahe fines second baseman Yank Robinson $25 for playing in a dirty uniform. Team threatens to strike.

Only a murdered umpire,
Only a bushel of bricks,
A can, and a cat, and such things as that,
And an umpire done with his tricks.
—from "The Krank, His Language and What It Means,"
by Thomas Lawson

You've heard about the Big Baseball Myth. Now you'll hear about the Big Lie underlying the big myth. Baseball was not invented in a cow pasture in Cooperstown in 1839 by General Abner Doubleday. That's totally false, a concoction of Albert G. Spalding, one of baseball's first pitching stars and later the founder of the famous sporting goods company. Spalding, who published an annual guide to the game, was a shrewd publicist. In 1904, he formed a blue ribbon committee to inquire into baseball's origins. This panel threw away the facts—that baseball was descended from the English game of rounders, that George Washington's soldiers had played a game much like baseball at Valley Forge, and that the urban game had grown steadily in popularity for at least forty years prior to the Civil War. Working from a clean slate, the committee issued a report describing the game's Immaculate Conception in Small Town USA. This set the stage for Cooperstown to become baseball's Bethlehem and established the proper tone for the marketing of the game.

And General Doubleday was its ultimate folk hero: it was he, after all, who had ordered the first shots fired in defense of the Union in the Civil War. For Spalding to tack the baseball creation tale onto the war hero's résumé was an act of inspiration. But the marketing ploy wrapped baseball in a graceful mantle that concealed the ugliness of the early game. In the years of repair that followed the Civil War, baseball's course almost paralleled the country's: both were big, raucus, exploding, exciting. And violent. Very, very violent. No mother wanted her son to become a baseball player, to hang around ballparks where the crowds teemed with "drunken rowdies, unwashed loafers, and arrant blacklegs," as a contemporary newspaper described them. Where vendors weaved through the throng selling bottles of spirits which, almost inevitably, once empty were heaved at umpires' heads. Where racketeers like John Morrissey, a U.S. congressman and owner of Manhattan gambling houses and the Saratoga, New York, racetrack, showed up with his entourage to bribe players, manipulate the odds, and make a killing.

Transcendental Graphics

Stone the manager too!

No mother wanted her son emulating the likes of Bill "Bull" Craver, a thick-bodied brute who played catcher for the Troy (New York) Haymakers. Craver was one of Boss Morrissey's favorites: the Bull would mug an opponent on the base paths—or off—to win a game for the Boss. Or, if the Boss so deemed it, Craver would nonchalantly blow a critical play to lose the contest. It was said that Morrissey, a former heavyweight boxing champion, played Craver and the Haymakers as if they were "loaded dice and marked cards."

No mother wanted her son walking in the steps of Bob "Death to Flying Things" Ferguson, a slick-fielding third baseman for the Brooklyn Atlantics. In 1873, the foul-tempered Ferguson umpired a game between the Baltimore Lord Baltimores and the New York Mutuals. When the Mutuals' catcher, Nat Hicks, mouthed off at the ump, Ferguson retaliated. He picked up a bat and pounded Hicks, breaking the catcher's arm in two places. But when a policeman tried to arrest Ferguson, Hicks minimized the injuries—which sidelined him for two months—and declined to press charges. He behaved like a modern gang member who refuses to snitch on an enemy.

That was baseball.

Much has been written about the sport being a "gentleman's game" during this period. But Mark Twain got it right when he called baseball "the very symbol, the outward and visible expression of the drive and push and rush and struggle of the raging, tearing, booming nineteenth century."

That's a fancy way of saying it was a violent game in a violent society. As the country moved west, cow towns popped up with their ramshackle saloons, whorehouses, and gambling joints. The cowboy's tough-guy mentality was romanticized in the popular dime novels of the era—just as movies and television romanticize violence today. People were reading about gunslinging and fisticuffs. Through the dime novels, the violence of the Wild West spread to the East, where it mingled with the tough, immigrant street life of the big cities, and rolled into the old wooden ballparks of the nation's national pastime.

The old ballparks were often found at the edge of town along with amusement parks, racetracks, and traveling circuses. In Cincinnati, baseball historian Dick Miller points out, one ballpark was at the end of a train line beside a racetrack, the other was at the end of a paddle wheeler line beside an amusement park. In New York, the fabled Knickerbockers played in an amusement park known as the Elysian Fields. All around the big cities, amusement park owners wanted baseball parks next door to draw the crowds, even though many of those who attended the games were regarded as riffraff. In almost every way, the ballparks were like the cow town saloons out West: wooden and impermanent, and often filled with tough cookies who fought, drank, and gambled.

In 1860, fifteen thousand people attended a championship game between the Brooklyn Excelsiors and their hosts, the Brooklyn Atlantics. It was a socioeconomic grudge match: the Atlantics' fans were working-class Irishmen, while the Excelsiors' followers were white-collar stiffs. The game was close, filled with controversial calls by the umpire, and the Atlantics' supporters became so threatening and abusive that the Excelsiors were driven from the field. The fans chased them into the streets, throwing rocks at the Excelsiors in their horse-drawn wagon. This became a familiar scene in baseball over the years: escaping ballplayers huddled in a wagon, besieged by rock-throwing "fans" who were more appropriately known as "bugs" or "kranks" during this period. One of the players on the Excelsiors' wagon was pitcher Jim Creighton, a handsome nineteen-year-old and baseball's first superstar. Two years later, in the final game of the 1862 season, Creighton walloped a home run and ruptured his spleen, collapsing and dying soon after of internal bleeding.

Out of this gore and chaos, organized baseball was born.

The first openly salaried professional team was the Cincinnati Red Stockings, who won sixty-four consecutive ball games in 1869 and another twenty-four in a row to open the

JAMES CREIGHTON,
Pitcher of the Excelsior Base Ball Club of Brooklyn, N.

Jim Creighton, baseball's first superstar. He collapsed and died after walloping a home run for the Brooklyn Excelsiors in 1862.

1870 season. The streak was spoiled by—you guessed it—the Brooklyn Atlantics, whose fans once more made the difference. You have to understand that at this time, and for much of the next thirty years, the crowd at a big game formed a circling mob around the players, standing behind ropes along the foul lines and on the outfield grass. On this day in Brooklyn, with the home team trailing by two in the eleventh inning, a fan leaped onto the back of Cincinnati right fielder Cal McVey as he tried to field a ball. The Atlantics went on to win by a score of 8–7.

William "Harry" Wright, the Red Stockings' player-manager and the so-called father of organized baseball, detested the rowdyism. So did journalist Henry Chadwick, another founding father of the game, who campaigned against the intrusion of violence and gambling. Yet betting odds were reported in the papers each day, and wagering at the ballpark grew even more routine as the John Morrisseys of the world expanded their influence. As the 1870s moved on, Albert G. Spalding admitted, "not an important game was played on any grounds where pools on the game were not sold. A few players became so corrupt that nobody could be certain whether the issue of any game in which they participated would be determined on its merits."

All this blew up in 1877 with baseball's first big betting scandal. That fall, the Louisville Grays fell apart on the field and lost the pennant. It was later discovered that team members had colluded with New York gamblers to throw games down the pennant stretch. Foreshadowing the punishments meted out to the Chicago Black Sox forty years later, four of the Grays were permanently expelled from baseball. One of the four was none other than Bill "Bull" Craver, Morrissey's pet from the old Haymakers club. After departing Troy in 1871, Craver had bounced from team to team. It's a good bet that he threw ball games from the redwood forests to the Gulf Stream waters before his corruption finally caught up with him in Louisville.

So much for the good, clean origins of the All-American game.

Which brings us to the 1880s.

'Twas a carefree time—with barbed-wire fences erected to prevent spectators from rushing the field to mob the lone umpire who officiated each game. It proved impossible to fully protect the man in blue as he raced from behind home plate to first base to second and on

When gambling controlled the game . . .

to third, huffing and puffing, desperately trying to arrive in time to make each call swiftly and accurately. Inevitably, the umpire blew a few calls, sometimes more than a few, and this made him a target for beer bottles and brutal tirades.

Umpire Billy McLean, a former Philadelphia boxer, responded one afternoon by hurling a bat at his tormentors in the stands, injuring a fan. McLean was arrested, and he apologized for letting his temper get the better of him. But was he really that far out of line? After all, umpiring was an almost suicidal career choice. The fans were sadists: "Stone the umpire!" they screamed. "Kill him! Skin him!" The players encouraged the spectators in their catcalling, and the owners encouraged the players to incite the fans, realizing that the whole violent cycle was a boost to attendance.

The most rabid umpire baiters were the St. Louis Browns. The club's owner was a saloonkeeper named Christian Von der Ahe who understood, better than anyone of his era, the entertainment value of rowdy play. Von der Ahe was an egomaniac who knew little about baseball. He made his athletes march behind him in single file on the way to the ballpark, and then turned the troops loose to sow destruction on the field. His ringleader was Charles Comiskey, the team's player-manager for four consecutive pennant-winning seasons from 1885 to 1888. Just as New York Yankees owner George Steinbrenner used the pugnacious Billy Martin to generate creative tension on their championship teams of the 1970s, Von der Ahe relied on Comiskey to agitate the Browns and everyone else on the diamond.

The "Noble Roman," as Comiskey came later to be known for his impressive profile, was the most incessant irritant in baseball in the 1880s. Coaching at third base, he ran up and down the baseline, cursing at the opposing pitcher, questioning almost every ball and strike called by the umpire, getting right up into the ump's face, stomping on the ump's feet with his spikes, making them bleed. Not a nice guy. In order to contain Comiskey, the rulemakers invented the coach's box in 1887. That was like jail to the Nobleman, whose antics paved the way for Cobb, McGraw, and the other criminals who followed in his spiked footsteps.

Yet, Comiskey wasn't the most despicable character in the game. The 1880s honor roll also included Terry Larkin, a pitcher and murderer; Arlie Latham, a third baseman and wife beater; and Tony Mullane, a pitcher and ne'er-do-well who was suspected of throwing ball games in piques over his salary. It included John Clarkson, a pitcher who supposedly smoked so much that he left nicotine stains on the bathtub; Paul Hines, a lifetime .301 hitter who became a pickpocket in Washington, D.C.; and Billy Gleason, the Browns' roughhouse shortstop, of whom it was written, "If he should someday break a limb or his neck, not a ballplayer in the American Association would feel the slightest regret."

But even beyond the personalities, this was an important, transitional decade:

—The game absorbed the Irish and other tough-nosed European immigrants who transformed baseball and set the stage for the raucous play of the 1890s.

—At the same time, organized baseball prepared to exclude those few blacks who were persistent enough to force their way into the game. On the base paths, black players were assaulted. Off the field, they were isolated. By the end of the decade, as Jim Crow laws proliferated, the color line was drawn and the All-American game was ready to become All-White.

—Owners moved toward total control of the game's salary structure. Money feuds between owners and players were played out through the press, much as they are today. One player, poor Yank Robinson of the Browns, cried to Von der Ahe, "You fine me enough to build a stone house."

Von der Ahe was just one of the wealthy men who came to control the game. All around the country, fortunes were being made—think of what was happening in the railroad and steel industries. In baseball, the owners wrested control from the players by forming the National League in 1876. They introduced the reserve clause to contracts to prevent players from "revolving" from club to club. Players still managed to sell their services to high bidders like modern-day free agents. But this happened less frequently as the lords of baseball tightened their grip, secretly introduced salary caps, and gradually turned the players into indentured servants.

Maybe this is why so many players lived on the bar stool.

Alcoholism was epidemic, consuming players and destroying their careers in much the same way that cocaine infected baseball a century later. Curt Welch, center fielder for the Browns, hid a pint of whiskey behind a sign in the outfield fence at Sportsman's Park in St. Louis. He'd snare a fly ball, sneak a drink, then return to his position. Players were plied with free drinks on the road, and no matter how hard management tried to break the pattern, writes historian Warren Goldstein, "the game never lost its association with that center of working-class culture, the saloon. . . . Drinking remained stubbornly . . . central to the culture of professional baseball players and their fans."

Let's flip through the sports sections of the time for more evidence of the alcoholic haze wafting through the game:

—In July 1882, the Philadelphia Athletics and Pittsburgh Alleghenies hired private detectives to shadow their players. Both teams had been playing wretchedly and attendance was falling.

—In July 1887, the Indianapolis team of the National League lost a game by the score of 24–0. The night before, the players had been "off on a big drunk."

—The same month, four Detroit players were suspended for drunkenness.

—The day before Christmas, the *Sporting News* ran a front-page editorial with the headline "Tommy Booze: Something About the Hardest Hitter in the Country." It suggested that Tommy lay off the liquor as a New Year's resolution.

It was inevitable that the game should change under the influence of these hard-drinking, fist-fighting men. It was in their time that pitching evolved from an underhand to sidearm delivery; this increased the velocity of pitched balls and put a new emphasis on the fear factor in baseball. In 1884, the overhand pitch was legalized and the intimidation war between pitchers and batters really began to escalate. Headhunters like Cincinnati's Tony Mullane were perfectly willing to throw at hitters. In fact, it was largely because of Mullane that the American Association—the National League's rival from 1882 to 1891—instituted the hit-batsmen rule. This is the rule that awards first base to the batter when he is hit by a pitch. A century ago, it was viewed with derisive humor. The National League thought it "sissified" the game and hesitated to adopt it. But throwing at the hitter was becoming too commonplace, too dangerous, and the NL was forced to follow the American Association's lead.

Let's end with a snapshot from mid-decade.

It's October 15, 1885, and the second game of the World Series between the St. Louis Browns and the Chicago White Stockings is being played at Sportsman's Park in St. Louis. Things are not going well for St. Louis.

Charles Comiskey is coaching at third base for the Browns. He is red in the face because his constant, bellowing remonstrations over calls are having no effect on the umpire. No, this ump is far too independent to suit Comiskey. So the leader of the Browns pulls his team from the field, and the hometown crowd, already seething with anger toward the ump, grows livid. Fans pour onto the field and head in one direction—towards umpire Dave Sullivan. He flees.

Sullivan sprints through the infield and across the outfield grass. The mob is at his heels now. Sullivan reaches the outfield fence, scales it, leaps!

And disappears from sight.

38

*The
Early
Game*

Gimme Gimme Gimme

You're tired of wealthy, whining ballplayers?
Tony Mullane was the original whiner.

A century before Rickey Henderson, Mullane was a superstar who ruined his own public image with his sulking and refusal to put out on the field.

Mullane was terrifically handsome—"Apollo of the Box," they called him. His good looks were said to be responsible for the introduction of Ladies' Days in Cincinnati. But because Mullane was always dissatisfied with his salary, the press was filled with details of his contract squabbles. The paper called him "the most avaricious and ungrateful player in the profession." Ennui set in with the public as Mullane went on sit-down strikes, threatened owners, and insulted his teammates.

Not many liked him.

In 1884, he jumped his contract with St. Louis to play with Louisville. He signed a contract to return to St. Louis, broke it, and jumped to Cincinnati, which offered him a salary increase and a $2,000 advance. He didn't play in Cincinnati, either. Mullane wound up winning thirty-seven games for Toledo, but was suspended for the 1885 season by the board of directors of the American Association.

"He sat on the seats at the Cincinnati Park the whole season, smoking cigarettes," one of the local papers complained, "and drew $3,200 out of the club treasury for so doing." This was a good chunk of change for the time. Charles Comiskey of the St. Louis Browns, among the highest-paid players in the game, earned about $1,000 more for playing every day. And Comiskey was the Browns' manager, too.

Mullane's suspension created a void in the midst of five consecutive seasons in which he won thirty or more games. He won 285 games in his career, so it's likely that the missed season ultimately prevented him from reaching the 300 mark.

He won thirty-three games in 1886, but was suspected of throwing

*The
Early
Game*

*The
original
whiner:
Tony Mullane
of Louisville.*

some of the twenty-seven games that he lost. His "queer work" on the field was exemplified by a game in June when he blew a 7–0 lead, giving up twelve runs in the eighth and ninth innings. When headlines of "Tony the Traitor" ran in the press, Mullane threatened libel, jumped his contract, and played ball in Montana mining camps.

Back in Cincinnati in 1887, Mullane demanded that club president Aaron Stern give him a $1,000 advance on his salary. Stern refused. When Mullane's turn in the pitching rotation came one day in May, he approached his manager in the dugout and told him, "You might as well put somebody else in. I don't intend to pitch." During a subsequent argument in Stern's office, Mullane threatened to beat the money out of the president. When Stern asked the park policeman to escort Mullane to the street, the pitcher threatened the cop.

"You leave go of me, or I'll put a bullet through you," Mullane said.

The amazing thing is that Mullane managed to keep winning ball games while all this was happening. He won thirty-one and lost seventeen in '87.

He was only twenty-eight years old, but his career began to fall off the next spring. Was he burned out by the fighting? The press had berated him for demanding special treatment from management. His teammates couldn't stand him: "He was the most unpopular member of the club. They don't want him back and declare they don't need him."

As time went on, no one could stomach Mullane.

In a game against the Chicago White Stockings in 1891, Mullane feuded with his Cincinnati teammates, then began pouring abuse on the opposition. Adrian "Cap" Anson came to bat for Chicago, Mullane kept ranting, and the batter finally blurted out: "Oh, shut up, you bloody Italian. Go and pitch your game."

Mullane gave Anson a look "as savage as a meat axe" and shut up.

He retired in 1894.

Baseball Apartheid

O h Cooperstown, hallowed be thy name.
Home of Cobb. Home of Ruth. Home of DiMaggio.

And home of Bud Fowler, whose image is not engraved on a bronze plaque and never will be, but who grew up in Cooperstown and threw rocks against the sides of barns and in the pastures where Abner Doubleday never walked, becoming perhaps the greatest second baseman in the country.

And what was Bud Fowler's fate? Why, to encase his legs in

Bud Fowler (top center) grew up in Cooperstown, New York.

wooden shin guards. He invented them to protect himself against white base runners who were intent on one thing—to spike the bejesus out of his black legs.

This is the real Cooperstown story. The story of the black man from the mythical hamlet who was denied his rightful place in the national pastime. "If he had a white face," the *Sporting Life* said in 1885, "he would be playing with the best of them. . . . Those who know, say there is no better second baseman."

Ah, but the next year, historian Jules Tygiel tells us, an even better second baseman entered organized ball. His name was Frank Grant. He, too, was black. And he, too, designed and wore wooden shin guards for protection against redneck base runners. Grant eventually moved to the outfield to rid himself of the problem. At the plate, he was a beanball target for pitchers. These routine attempts to rip up and knock down Grant, these baseball lynchings, were harbingers of the rough treatment that Jackie Robinson would receive sixty years later upon joining the Brooklyn Dodgers.

Grant batted .366 in the International League in 1877. His mark led the league, and one might guess this would have marked him as a potential major leaguer and won him the approval of teammates and International League executives.

In fact, Grant had no chance of advancing to the majors, for the National League already had an unwritten racial code barring blacks. His teammates shunned him. And the owners? During the '87 season, they met in Buffalo to adopt an apartheid law stipulating "no more contracts with colored men," a newspaper matter-of-factly reported. This new policy scattered the black players and ensured that by the turn of the century no black man would play alongside whites.

How did baseball apartheid come about?

National Baseball Library

Second baseman Frank Grant designed wooden shin guards to protect himself against racist base runners.

In 1883, a black catcher named Moses Fleetwood Walker joined the Toledo club of the Northwestern League. When Toledo joined the American Association in 1884, Walker became the nineteenth century's first black major leaguer. There were only two. The other was his brother Welday, who briefly joined the club that year. The next season the brothers were gone, and that was the end of black major league baseball in the nineteenth century.

The sort of abuse that Fleet Walker suffered is undeserved by anyone. But it must have been particularly hard for Walker to stomach. He was from a privileged background, the son of a doctor. He had spent three years at Oberlin College in Ohio, studying Latin, Greek, trigonometry, botany, zoology. He chucked academics for a career in baseball alongside ballplayers who couldn't begin to match his social pedigree and education. And he held down the most brutal, injury-prone job on the diamond, that of catcher in an era when catchers played barehanded. He suffered routinely through mashed fingers and a multitude of welts and bruises. And what did it get him?

When Adrian "Cap" Anson brought his champion Chicago White Stockings to Toledo for an exhibition match in 1883, he threatened to cancel the match if Walker played. The game went on: the Toledo manager called Anson's bluff by inserting Walker in the middle innings. But Anson, a superstar and role model to boys all over America, a man who had baseball bats and candy bars named after him, had set a precedent.

By 1887, Walker was playing for Newark in the International League. The team traveled to Hamilton, Ontario, where a sportswriter tagged him "the coon catcher." All around the league that year, blacks caught it from fans, teammates, and the press. Frank Grant, whose Buffalo teammates had refused to pose for a team photograph with him the year before, was taunted by rowdies who yelled, "Kill the nigger!" Fowler was released by the Binghamton club when his teammates refused to take the field with him. Robert Higgins, a black pitcher with Syracuse, was undermined by teammates who committed a slew of intentional errors, hoping to humiliate Higgins and drive him from the team. And then, joining the movement, they refused to pose for a team photograph with Higgins.

The climactic event of 1887 occurred on July 14 in Newark when

Moses Fleetwood Walker, the first black major leaguer. He ran up against the game's color line in 1887.

Anson arrived once again with the White Stockings. This time his threats resulted in the removal of Fleet Walker from the game along with Walker's black battery mate, a pitcher named George Stovey.

That same day in Buffalo, the team owners agreed informally to institute the color line. It was probably a coincidence. But Anson was a barometer for the country's racial climate. The actions of Anson and the International League owners were only "a small part of what happened in almost every area of the country in the 1880s and 1890s," explains historian Charles C. Alexander. "It was around 1889 that the State of Mississippi adopted statutes prohibiting black people from voting. . . . State and local laws were passed establishing segregation in every aspect of Southern life, even extending to the use of separate Bibles for blacks and whites when they were sworn in in court. There was a tremendous upsurge of racial violence. If you look at statistics kept by Tuskeegee University, in the 1890s you're averaging about 250 lynchings in the U.S. each year, and almost all against black people. What's happening in baseball is a part of that pattern."

As the new century approached, blacks were barred from unions and professional organizations and discriminated against in other sports. Major Taylor, a black man who dominated competitive cycling, was barred from participating in important races. When blacks were excluded from baseball, it was no surprise. It was just one more item to tick off on the national racist agenda. Few whites lifted an eyebrow.

A handful of blacks managed to play alongside whites through the 1890s, and a few black teams even survived in otherwise white professional leagues. But integration was on its way out. By 1900, blacks were gone from "organized baseball." They were forced in coming years to play in their own leagues, in front of their own black fans, their accomplishments reported almost exclusively in their own black newspapers. They vanished from the national scene. And they wouldn't be back until the emergence of Jackie Robinson nearly half a century later.

Macho Men:
Arlie Latham and Tommy Foster

In the 1930s, Arlie Latham, a rough and colorful former third baseman for the Browns, met at Yankee Stadium with his friend Tommy Foster, a retired outfielder of the same vintage. The two tough guys reminisced about the baseball wars of the 1880s:

Latham: "It's a wonder we weren't both killed—the way they used to fire the ball at our heads, Tommy."

Foster: "Yes, and they wouldn't even let us take our base when we were hit. The pitcher was fifteen feet nearer the batter than he is today, and the rules let him jump around in the box before delivering the ball. He would run up on you and let go. Lem Sowders hit me flush on the jaw one day and broke the hoop of it. Funny part of it was I didn't know I was hurt until I tried to talk—and then I couldn't say anything."

Latham: "Say, Tommy, do you remember Curt Welch of the St. Louis Browns? He was the original Iron Horse. You could hit him anyplace with the ball."

Foster: "I remember Tony Mullane. He was always trying to bean you. Uncle Robbie [Wilbert Robinson] used to say, if you got three hits one day, they'd hit you the next. Baseball was like that when we were young, Arlie."

Latham: "Huh! I was never scared of Mullane. I used to dare him to hit me—if he could. I'd get him mad by telling him he couldn't do it, because I'd learned how to protect myself boxing. No, Tony couldn't hit me no matter how hard he tried."

National Baseball Library

Arlie Latham bragged that he dared pitchers to throw at his head.

Criticals

John Glenn—A mediocre outfielder and first baseman for the Chicago White Stockings, he retired in 1877 and was arrested for robbery about a year later. After doing time in a Rochester prison, he visited the small town of Glens Falls, New York, where he hid behind an outhouse, grabbed a twelve-year-old girl, and raped her. He was attacked by a mob that chased him down the street, and killed by the discharge of a police officer's gun. The cop had been trying to protect him from the mob.

Terry Larkin—Larkin was a pitcher and teammate of Glenn's who is best known for the outrageously violent series of crimes he committed after retiring in 1880. Larkin went berserk, shot his wife and cut his own throat (both lived). Committed to a mental institution, he tried to kill himself by jumping headfirst off a bed into a cast-iron radiator. His wife nursed him back to health at home. Ever grateful, Larkin killed her father, and committed suicide with a razor in a mental hospital.

John Clarkson—A pitcher who won fifty-three games for the Chicago White Stockings in 1885, Clarkson later slashed his wife to death with a razor. This didn't stop him from being elected to the Hall of Fame. Pete Rose, take notice.
    —*Compiled with the assistance of Richard Topp*

Drinking Man: Pete Browning

"Ol' Pete" Browning, as he liked to be called, batted .341 in thirteen seasons in the old American Association and National League. That's the twelfth-highest batting average in the history of baseball, a single percentage point behind Babe Ruth. In his own era, Browning's career average stands second only to that of Dan Brouthers. His achievement is the more remarkable because Browning was almost continually drunk both off the field and on.

"What is it that so often gets Pete Browning into trouble?" the *Sporting News* asked. "Why, booze."

Browning was prone to making "extraordinary foozles" in the outfield of the Louisville Eclipse, for which he played from 1882 to 1889. In the fall of 1887, he missed the first game of a series in Cincinnati because he was "too intoxicated to find his way to the train." Browning, still drunk, arrived for game two and doubled to start a rally. Then he took a fifteen-foot lead off second base, the newspapers reported, and fell asleep. The second baseman "walked up and put him out, to the intense disgust of the spectators."

Perhaps it is because of this sort of story, one of many, that Pete Browning has never been elected to the Hall of Fame.

"I can't hit the ball until I hit the bottle," he once said.

This may sound amusing, but it points to the insidious relationship between baseball and boozing that has existed for over a century. The Eclipse belonged to the American Association, which allowed the sale of alcohol during games, earning it the sobriquet "Beer-Ball League." Historian Dean Sullivan, an expert on the Louisville franchise, says the team was led by a distillery executive. The Eclipse depended on alcohol sales to boost attendance. When there were complaints of drunken behavior "in the presence of the ladies," management cracked down only halfheartedly. This was despite public concern that rowdy fans threatened to spoil the game's carefully nurtured upright image. But Louisville was a drinking town. The fans, by and large, wanted their beer, and the fact that Browning was a drunk didn't affect his popularity.

Browning is one of those simple, childlike characters from baseball's early days—Rube Waddell is another—whose behavior makes you wonder if they suffered from mental retardation. Could the press have covered for them? In recent years, writers have speculated that Browning suffered from an untreated mastoid infection and brain damage caused by excessive alcohol consumption to alleviate the pain. Whatever the reason, "his mind was not attuned to greatness," to quote a reporter who knew him.

During a road trip to Kansas City, Browning went fishing in the gutter outside his hotel. This was during a torrential rainstorm.

"He lighted a long black cigar, took a lounging chair from the hotel and fished in solitary grandeur," the writer, John B. Foster, recounted years later. "Curious-minded persons by the score watched him and giggled. Oblivious to all, soaked to the skin, keeping his cigar alight against the water that was falling and wind that was blowing, Pete cast his line and swept the current; rebaited his hook, amused himself until he was tired of it and finally withdrew in discomfiture because of his ill luck."

When Browning returned to the hotel, the team's manager looked at him derisively and said, "Pete, you old damn fool."

"No luck," was the uncomprehending Browning's reply. "They ain't runnin' very well today."

In 1890, Browning jumped to the Cleveland team in the short-lived Brotherhood league, predicting he would bat .400. The night before the final game of the season, he spoke to a reporter.

"Any good news for Petey?" Browning asked. "How about the .400?"

The reporter told Browning, who won the batting championship with a .373 average, that he was substantially short of his mark.

"Don't fool Petey. Don't fool him," Browning answered, then broke down sobbing in the middle of the busy hotel lobby.

"What's the matter, Pete?" a teammate asked. "Somebody sick at home?"

"Hell, no," Browning answered. "Can't make .400. Beer."

Committed to an insane asylum near the end of his life, Browning died in 1905 at the age of forty-four.

Der Boss President

In the beginning there was Christian Von der Ahe, the first bad-news club owner in baseball history. A spiritual ancestor of George Steinbrenner, he was an overbearing, interfering owner who ran through managers like a piranha through schools of defenseless fish.

In his seventeen seasons as owner of the St. Louis Browns, Von der Ahe (pronounced Ah-hay) changed managers thirty-two times. Steinbrenner, in his first seventeen years running the New York Yankees, did it only nineteen times. Both paid megabucks to key players, then feuded with the recipients. Both won pennants early in their careers, then watched the franchises stumble. Both were great guys until you worked for them.

Von der Ahe called himself "Der Boss President."

He sat in the stands with a bugle in his lap. He blew the horn whenever he needed assistance from a park policeman.

He thought he knew everything about baseball and fined his players accordingly. If someone dropped a fly ball, Von der Ahe fined him. If the team played sloppily, he threatened to fire the whole squad. He told his managers who to play and who to pitch. One time in New York, he shouted from his seat, *"Change pitchers!"*

And that's why his managers quit.

Von der Ahe was born near Hanover, Germany, in 1851 and came to St. Louis around 1870. He opened a saloon a block and a half from the Grand Avenue park where a National League baseball team played in 1876–77. After the ball games, fans stopped by to drink and made Von der Ahe, who spoke with a thick German accent, a rich man: "Five thousand tamn fools," he supposedly declared as he surveyed his busy establishment, "und one wise man. Und dat wise man iss me—Chris Von der Ahe."

In 1881, he rebuilt Sportsman's Park. Then he took control of St. Louis's new American Association team, the Browns, which played its

first season in 1882. One of Von der Ahe's players was twenty-one-year-old Charles Comiskey, the son of a Chicago alderman. In 1885, Comiskey became player-manager and led the Browns to four consecutive pennants. Von der Ahe needed the combustible Comiskey to win, just as Steinbrenner needed the pugnacious Billy Martin.

But that's where the Steinbrenner parallels end.

Von der Ahe was not mean-spirited like Steinbrenner. He was just a pain in the ass. And a show-off.

And because he was an immigrant with an accent, he was treated like a buffoon by players and the press. Their condescension and cruelty matched his *nouveau riche* pretensions.

The newspapers alternately glorified and vilified him, labeling him the "Tricky Teuton" and the "wooden-shoed Dutchman."

Rival owners got into the act. Charles Byrne, owner of the Brooklyn Bridegrooms, feuded with Von der Ahe and chalked up their differences to "a case of abnormal enlargement of the cranium in a mentally small man."

Von der Ahe was rotund and had a large strawberry nose, and when he walked, he waddled. The Browns' third baseman, Arlie Latham, used to walk behind him, mimicking the boss's clumsy movements and eliciting peals of laughter from the crowds.

When Von der Ahe wore a loud, salmon-toned mackintosh to a league meeting, the press mocked him: "It was several folds too wide for Chris in spite of the recent addition to his chest, and it fit him much after the style of the late Julius Caesar's cloak. But the St. Louis magnate expects to continue to grow, and he will yet fill out the mackintosh as the stuffing of a balloon fills out the silk bag."

Latham joked that Von der Ahe hated it when his players hit fly balls.

"Shtop hitting them high-fliers," he yelled. "Don't you know them fielders can gatch dose high vuns?"

Sometimes he sat on the bench with the players, holding a small telescope. When a fly ball was hit, he followed it with the telescope, grunting and contorting his body as if this could change the ball's course and force the opposition to misplay it. The routine inevitably ended with Von der Ahe losing his balance, toppling from the bench, and crashing to the floor.

One hundred years before George Steinbrenner, there was Christian Von der Ahe, the unbearable owner of the champion St. Louis Browns.

Der Boss President

The players tried not to laugh, for fear of being fined.

Von der Ahe fined second baseman Yank Robinson $25 in 1889 for playing in a dirty uniform. Now, Robinson was not a big star. He earned maybe $1,000 or $1,500 per year, and $25 was a lot of money. His teammates resented the owner's dictatorial manner: Von der Ahe prorated their paychecks when they missed games due to illness, and insisted that they cover expenses on the road. To protest the owner's treatment of Robinson, they refused to travel to Kansas City for a series. Comiskey persuaded them to catch a late train, but they lost three games in a row to a weak K.C. club. There was suspicion that they threw the ball games.

That's when Von der Ahe decided to return the $25 to Robinson. The Browns won the next game.

Player relations were not his forte. But he was a great promoter, the Bill Veeck of his times.

He introduced Sunday baseball to St. Louis and built a beer garden beyond the right field grass. It was separated from the playing field by ropes. In the beer garden, people toasted one another at picnic tables. They played lawn bowling and handball.

If a baseball was hit into the beer garden, the outfielder jumped over the ropes and ran among the picnic tables to retrieve it. This was a ridiculous spectacle, yet the excitement it engendered got people talking and brought them out to the ballpark.

Eventually, though, Von der Ahe crossed the line between promotional innovation and hucksterism. After Comiskey left the team at the end of the decade—he "could not endure the pickled disposition" of his boss—the Browns' performance crumbled and never recovered. The revolving door spun even faster for managers. Von der Ahe managed two games himself and lost twice.

Attendance dropped, and a desperate Von der Ahe nearly turned the ballpark into an amusement park. There was horse racing after games and when the Browns were on the road. There was a shoot-the-chute. He moved in the fences and built a small lake beyond the left field wall for paddle boats and water games.

It was too much for St. Louis sportswriters like Charles Spink, editor of the *Sporting News,* who accused Der Boss of turning baseball into a circus at a time when it needed respectability. We've heard that one before and we'll hear it again. In any event, the amusement park idea didn't work out.

Sportsman's Park burned to the ground in 1898. All of Von der Ahe's memorabilia from the championship teams of 1885–88 were destroyed. He was devastated, went bankrupt, and returned to his saloon, where he was reduced to taking handouts from Comiskey, now a baseball magnate in Chicago, when his ex-manager visited St. Louis.

Von der Ahe died in 1913, and Comiskey paid for Der Boss President's funeral and gravestone.

The
1890s

Kill the umpire!

Mother, may I slug the umpire,
May I slug him right away?
So he cannot be here, mother,
When the clubs begin to play?

Let me clasp his throat, dear mother,
In a clear, delightful grip
With one hand, and with the other
Bat him several in the lip.

Let me climb his frame, dear mother,
While the happy people shout;
I'll not kill him, dearest mother,
I will only knock him out.

Let me mop the ground up, mother,
With his person, dearest, do;
If the ground can stand it, mother,
I don't see why you can't too.

Mother, may I slug the umpire,
Slug him right between the eyes?
If you let me do it, mother,
You shall have the champion prize.
   —*Rhyme of the era*

58

*The
1890s*

1890
- The Players League, which shared profits with players, fails after its first season.

1891
- John McGraw plays his first major league ball game. His Baltimore teammates shove him off Orioles' bench. McGraw fights.
- The American Association goes bankrupt.

1892
- Expanded National League establishes twelve-team monopoly. Owners slash player salaries.

1893
- McGraw curses manager of Savannah team in exhibition. Manager knocks him down.
- The next week, McGraw's roughhouse tactics cause near-riot in Chattanooga.
- Boston Beaneaters stoned in horse-drawn wagon after winning championship game in Pittsburgh.

1894
- Baltimore Orioles pitcher E. J. McNabb fatally shoots actress Louise Kellogg, his mistress and wife of Seattle ice merchant. He shoots himself twice in the mouth and dies at Pittsburgh hotel.
- South End Grounds burn in Boston while McGraw and Tommy Tucker fight at third base.

1895
- McGraw harasses rookie umpire Tim Keefe, calling him a drunkard. Keefe quits umpiring because it is "absolutely disagreeable."
- Cleveland Spiders defeat Baltimore Orioles in championship. Patsy Tebeau plays series in agony with boil beneath groin. Spiders are stoned in horse-drawn wagon in Baltimore streets.

1896
- Umpire Tim Keefe, back behind plate, has eight members of Cleveland Spiders placed under arrest during June game.
- Upset by abuse from New York Giants and St. Louis Browns, Keefe refuses to officiate a July game past fifth inning. Two players officiate final four innings.
- Amos Rusie of New York Giants sits out 1896 season. Dispute with owner Andrew Freedman is over $200.
- Drunken Patsy Tebeau beats up newspaper reporter who wrote unflattering stories.

1897
- McGraw and Willie Keeler in naked locker-room brawl. Keeler can't stand McGraw's constant belittlements.

1898
- National League owners set strict $2,400 salary cap. League tries—and fails—to control chronic brawling and filthy language through "Brush Resolution."
- Syndicate ownership agreements strip Cleveland Spiders of best players and send them to St. Louis.
- Baltimore's Keeler makes lunging outfield catch in Washington and is caught on barbed wire. He is left dangling by his uniform.
- Baltimore's Ducky Holmes calls New York Giants owner Andrew Freedman a "Sheeny."
- Freedman makes ninth managerial change in four seasons.

1899
- Cleveland Spiders, gutted by syndicate deal, are the worst team in baseball history. They win twenty games, lose 134, and finish last, eighty-four games out of first place.

Sportsmanship and easygoing methods are all right, but it is the prospect of a hot fight that brings out the crowds.
—John McGraw

Fight, fight, fight.

That's the way they played the game in the '90s, the punks who took over baseball. Players fought players. Fans fought fans. Fans fought players. And everybody terrorized the umpire, whose vilification was completed in this decade. You remember the umpire Billy McLean, the former prize fighter from Philadelphia, who hurled a bat at an abusive crowd in the glorious '80s? Well, this time around frustrated Billy stands before an entire grandstand and challenges everyone to come down onto the field and fight him. The most famous umpire of the '90s, a brawler named Timothy Hurst, once drew a pistol from his belt and fired it in the air to send a message to the hostile crowd. Another umpire, Tim Keefe, had eight members of the Cleveland Spiders ball club placed under arrest during a game in June 1896. The historians say young Keefe was thin-skinned. I say he was smart.

It was dangerous out there. A popular rhyme of the day was "Mother, May I Slug the Umpire?" Fans threw bottles and brickbats and beer mugs at umpires: "The umpire stands there as one defenseless man against thousands of pitiless foes," wrote the crusading journalist Henry Chadwick. To contain the fans and their barrages, the clubs built more of those tall barbed-wire fences in front of the grandstands—sort of the way we build better prisons today to keep prisoners at bay. Then in 1894, West Side Park in Chicago went up in smoke during a game and the fans were trapped between barbed wire and burning exits. Players had to hack the barbed wire down with baseball bats so the fans could escape.

This was anarchy.

*And take that!
Player belts
fan in Louisville.*

You recall the gambling and drinking of earlier decades?

Now it was worse. The boors were in power. Women wouldn't go near the ballpark.

You remember the aggressive play of Comiskey and the St. Louis Browns?

That was nothin' compared with the dirty, cheating, vicious brand of baseball that was perfected and popularized by the Cleveland Spiders and McGraw's old Baltimore Orioles. You only have to look at some of the nicknames from this period—"Dirty" Jack Doyle, "Scrappy" Bill Joyce, "Rowdy" Jack O'Connor—to get a feel for what was happening on the ball field.

A number of factors contributed to the ascendance of rowdy

baseball—"hoodlumism," journalist Chadwick branded it. These included the lack of central authority in baseball and the horrendous behavior of the many cheapskate owners who called the shots a century ago.

But before discussing these matters, I would like to propose another reason for the change. I don't mean to cause any problems in doing this, for I realize some may find my proposition to be insulting.

But let the truth be spoken: baseball changed because it was taken over by arrogant little men.

Facts are facts.

The stars of the 1880s tended to be large lumbering fellows:

Adrian "Cap" Anson stood six feet tall and weighed 227 pounds.

Dan Brouthers was six feet two and weighed 207 pounds.

Ol' Pete Browning was six feet tall and weighed a still substantial 180 pounds.

Now check out the shrimps—I mean, the stars—of the '90s:

John McGraw, foul-mouthed bullier of umpires, was all of five feet seven and 155 pounds.

"Wee Willie" Keeler, his hustling teammate, was a smidgeon over five feet four and a measly 140 pounds.

Oliver "Patsy" Tebeau, McGraw's clone on the Spiders, stood five feet eight and weighed 163 pounds.

Jesse "the Crab" Burkett, a three-time .400 hitter who played outfield for the Spiders, was five feet eight and 155 pounds. In one doubleheader, he started three fights, was thrown out of both games, and needed a police escort out of the stadium.

These cocky little guys with Napoleon complexes—McGraw was even known as "Little Napoleon"—changed the way the game was played. The "scientific game" emerged, dubbed "inside baseball." It was a game in which the opposing teams scratched and clawed their way to every run, looking for every possible advantage, no matter how slight. In fact, it was a game of survival and formed a neat metaphor for the hard-bitten life on the streets outside the ballpark. In 1893, there was a major depression which coincided with one of the Irish potato famines. Tremendous numbers of poor people were arriving in this country, and ballplayers were fighting for the same nickels to get by.

Inside baseball was a fast, aggressive game: set the runners in motion, steal bases, upset the defense. The hit-and-run play was popularized: historians like Bill James credit the Boston Beaneaters with its development, though it has often been attributed to McGraw, Keeler, and the Orioles. The "Baltimore chop"—by which the hitter deliberately chops the ball into the ground and runs like hell to first base to beat the throw—was a hallmark of the Baltimore offense and spread through the game. (The Orioles reputedly buried cement in front of home plate to affect a higher chop). Suddenly everybody was sliding hard, breaking up double plays, blocking home plate.

Pitchers were showing more sophistication: throwing rising curve balls, "in-shoots" and "out-shoots," pitches that dipped, broke, and hugged the corners, particularly the inside corner. They were tossing beanballs by the bundle. In 1899, James has computed, ninety-one batters were hit by pitches for every hundred games played. That's double the rate of hit batsmen that occurred in 1968; astounding inasmuch as '68 represented the zenith of pitcher dominance in modern baseball with intimidators like Bob Gibson and Juan Marichal in full force.

And so with inside baseball, we see the rise of a fast, aggressive, heavily strategized game.

Now add one more layer to it: the dirty stuff.

If a batter reached first base, he had a hard time getting around the bases to score. It was like running through a war zone. Particularly if he was playing against Cleveland or Baltimore.

There was still only one umpire officiating each game, and this wouldn't change until the first decade of the new century. Consequently, when the umpire wasn't looking, infielders blocked and tripped base runners and threw whatever obstacles they could find in front of them.

Intimidation ruled. Cleveland, a talent-rich club that could never quite win a pennant, had a shortstop named Ed McKean who excelled at "giving the runner the hip," according to a contemporary newspaper account. He once put a neck hold on an opponent "and threw him so hard that . . . his eyes stuck out of their sockets like doorknobs."

Kid Gleason, who played shortstop for the pennant-winning

Orioles in 1895 and went on to manage the 1919 Black Sox, liked to "low-bridge" the runner. In other words, he enjoyed throwing the ball directly at the forehead of anyone who tried to break up a double play.

McGraw, the Orioles' third baseman, was known for stepping on the feet of sliding base runners with his high-topped spiked shoes. He excelled at holding runners by the belt as they rounded the bag and headed home. If he was caught by the ump, McGraw would flip out.

"Who, me? Why, you yellow-eyed cur, I'll . . ."

Consider the fights that erupted under these conditions.

McGraw and Boston's Tommy Tucker once settled a score by squaring off at a distance of ten feet. Each held three balls which he then hurled at the other as hard as he could.

John Heydler, an ump who later became National League president, remembered the Orioles as "mean, vicious, ready at any time to maim a rival player or an umpire, if it helped their cause. The things they would say to an umpire were unbelievably vile, and they broke the spirits of some fine men. I've seen umpires bathe their feet by the hour after McGraw and others spiked them through their shoes. . . . I feel the lot of the umpires never was worse than in the years that the Orioles were flying high."

It sounds nightmarish and it was. "The baseball diamond is not supposed to be a gladiatorial arena," the *Sporting News* declared, "and spectators do not go to games to see men make brutes of themselves."

The irony is that the decade began with sweet dreams.

The Brotherhood, or Players League, was born in 1890. This rival to the National League attempted to cut players a better deal by paying them fair wages and sharing profits with them. Charles Comiskey, who would later metamorphose into the skinflint owner of the Chicago Black Sox, was among the superstars of the day who risked their livelihoods by joining the Brotherhood. The new league managed to set up franchises in many National League cities, and it outdrew the "big league" clubs over the course of the season.

On the field, the Brotherhood's high salaries assured aggressive, heads-up play and a minimum of violence—much like the millionaires who compete today, the well-compensated players of the Brotherhood didn't go out of their way to injure one another. Gambling was less of a temptation, because the players were satisfied with their paychecks. All in all, the Brotherhood represented a step forward for the game. But financing was shaky, and it went bankrupt after one year.

This left the National League with a single rival, the American Association. But not for long. The National League owners began bribing AA players to break their contracts. Players were constantly jumping from league to league. There was such confusion that when two members of the St. Louis Browns failed to show up for a game, their teammates assumed they were simply in transit to a new team in the other league. In fact, they were out on a toot with demon rum. One of them, Jack Stivetts, later said he didn't give a "continental dang" what the owner thought.

The next season, the entire St. Louis team *did* change leagues. This happened because the American Association went bankrupt. Four of its teams disappeared. The other four—St. Louis, Baltimore, Louisville, and Washington—were absorbed by the National League.

And that's how the National League became a twelve-team monopoly starting in 1892. It was the age of monopolies: Rockefeller, Carnegie, J. P. Morgan. Why shouldn't baseball get into the act?

The owners got nasty and started turning the screws. They cut salaries and later established a strict $2,400 salary cap. In the 1880s, lots of players had managed to circumvent salary caps by reaching agreements for under-the-table bonuses. This was no longer possible, because the club owners of the 1890s ruled like feudal lords. The players were their serfs and were paid the chintziest salaries in the game's history.

This was the worst time to be a major league ballplayer. Ever.

The players were desperate to improve their lot. They designed strategies to make names for themselves with the public and the press. They plotted how to coax a few extra dollars from cruel owners who were otherwise impossible to impress.

There was only one way to do it: by getting rowdy.

And as it turned out, the owners loved it, encouraged it. Here was a way, they thought, to increase gate receipts: Take Me Out to the Brawl Game!

There was no central authority in baseball to control the

rowdyism. The National League president was a mere figurehead. In this vacuum, the players were free to punch, kick, swear, and basically behave like criminals on the diamond.

Even Connie Mack, mythologized as the game's ultimate gentleman, caught the disease. At mid-decade, Mack's Pittsburgh pitching staff included Frank Killen and Pink Hawley, two of the supreme beanballers of the day. Mr. Mack, despite his lily-white image, condoned rough tactics throughout his career. And he cheated. He froze baseballs—about as easy to hit as wooden croquet balls—and snuck them into the game when his pitchers took the mound. He hid a spy inside the center field scoreboard to steal signs from opposing catchers. And he was caught.

Baseball was at war with itself. Once again, even as they let the game go to the dogs, the owners tried to achieve a measure of respectability. The New York teams scheduled 4 P.M. ball games to attract the well-heeled Wall Street crowd. "Suburban day" promotions were held by various clubs to draw a gentler breed of fan. A hundred years later, academics still argue about the composition of the fans in the stands. Were they predominantly middle-class? Blue-collar?

What's the difference? Given the brand of baseball promoted on the diamond, the fans were going to riot regardless of their backgrounds.

In 1893, the Boston Beaneaters were stoned in their horse-drawn wagon after winning a championship game in Pittsburgh: "Pitcher Kid Nichols was struck six times about the head and outfielder Hugh Duffy was hit in the face," writes the scholar David Q. Voigt. The Cleveland Spiders, he notes, were mobbed twice after a championship game in Baltimore in 1894: first the mob drove the Spiders from the field, then the fans stoned the team as its carriage left for the hotel. It was the normal state of affairs for John McGraw to incite the near-homicidal behavior of Baltimore Kranks: "McGraw was accused of inciting Baltimore fans to hurl beer glasses at rival outfielders. And Chicago manager Pop Anson lamented, 'I don't see how any team can win in Baltimore.'"

The All-American Anson got with the spirit before too long, though. When a rival player slid safely into first base during a game in 1897, Anson reached down and punched the prostrate man in the head.

"What is the game coming to when a player like Anson acts disgracefully on the ball field?" one reporter asked after the incident. "How can the tough element be expected to behave when a manager and captain, who is held up to them as a model in deportment on and off the field, sets them a bad example?"

The owners attempted to salvage things by instituting a system of fines and suspensions for chronic brawlers and brayers of "villainously filthy language." This was called the "Brush Resolution," after Cincinnati owner John T. Brush. It didn't work. Fans had tired of the violence and obscenity, but the players were incorrigible. The fire at Sportsman's Park in 1898, only one in a series of ballpark blazes, injured a hundred fans and raised safety concerns about the game.

Attendance was dropping badly.

The game was going downhill.

We will finish with an image of John McGraw, drawn from his biography by Charles C. Alexander.

In mid-September 1899, McGraw was newly widowed; barely two weeks had passed since his twenty-two-year-old wife, Minnie, died from a ruptured appendix. But McGraw was already back at work, coaching at third base for Baltimore in a game against Brooklyn. The Orioles had a runner, Bill Keister, on first base

Now McGraw called to Brooklyn pitcher Bill "Brickyard" Kennedy to "let him see the ball. The unthinking Kennedy threw over to McGraw, who smilingly stepped aside and watched the ball roll to the grandstand fence. Keister ran to second and then scored."

Up yours, friend.

National Baseball Library

Adrian "Pop" Anson helped instigate the game's first color line and wasn't above punching a sliding base runner in the head.

Chadwickisms

Henry "Father" Chadwick pioneered baseball journalism. He wrote the first history of the game. He devised the box score. He essentially invented the method of scoring that you and I still use whenever we open a scorecard and record the progress of a ball game.

The British-born Chadwick was also the national game's first stalwart guardian. He witnessed the birth of professional baseball, helped guide it through adolescence as a member of various rules committees, and came to fear for the game as it entered adulthood.

As editor of the *Spalding Guide* from 1881 to 1908, Chadwick railed against gambling, drunkenness, meddling owners, and rowdy players. He was offended by the endless "kicking" against the umpire—the constant bellowing against every unpopular call—and the vile language that was part of it.

His 1895 edition of the *Spalding Guide* was a classic. It's hard to say whether his reference to the killings of umpires is real or apocryphal—apparently at least one ump was fatally assaulted in the minor leagues in the last century. Perhaps Chadwick knew more than we do today.

Here are some excerpts.

ON THE DANGERS OF UMPIRING

"There he stands, close behind the catcher and batsman, where he is required to judge whether the swiftly thrown balls from the pitcher, with its erratic "curves" and "shoots," dart in over the home base, or within the legal range of the bat. The startling fact is never considered that several umpires have been killed outright while occupying this dangerous position. Neither does any one reflect for a moment that the umpire occupies this perilous position while regarded as a common enemy by both of the contesting teams, and as a legitimate object for insulting abuse from the partisan portion of the crowd of spectators. In fact, the umpire stands there as the one defenseless man against thousands of pitiless foes."

ON ROWDY PLAY

"There was but one drawback to the creditable success of the entire championship campaigns of 1894, and that was the unwonted degree of 'hoodlumism' which disgraced the season. . . .

"Much of the 'hoodlumism'—a technical term applicable to the use of *blackguard language; low cunning tricks,* unworthy of manly players; *brutal assaults* on umpire and players; that nuisance of our ball fields, 'kicking,' and the dishonorable methods comprised in the term *'dirty ball playing'*—indulged in in 1894 was largely due to the advocacy of the method of the so-called *'aggressive policy,'* which countenanced rowdy ball playing . . . such as spiking or wilfully colliding with a base runner; bellowing like a wild bull at the pitcher. . . .

"Managers and captains were alike guilty. . . . Is it any wonder that the season of 1894 stands on record as being marked by more disgraceful kicking, rowdy play, blackguard language and brutal play than that of any season since the League was organized?"

ON MEDDLING OWNERS

"There is a class of club officials in the League who, for the life of them, cannot keep from interfering with the club's legitimate manager in his running of the team. Some of them have the cool effrontery of stating that 'the manager of our team is never interfered with in any way.' . . . It is all nonsense for a club to place a manager in the position with a merely nominal control of the players and then to hold him responsible for the non-success of the team in winning games."

ON DRINKING

"Year after year drinking offenses are condoned by the club officials, and old time drunkards re-engaged for the coming season. . . . Why managers cannot perceive the folly of re-engaging such men is a mystery. No matter what their skill at the bat or in the field may be, their drinking habits, with the demoralizing effect on the teams at large which follows, more than offset the advantage of their alleged ability in the field. Despite this obvious fact, however, club officials . . . still blunder on in having these drunkards on their teams, even after condoning their offenses time and again, on the promise of reform, which in no single instance has ever taken place that I am aware of."

The 1890s

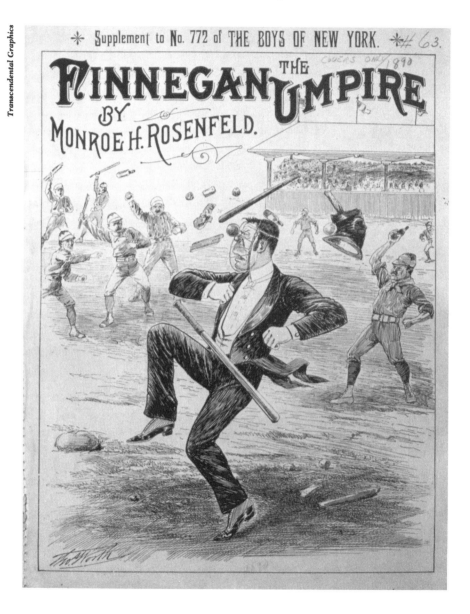

John McGraw was a thug: the nastiest, most pugnacious, lying, irascible SOB you can imagine.

He grew up in a small upstate New York town, Truxton, one of nine brothers and sisters. When he was eleven, a diphtheria epidemic rolled through town. By the time it left, McGraw's mother and four siblings were dead. His father, John McGraw, Sr., was an Irish immigrant, fairly well educated, hard pressed in his dead-end job as a railroad maintenance worker. When John Jr. collected stones from the railroad bed and pounded them with a stick to hone his batting skills, his father whipped him for wasting time better spent on chores.

Baseball was an escape, but it brought punishment.

During his forty years as player and manager in the major leagues, McGraw played a punishing brand of baseball and taught his teams to do the same. With the possible exception of Ty Cobb, he was the most dominant figure in the professional game's first half century. His importance—or notoriety—rests on his dual role as strategist and teacher, and on his total willingness to test the limits of acceptable behavior on the ball field. And for McGraw, rest assured, there were very few limits that mattered as long as his actions helped to score a run or win a game. Ty Cobb was famous for saying baseball was a war. But if Cobb was a lone commando, McGraw was a guerrilla leader: "Show me a team of fighters," he declared, "and I'll show you a team that has a chance."

In his first game with Baltimore in 1892, his teammates pushed him off the Orioles' bench. McGraw, who didn't like to be mocked, came up swinging. The next spring, in an exhibition game in Chattanooga, according to Charles C. Alexander's excellent biography, "McGraw, playing shortstop, held a runner by the belt to keep him from advancing on a fly ball, spiked the opposition shortstop sliding into second, and slapped a sliding Chattanooga runner in the face with the ball, bloodying his nose. By the time the game ended, a good portion of the crowd was ready to assault the tough kid with the Baltimores."

McGraw became the club's exemplar as it institutionalized violence on the diamond through the '90s: "McGraw eats gunpowder every morning and washes it down with warm blood," commented Arlie Latham. The sharpened spikes of McGraw, Jennings, and Keeler exemplified the scrappy, rough-hewn playing style—later extended to a further extreme by Cobb—that dominated the game until the advent of Babe Ruth and the long ball around 1920.

McGraw was unscrupulous. He publicly accused a rookie umpire, Tim Keefe, of being drunk during games. It wasn't true, but that meant nothing to McGraw, who got his satisfaction when Keefe, twenty-five, quit his job rather than face such an aspersion again. McGraw insulted everybody, including his own teammates. His persistent beratement of Willie Keeler led to a naked brawl between the two on the floor of the Baltimore locker room. There was a savage confidence about McGraw. Predicting success for himself early in his Baltimore career, he wrote to a friend, "Just give me a little time and I have got 'em skinned to death."

But lost amid the discussions of McGraw's violence are his talents as a player. He batted .300 or more for nine straight seasons. From 1894 to 1896, when the Orioles won successive pennants, he batted .340, .369, and .325. McGraw's lifetime .460 on-base percentage is the highest of any nineteenth-century ballplayer—and the third-highest in the history of the major leagues after Ted Williams and the Babe himself.

He was a valuable man to have around. But he also missed a lot of games because of injuries and sickness. In fact, McGraw played only three complete, or nearly complete, seasons in his sixteen-year playing career—surprising for someone who did so much to promote the macho play-with-pain mystique of the old-time ballplayer.

How do you solve a puzzle like McGraw?

As a young man, he seemed to be two people: the good Catholic boy who attended St. Bonaventure College in the off-season and the reckless, whooping mugger of the ball field.

If you read the various biographies of McGraw, if you immerse yourself in old news clippings about him, you will find stories of his loyalty and compassion in the later years, giving pocket money and jobs to down-on-their-heels old-timers, trying to reform the drunken sots who played for him.

But that all forms a subtext to the predominant truths about McGraw: that his friends were gamblers and criminals; that his racetrack obsession rivaled his love of the ballpark; that he was often mean and violent, an umpire baiter who brought people to tears, and whose life was characterized by brawls, mob scenes, and crude behavior.

You've read about how McGraw contributed to the development of the strategies of "scientific" baseball. When to steal. When to bunt. When to hit the cutoff man. It was a detail-oriented

Meet John McGraw, whose rowdy play epitomized what went wrong with the game in the 1890s.

approach, designed to fit the situation at hand; here was the beginning of modern baseball strategy by which a manager like Tony LaRussa attempts to consider all variables in a given situation before making even the most inconsequential decision in a ball game.

But McGraw extended the "scientific" approach to matters that La Russa would never even consider: the verbal and even physical abuse of opponents, fans, and umpires. Truly a psychologist, "Mugsy" McGraw learned how to push an opposing player's buttons like *so*. How much taunting could this particular pitcher take and when might it become counterproductive? How could he tweak a rival crowd to increase ballpark tension and give his team a rush of adrenaline? How far could he push an umpire? Could he tease him? Step on his shoes? Spit in his face? How would the spectators react?

This became a science like any other aspect of the game for McGraw. "He has the vilest tongue of any ballplayer," a reporter complained. "He adopts every low and contemptible method that his erratic brain can conceive to win a play by a dirty trick."

The umps hated him. The fans outside Baltimore hated him. He had enemies among players throughout the league. Quite a few would literally have liked to kill him.

McGraw opposed all fraternization with the opposition. If you were on the other team, you were the *enemy*. He carried this attitude over into the next century. Be warned: his New York Giants were wild men, reminiscent of the old Orioles. You will meet them in another chapter.

Patsy Tebeau

History has shortchanged Oliver "Patsy" Tebeau.
His star was eclipsed over the decades by John McGraw's,
even though he was McGraw's nemesis and played an equal role in the
trashing of the game. Maybe that's because Tebeau's Cleveland Spiders
finished a perennial second to McGraw's Baltimore Orioles during the
years that their scrapping, cursing brawl clubs dominated baseball. Or
maybe it's because McGraw's legend kept growing during his
thirty-one-year ride as manager of the New York Giants, whereas
Tebeau's faded in St. Louis, where he retired to run a saloon shortly
after his playing days ended and eventually killed himself.

But in their heyday, Tebeau and McGraw enjoyed almost
interchangeable reputations as revolutionary cutthroats, the
Robespierre and Danton of baseball. Innovators of the new rowdy
game, each was field captain of his renegade club, and when the two
teams met, "wild war raged up and down the field."

Tebeau belonged "to the blood and iron brigade of baseball," his
obituary read, "and was in his glory when the game was not for
weaklings, either of heart or muscle." In 1895, the second-place
Spiders took on the first-place Orioles in the Temple Cup, the World
Series of the time. During game one in Cleveland, fans "threw
vegetables at the Orioles as they tried to catch fly balls," author Charles
C. Alexander tells us, "and stood behind McGraw shouting 'Dirty
McGraw,' 'Hoodlum,' 'Tough.' " Cleveland won, then traveled to
Baltimore for game two, where street toughs showered their carriage
with rocks and bricks. The Spiders lay on the floor "with their mitts
over their heads" for protection. On the field, during a play at third
base, "McGraw slammed the ball into Tebeau's face and split his lip.
'Good boy, McGraw!' yelled the bleacher kranks."

The Spiders won that game, too, and went on to take the series
four games to one. Tebeau demonstrated his fortitude, the newspapers
later reported, by playing "with a boil that had broken under his groin.

76

*The
1890s*

*Leader of
the brawling
Cleveland
Spiders,
Oliver "Patsy"
Tebeau did
as much to trash
the game as
his nemesis
McGraw.*

COPYRIGHTED 1888 BY
GOODWIN & CO. N.Y.

Oliver Tebeau, 3 B. Cleveland

OLD JUDGE CIGARETTES Goodwin & Co., New York.

Every move was agony. Each day when he went to the clubhouse his uniform was clotted with blood."

Tebeau, like McGraw, truly hated his opponents. The fanny-patting that goes on today in baseball would have been an affront to him. Nor did he sidle up to rival crowds; "friendliness by fans in the opposition city indicated to his mind that his team wasn't putting up the battle it should." Better that enemy fans should "throw pop bottles at him throughout the entire games," one reporter wrote in an appreciation following Tebeau's death. The unshakable Tebeau "would not deign to turn his head to satisfy an assailant."

Nor did he approve when Cleveland second baseman Cupid Childs, who lived in Baltimore, was honored by friends during a game at the Orioles' park. Between innings, with Cleveland ahead by six runs, Childs's chums presented him with a big horseshoe of flowers. Tebeau "took in the scene with a frown, grumbling under his breath," the writer recalled. When the Orioles scored eight runs in the next inning, partially because of Child's blunders at second, Tebeau "rushed to the bench, grabbed Childs's floral horseshoe and tearing it asunder threw the mutilated emblem with all his force into the grandstand right among Childs's friends.

77

Patsy Tebeau

" 'There's your flowers,' " he roared, " 'and the next bunch of (blank) that give flowers to one of me players I'll—I'll fire the player off me club and his damn friends can keep him if they like him so well.' "

But Patsy had his tender moments.

From time to time in the history of the game there have been Jekyll-Hyde characters who carry on like terrorists on the field, but behave like gentlemen outside the ballpark, eager to give a child a pat on the head and maybe even an autograph. Eddie Stanky, years later, was this type of ballplayer. And so was Tebeau in his time: one purple obituary described him as "so lamblike of demeanor that one would hardly single him out for the doughty warrior whose sultry diction, frescoed in sulphurous blue, has started the wheels revolving 'neath the cap of many a twirler."

He was born in St. Louis in 1864 and grew up in the Goose Hill district which became famous for spawning ballplayers. Tebeau's childhood friends included "Scrappy" Bill Joyce and "Rowdy" Jack O'Connor. One wonders: would a nine-year-old dare to low-bridge the runner? It could have happened in Goose Hill.

Tebeau's minor league career started in 1885. Two years later, he caught the attention of Cap Anson of the Chicago White Stockings and

Tebeau joined the club. But a line drive straight into his gut finished him for the season, and it wasn't until 1889 that Tebeau returned to the National League with Cleveland. He started as a third baseman but switched to first base, where, despite his shortness, he became an exceptional fielder. Tebeau was a fiercely aggressive base runner, given to flashing his sharpened spikes, and a more than passable hitter, with a .280 lifetime batting average.

He was also the Spiders' manager for eight years, starting in 1890. When he led the team to the World Series in 1892, there were only eleven men on the squad. Try to imagine the injuries they were forced to endure, with only two reserve players sitting on the bench. Tebeau set the tough tone for the team, browbeating opposing pitchers, hurling baseballs out of ballparks in fits of anger, once threatening to put an ump in the hospital if he didn't leave the park for making an unpopular call. The ump said he "wouldn't officiate any longer for hoodlums" and left.

All of this sat well with the fans for a while, and Tebeau won the affections of "every red-blooded man who loved a fighter."

But the inevitable backlash came as the decade wore on. Fans tired of the circus and journalists rendered stern judgments.

The aging Henry Chadwick wrote in 1896 that Tebeau degraded the game more than any player of the previous quarter century. Patsy represented "evil in the ranks which aims a death blow at the permanent existence of the league itself." Chadwick chastised Cleveland owner Frank Robison for resisting league efforts to punish Tebeau for his antics. And he accused the magnate of promoting rowdyism by aligning himself "with mad furor on the side of blackguardism."

In 1898, the league tried to muzzle Tebeau and other "bench jockeys" who teased and cursed their opponents to the point of distraction with "sulphurous blue" epithets. "My esteemed friend Chadwick," Tebeau conceded, tongue in cheek, "used to indulge in considerable flower-tossing at my expense, charging that I abused the young pitchers by word-of-mouth inelegancies." Such "inelegancies" were the target of the "Brush Resolution," which levied heavy fines and suspensions on big-mouth players. Its short-term effect was to silence Tebeau and the other culprits: "I figured that the restriction would save me a heap of unnecessary conversation," Tebeau joked. "I was led to believe the patrons wanted a change and were in favor of quiet speechless ball, something after the fashion of a deaf mute reunion."

But the players soon returned to old habits.

Tebeau was sent home to St. Louis to play for the Cardinals in 1899. The following year, his last, he managed John McGraw, who was his third baseman for a short while. The arrangement didn't work out. Tebeau was convinced that a "double-cross" was in the works to ease him out as manager and bring in McGraw. He quit, even though this wasn't the case, and never returned to baseball. Friends tried recruiting him to the front office of one team or another, but he always resisted. "I'm not one of those fancy guys," he explained. "They'll never put me on one of those swinging chairs."

Patsy Tebeau

He opened his saloon instead. It was a respectable joint in the financial district that catered to bankers and closed early. Over the years, Tebeau became a successful businessman, and he was always a figure of note in town. But when his wife left him, moving to Cleveland with their children, he became morose.

The night of May 14, 1918, he shot himself in the head. His body was found in the saloon the next morning. Tebeau, 53, left a suicide note, describing himself as "a very unhappy and miserable man."

His death was announced in the local paper under the headline "Patsy Tebeau Acts as His Own Umpire."

Andrew Freedman

If you were to travel a century back in time, you would find a man who behaved as if he were George Steinbrenner's previous incarnation. And you would find him in New York. His name was Andrew Freedman and he owned the New York Giants. Like Steinbrenner, Freedman knew nothing about baseball; like Steinbrenner, he insisted he knew everything about baseball. Just like Steinbrenner, Freedman befriended crooked politicians; fired managers willy-nilly; bullied his players; bullied the press; poisoned the loyalties of long-time fans; and wound up the most hated man in New York City.

Freedman was born in 1860, worked in his parents' grocery business, and became a successful real estate investor after graduating from college. He joined Tammany Hall, the Democratic political organization, while in his early twenties and astutely penetrated the machine. The close connections Freedman established with Tammany honchos ensured his later success as a financier. He made the bonding arrangements for construction of the New York City subway. This was probably his crowning achievement, although there was another that might have equaled it: using his political muscle, he stopped the American League from establishing a New York franchise to compete with the Giants while he owned the club.

He had bought a controlling interest in the Giants in 1895 and attempted to apply his high-powered, bottom-line business practices to the club. "He was a genius for construction and success," wrote Pittsburgh reporter A. R. Cratty, "and . . . couldn't brook restraint. He sought to conduct a ball team on the same lines as other business ventures. Whenever a man's work didn't suit him it was off with his head."

Freedman's first victim was the team's best pitcher, Amos Rusie, a superstar. They feuded over $200 in fines. Freedman, whose penny-pinching became the talk of the city, refused to clear the matter up, Rusie had the most disappointing season of his career, and the team fell from second place to ninth. Rusie refused to play the next season and the team finished seventh. He returned in 1897 and guided the Giants back to third place. But the team never won a championship while Freedman was owner, for the club experienced constant upsets and emotional turmoil.

In his seven years as owner, Freedman fired managers sixteen times. His capriciousness led to fighting with journalists, whom Freedmen then barred from the Polo Grounds; one reporter, Charley Dryden, bought a ticket to the grandstand and was still denied entrance. The owner was difficult to interview, for he "never let you get away from the idea that he was a New Yorker," complained Cratty. "His whole attitude demanded sort of homage because he was from the big burg on the island."

By 1898, Charles C. Alexander writes, "Freedman had become the storm center of the National League." The other owners despised him, though they were not really very different in their management styles. Freedman's high-handed bearing, infernal meddling, and personality clashes all served to alienate the New York public: "Freedman is held responsible for ruining the game in the metropolis through his arbitrary methods," the *Utica Globe* stated in 1899, "and many believe that with another man at the helm the game could regain its old-time prestige there."

Freedman's outsider status as a Jew certainly had something to do with the controversy around him. It didn't make him unique: Pittsburgh owner Barney Dreyfuss was Jewish, as were the co-owners of the Brooklyn club. And Freedman appears to have been forthright in demanding respect for his

Andrew Freedman

Transcendental Graphics

The most hated man in New York circa 1895: Giants owner Andrew Freedman.

religious background. There was a famous incident in which Orioles outfielder Ducky Holmes, formerly a Giant, returned to the Polo Grounds and shouted to an old teammate, "I'm glad I'm not working for a Sheeny anymore." Freedman, hearing this while seated in his box near home plate, asked the ump to eject Holmes. Getting no satisfaction, he pulled the Giants off the field and forfeited the game.

Joe Vila, a popular sportswriter for the *New York Morning Sun,* detested Freedman. He had plenty of reasons to do so that had nothing to do with religion. But the underlying message in the following dispatch seems to be that Vila was disgusted by Freedman's Jewish features and viewed the owner stereotypically as an insincere conniver:

"Freedman went to the races the other day. He carried a pair of field glasses that looked like a couple of ten-inch guns. He was using that old con smile of his on all sides when suddenly he caught sight of yours truly. The transformation was wonderful. His eyes bulged like hard-boiled eggs, the froth came from his ruby lips, and the snorting from his nose sounded like a new automobile out for a spin. But he won $2 on the next race and his anger disappeared."

Freedman hadn't many friends in the baseball business during his final two years as owner of the Giants. His plan to enact syndicate control over the National League was killed by the other owners during the winter meetings of 1901–1902. Then Freedman shifted focus to fight with Ban Johnson, president of the newly formed American League. Johnson was looking for a site to build a ballpark for the AL's New York Highlanders, who would later become the Yankees. Through his Tammany influence and real estate connections, Freedman scoped out all the potential sites and threatened to have streets built through the middle of them.

But he was outmaneuvered after the Tammany crowd suffered election losses to a new reform slate. By courting the new folks in city hall, Johnson found a site up on 168th Street, across the Harlem River from the Polo Grounds.

Freedman got back at Johnson anyway.

The Baltimore Orioles were an American League team now. Their manager was John McGraw, whose rough-and-ready play was exactly what Johnson didn't want in the new league. McGraw and Johnson hated each other. And McGraw was sure he would be booted from the league after the 1902 season.

Freedman, always politically aware, put out feelers to see if McGraw might want to come and manage the Giants in the National League. The two met privately. And in July 1902, Freedman pulled one of his most outrageous maneuvers: he bought just over 50 percent of the Orioles' stock. To use today's terminology, he pulled a corporate takeover. Freedman granted unconditional releases to Baltimore's best players, including McGraw, put them on a train to New York, and signed them to midseason contracts with the Giants. The Orioles were left with five players—they couldn't even field a team.

Ban Johnson, who took a proprietary interest in every club in the American League, looked like a chump. And thanks to Freedman, McGraw was ready to terrorize the National League for another thirty-one years.

Later that summer, Freedman sold the Giants to former Cincinnati Reds owner John T. Brush. There are two theories about this: one says that Freedman was forced out of the league because the other owners had come to view him as a menace; the other says he simply wanted to move on to the big subway bonding deal. A thorn in Johnson's butt to the end, he almost blocked construction of the 168th Street station.

Freedman died in 1915 at age fifty-five, a lifelong bachelor with a $7 million fortune.

83

Andrew
Freedman

Amos Rusie

What is it that makes a pitcher scary? A bullet fastball? A knockdown pitch?

I asked Pat Jordan, the former minor league pitcher turned sportswriter and journalist. He answered that speed helps. But a good major league batter will hold his own against almost anyone—except a pitcher who is consistently a little bit wild. That, Jordan said, is the type of pitcher who makes a batter think to himself, "Hey, this xxxx guy doesn't know *where* the ball's going."

Which brings us to Amos Rusie. Batters feigned injuries to avoid hitting against this man.

He was fast.

And man, was he wild.

First, Rusie's speed. People paid to watch him throw baseballs through the panels of a wooden fence at the Tennessee State Fair when he was in his mid-teens. In 1889, at the age of seventeen, the Hoosier Thunderbolt, as he was known, made the majors. His first catcher slipped a slab of lead covered with a handkerchief and sponge inside his glove for protection against Rusie's heat.

Rusie's fastballs were legend: "You can't hit what you can't see," said John McGraw. When one of his fastballs hit McGraw's Baltimore teammate Hughie Jennings on the head, the batter dropped to the ground, Rusie's own wife testified, "like a sack of cornmeal. Everyone in the park thought he was dead."

It was largely because of Rusie that the National League, in 1893, increased the distance between batter and pitcher from fifty feet to the present sixty feet six inches.

Now, Rusie's wildness. In nine full seasons, eight of them spent with the New York Giants, he was the league's strikeout leader five times. More important, each year he walked nearly as many batters as he whiffed, sometimes more.

Here are some numbers:

1889: 109 strikeouts; 116 walks
1890: 341 strikeouts; 289 walks
1891: 337 strikeouts; 262 walks
1892: 288 strikeouts; 267 walks
1893: 208 strikeouts; 218 walks
1894: 195 strikeouts; 200 walks
1895: 201 strikeouts; 159 walks
1897: 135 strikeouts; 87 walks
1898: 114 strikeouts; 103 walks

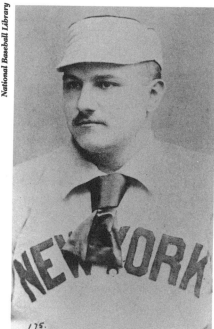

National Baseball Library

Amos Rusie

**Hitters were terrified
of Amos Rusie's fastball.**

Rusie kept those batters loose.

His combination of speed and wildness—and his ill-tempered, taciturn disposition—made him the most terrifying pitcher of the era. And one of its most successful. Rusie won a total of 245 games and lost 174. After Kid Nichols and Cy Young, he was probably the best pitcher of the 1890s.

His career ended in 1901 when the Giants traded him to Cincinnati for Christy Mathewson. Rusie pitched three games for the Reds, then retired to a life of odd jobs, booze, and bankruptcy. In 1930, twelve years before his death, he was jailed for driving his invalid wife into the street outside their home in Seattle and threatening to kill her.

But Rusie's character flaws were long forgotten by 1977 when he was posthumously elected to the Hall of Fame.

The Amos 'n' Andy Show

A mos Rusie won thirty-six games against thirteen losses in 1894. His 2.78 ERA was about half that of the National League average of 5.32. He led the team to victory in the Temple Cup championship series against Baltimore, winning two more games in a four-game sweep.

Then in walked Andrew Freedman, who bought the Giants in 1895.

You remember the disagreements between New York Yankees outfielder Dave Winfield and owner George Steinbrenner a few years back? The antipathy between Rusie and Freedman was similar. The papers hotly covered the escalating dispute. And Freedman, like Steinbrenner, wouldn't back off, even though it hurt the team.

First Freedman fined Rusie $100 for a curfew violation. Rusie insisted he'd been in bed by 11 P.M.

Then Freedman fined him another $100 for thumbing his nose at the owner from the mound. Rusie said he didn't do it.

Small potatoes. But the pitcher's performance fell off. He won twenty-three and lost twenty-three, and his ERA jumped to 3.73 that year.

When Freedman mailed him a contract for the 1896 season, Rusie asked for his $200 in fines back.

Freedman refused, so Rusie refused to sign, and proceeded to sit out the 1896 season.

Then Rusie sued Freedman in federal court for $5,000, which didn't faze Andy. The league's other owners, however, were horrified. They feared the court would invalidate Rusie's contract, dissolving the reserve clause that bound him to the Giants. Were this to happen, the entire reserve clause system would be called into question, potentially undermining the salary structure of the game.

"Look, why don't we settle this matter sensibly?" the owners asked Rusie, pooling their money, and handing the pitcher his $5,000.

Freedman didn't contribute a dime.

Rusie returned to the Giants in 1897 and pitched well. He was a young man, only twenty-six, and should have been entering his prime. But after another season, he began a slow fade from the game.

As for the Giants, they never regained their equilibrium after the dispute. With Freedman as navigator, the team went into the toilet and didn't reemerge until after he sold the club in 1902.

The Amos 'n' Andy Show

Macho Man: Umpire Timothy Hurst

Umpire Timothy Hurst knew how to intimidate Patsy Tebeau and the old Cleveland Spiders. Those rowdy men liked to argue boisterously, stick their pusses in an umpire's face, and step on his feet with their spikes. "Hurst broke up that practice," *Sporting Life* magazine said. "A couple of the infielders were large, fat men with overlapping stomachs. When one of these athletes attacked him verbally, Tim would reach forth and nip a roll of fat between the second joints of his index and middle fingers and twist.

"Tim used to practice this grip on the mattress in his room until he could twist a piece out of the ticking. Persons in the stand used to wonder why Ed McKean, Tebeau, and Cupid Childs should bend double and hop backward. Hurst made no violent demonstration with the corkscrew hand and the other was usually held up in a warning manner. At the same time he had nipped off a chunk of meat sufficient to feed a lapdog.

"Sometimes an athlete forgot the first treatment and tackled Tim on another occasion. The second was a complete cure."

Outfield Encounters

The Brooklyn Bridegrooms of 1891 included Scissors Foutz at first, Hub Collins at second, and Oyster Burns in right field. Good names or what? When a fly ball looped over the heads of Scissors and Hub toward Oyster during a game with the New York Giants in July 1891, two of these men fell.

The papers reported that Roger Connor of the Giants hit the fly "to short right field, and Collins and Burns ran for it. A screeching Long Island engine rushed past just outside the grounds, so it could not be heard which player Captain Ward ordered to take the ball.

"Take it, Hub," yelled Burns.

Collins started full speed for the ball.

"They came together face to face with a crash, and a cry of horror went up as both men fell to the ground as if each had been struck by a mammoth club. Each man lay unconscious, while blood spurted from their eyes, nostrils, and ears.

"Women shrieked and the other players rushed to aid their comrades. They were still unconscious and were tenderly carried from the field and physicians summoned."

And what happened to the injured parties? Those boys were tough. The odds say they were back in uniform the next afternoon.

The Hall of Flame

Major league ballparks burned eight times during the 1890s. This was the era of wooden grandstands, and fires were almost an accepted part of the business. The grounds crew would roll up an oil-soaked tarpaulin and store it beneath the stands. A gentleman in the crowd would drop his stogie and—whoosh! There went the stadium. No big deal. The old wooden parks were rebuilt quickly and at relatively small expense.

The tradition of baseball conflagrations reached back to Chicago's Great Fire of 1871, which destroyed the White Stockings ballpark along with much of the city. In 1892, lightning struck League Park in Cleveland during a game between the Spiders and Chicago Colts. The stadium flared and the game was canceled; I don't know about rain checks. In 1894, things really got hot. Three parks burned in the course of three months, and two on consecutive days, feeding false rumors that a baseball arsonist was moving from city to city.

On May 15, fire broke out in the right field bleachers at Boston's elegant South End Grounds—the most celebrated stadium of its day. The flames crept around the park and consumed the ornate, multispired grandstand behind home plate while John McGraw and the Beaneaters' Tommy Tucker slugged it out at third base. This fire *was* started by an arsonist, feeding the aforementioned rumors.

The second blaze of 1894 occurred at West Side Park in Chicago on August 5. Here's how historian Lloyd Johnson, formerly senior researcher at the National Baseball Library in Cooperstown, described the episode: "A cigar stub carelessly tossed into rubbish ignited the blaze and consumed the side stands. About 1,600 fans were imperiled as they rushed to the top of the stands to get a better view of the flames. The spectators soon realized they were hemmed between the fire and the high barbed-wire fences that kept people from encroaching on the diamond. The Chicago Colts' Jimmy Ryan and Walt Wilmot came to the rescue. Using baseball bats, they hacked through the fence to make a passageway onto the field. Flames completely engulfed the stands as the last man jostled through the opening. After fencing off the burned portion, the grounds were used the next day."

The next day, August 6, a plumber's stove ignited a fire that consumed the Philadelphia Baseball Grounds, home of the Phillies. At this point, the arson hotline must have gone haywire.

Public confidence was once more undermined on April 16, 1898, when a fast-moving fire destroyed Sportsman's Park, home of the St. Louis Browns, in half an hour. Lloyd Johnson recounts the disaster: "An angry flame was spotted beneath the grandstand during the second inning. A man yelled, 'Fire!' and panic from the 400 women seated in the main stand ensued. 'Without hesitation the men had caught the women up in their arms and hurled them over the railing into the field. Most of them were caught,' writes *Sporting Life*. A lit cigar tossed by a careless fan into a mass of tarpaulins that was lying beneath the grandstand was the suspected cause of the blaze. The fire destroyed St. Louis Browns owner Chris Von der Ahe's apartment, saloon, and memorabilia of the team's championship years. No one was fatally injured."

However, about a hundred fans were hurt, making this baseball's worst fire disaster.

Sportsman's Park was replaced by Robison Field as the new home of the Browns, who were renamed the Cardinals in honor of their bright red uniforms. In the bottom of the tenth inning on May 4, 1901, the Cardinals were rallying against Cincinnati when flames erupted in the grandstand. Fans lifted the crippled Cincinnati owner John T. Brush in his wheelchair and carried him hand over hand to safety. Remarkably, no one was injured by the fire, which was ignited by a lighted cigarette tossed into a rubbish pile. But there was a dramatic escape scene, Johnson writes, as "the Lindell Avenue street car line plunged through a sea of flames as it carried fans away from the burning structure. Umpire Dwyer lost a suit of clothing and a roll of money in the flames."

Baseball fires didn't subside until the new generation of big concrete-and-steel stadiums was built. Parks like Forbes Field (1909), Shibe Park (1909), and the Polo Grounds (rebuilt in 1911) were less cozy and intimate than their predecessors. They increased the distance between players and fans, decreased the chances that kids would get to know their heroes, and generally accelerated the depersonalization of the game.

But at least they didn't burn.

And now, the roll call of the Hall of Flame:

League Park, Cleveland (Spiders), May 29, 1892, Lightning
Eclipse Park, Louisville (Colonels), September 27, 1892, Cause not known
South End Grounds, Boston (Beaneaters), May 15, 1894, Arson
West Side Park, Chicago (Colts), August 5, 1894, Cigar
Baseball Grounds, Philadelphia (Phillies), August 6, 1894, Plumber's stove
Union Park, Baltimore (Orioles), 1894, Cause not known
Sportsman's Park, St. Louis (Browns), April 16, 1898, Cigar
Eclipse Park, Louisville (Colonels), August 12, 1899, Cause not known
Robison Field, St. Louis (Cardinals), May 4, 1901, Cigarette

> —*Compiled by Lloyd Johnson,*
> *formerly senior researcher,*
> *National Baseball Library*

1900
to
1910

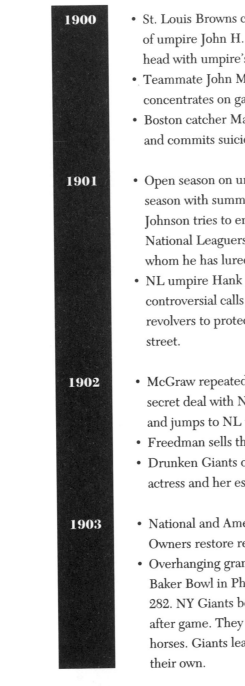

94

*1900
to
1910*

1900

- St. Louis Browns catcher Wilbert Robinson hurls ball at legs of umpire John H. Gaffney, who slugs "Uncle Robby" in the head with umpire's mask.
- Teammate John McGraw, injured half the season, concentrates on gambling at nearby racetrack.
- Boston catcher Marty Bergen, twenty-eight, slaughters family and commits suicide.

1901

- Open season on umpires: American League begins first season with summer-long spate of player suspensions. Ban Johnson tries to end umpire abuse and rowdyism by former National Leaguers, including McGraw and Clark Griffith, whom he has lured to new league.
- NL umpire Hank O'Day badly beaten by St. Louis fans after controversial calls cost Cardinals a game. Police draw revolvers to protect O'Day, who is later pelted with rocks in street.

1902

- McGraw repeatedly suspended for umpire-baiting. Makes secret deal with New York Giants owner Andrew Freedman and jumps to NL to become Giants' manager.
- Freedman sells the Giants after seven stormy years.
- Drunken Giants outfielder "Turkey Mike" Donlin beats up actress and her escort outside Baltimore theater.

1903

- National and American Leagues make peace agreement. Owners restore reserve clause.
- Overhanging grandstand collapses during Phillies game at Baker Bowl in Philadelphia, killing twelve fans and injuring 282. NY Giants beat up driver of team's horse-drawn wagon after game. They were displeased that he stopped to water horses. Giants leave him in street and drive wagon to hotel on their own.

- Washington Nationals slugger Ed Delahanty, thirty-five, threatens train conductor with razor. He is put off train and plunges to death from bridge over Niagara River outside Buffalo, New York.
- Detroit pitcher Win Mercer, twenty-eight, commits suicide by inhaling poison gas.

1905

- Ty Cobb, most violent player in game's history, joins Detroit Tigers.
- Hal Chase, most corrupt player in game's history, joins New York Highlanders.
- NY Giants pitcher Christy Mathewson, moral paragon, punches boy at game for insulting remark.

1906

- Rookie umpire Billy Evans, twenty-two, struck in head with bottle thrown by St. Louis fan. Undergoes lengthy hospitalization for skull fracture.
- Ty Cobb viciously beats and kicks Detroit pitcher Ed Siever in hotel fight. Worn out from emotional abuse by teammates, Cobb retires briefly to sanitarium.
- Gun-wielding "Turkey Mike" Donlin terrorizes trainload of passengers near Troy, New York.

1907

- Giants fans disrupt Opening Day by throwing snowballs. Giants forfeit.
- Bottle thrown by Brooklyn fan nearly beans Chicago Cubs manager Frank Chance. Chance hurls it into stands, badly injuring a child and inciting a small riot.
- Prominent Chicago lawyer Robert Cantwell, member of the White Sox Rooters Association, runs onto field and slugs umpire to protest call.
- Boston manager Chick Stahl, thirty-four, kills himself by drinking carbolic acid.

1908

- Hal Chase suspected of throwing ball games to Yankees' opponents. Ban Johnson, American League president, clears Chase, a box-office draw. Manager George Stallings is scapegoated and fired.
- Cobb attacks black construction worker in Detroit street.

1909

- NY Giants fans batter down outfield fence at Polo Grounds to gain entry to one-game play-off with Chicago Cubs. After Cubs' victory, mob chases them to clubhouse, where NL champions take refuge for three hours.
- McGraw invests in Manhattan pool hall with silent partner Arnold Rothstein, powerful mobster.

- NL president Harry Clay Pulliam fatally shoots himself through right temple.
- NY Giants suspend pitcher Bugs Raymond, a chronic drunk.
- Cobb attacks black porter in Cleveland hotel.
- Detroit plays Pittsburgh in World Series. Cobb, reaching first base, warns Pittsburgh shortstop Honus Wagner, "Hey, Kraut Head, I'm comin' down on the next pitch."
- Umpire Timothy Hurst spits in face of Philadelphia Athletics star Eddie Collins for protesting call. Hurst is thrown out of American League and never returns to major league baseball.

Baseball is a red-blooded sport for red-blooded men. It's no pink tea, and mollycoddles had better stay out of it. It's . . . a struggle for supremacy, a survival of the fittest.
—*Ty Cobb*

This is the decade, we're told, when baseball finally cleaned up its act.

We'll see about that.

We'll see how you feel about Ty Cobb's bloody assaults on players and citizens, Norman "the Tabasco Kid" Elberfeld's assault on Ty Cobb, Napoleon Lajoie's assault on Kid Elberfeld, and . . .

But wait.

In all fairness, improvements were made. Events in the National League had gotten out of hand. There was too much violence, and the average citizen had grown wary of the lowlifes drawn to the ballpark by that violence. The pendulum had swung too far toward anarchy. It was time for a reaction.

Witness the emergence of Byron "Ban" Johnson, a revolutionary, who was convinced that large numbers of fans were turned off by rough play, profanity, and assaults on umpires. Brother Ban wanted to make the ballpark a place where a man could bring his wife and children. He wanted to refashion the rowdy game into the family game. And so he founded the American League with the specific purpose of reclaiming baseball for the good, church-going American masses.

Johnson, a sportswriter and editor in Cincinnati, had long been distressed by rowdiness and umpire abuse. He became president of the Western League around 1893 and made it a forum and test case for clean baseball. The Western League was one of innumerable minor leagues that flourished around the country. Under Johnson's guidance, its umpires were unfailingly supported in their efforts to discipline the unruly; punitive rules were enforced, suspensions and fines upheld. The league's prestige grew.

His experiment a success, Johnson decided to market the concept nationally—to turn profits from probity.

In 1900, he announced that the Western League was changing its name. Henceforth, it would be known as the American League.

In 1901, he declared the American League to be the second major league, putting it on an equal footing with the National League. His hope for baseball was "to make ability and brains and clean, honorable play, not the swinging of clenched fists, coarse oaths, riots, or assaults upon the umpires, decide the issue."

All hell broke loose.

The National League owners were toying with the idea of syndicate-controlled baseball. For Johnson to come along and challenge their monopoly at this juncture—just as they plotted to extend control of the game and maximize profits—was not acceptable.

A war broke out over players, with Johnson raiding National League rosters and National League owners bribing players to stay or return with higher salaries. Hippity hop. The players were jumping back and forth like hares.

Cy Young, who won 511 games in his twenty-two-year career, jumped from the National League to the American and stayed. Ban Johnson's venture was a risk. Yet Young, one of baseball's biggest stars, put his career on the line and joined it for a mere $500 increase in his 1901 salary. His disillusionment with brutal conditions in the NL was total.

John McGraw jumped too. But the

Baseball's savior?
Ban Johnson detested the rowdiness
of the National League and founded the
American League as a "clean" alternative.

cornerstone of Johnson's new league was respect for the umpire. McGraw couldn't stomach this, and Johnson couldn't stomach McGraw. He quickly returned to his raunchy National League homeland, where the umpires were short and combative, just like McGraw, and more willing to take his infernal guff.

The war between the leagues went on for two years, and when the dust settled, peace remained elusive.

There is no point in prettifying events.

Ban Johnson had spent the summer of 1901 suspending one player after another for cursing and assaulting umpires and spitting tobacco juice in their faces. Most of the perpetrators were former National Leaguers who were accustomed to the NL's laissez-faire attitude. But Ban wouldn't put up with it.

This is why McGraw bolted to the National League in 1902 to manage the New York Giants. He made them the most reviled team in baseball. Arrogant, spoiling to fight, they strutted onto the opposition's ball field to incite the crowd. There were riots in Philadelphia, Brooklyn, Pittsburgh. And it all suited McGraw perfectly, for he "was a showman and a promoter and he knew the more people hated the New York Giants, the more people were going to show up to see 'em," says McGraw biographer Charles C. Alexander. "He knew he was selling a product. It's interesting to compare his attitude with that of today's players who look out for their own money. They're not interested in generating money for the team. They don't have the same sense of being performers: that if fans hate 'em in Pittsburgh, it's *good* for the team."

In Brooklyn, fans stationed themselves atop apartment houses adjacent to the ballpark when the Giants came to play. They fashioned spears from umbrella spokes and threw them at the Giants' outfielders. For two reasons. One, the Brooklyn fans were crazy—one old player said he would rather hoe cotton in Alabama than "run the gauntlet" of kranks in Brooklyn. And two, the Giants were bad guys. Even Christy Mathewson, who has been handed down through decades of baseball lore as Mr. Clean. He baited umpires. He threw at opponents' chins. He once punched a kid in the mouth for making an insulting comment while selling lemonade near the Giants' bench.

And he was the best of the bunch.

Baseball was littered with social rejects like the American League's Norman "Kid" Elberfeld, an itty-bitty mountain man from Tennessee who smashed dishes to the floor in restaurants if he didn't like the service and once hit a waiter over the head with a bottle.

Like Johnny "the Crab" Evers, one-third of the Chicago Cubs' "Tinker to Evers to Chance" double-play combination that was later immortalized in the refrain of the poem by F. P. Adams. In their day, these men did not even lead the league in double plays. They were better known as brawlers.

The Cubs fought anyone on the field, and after the game they fought each other in the locker room. They feuded with opposing teams and the opposing teams' towns. And when they beat the Giants in a one-game playoff at the Polo Grounds to capture the 1908 pennant, the Cubs barely got away alive. A mob of Giants fans chased them to the center field clubhouse and tried beating down the doors. For three hours, the Cubs were prisoners until enough police arrived to clear away the crowd.

And then there is the matter of umpires being shot. In the years leading up to World War I, it happened several times in the minor leagues. Shot! And one umpire fired his pistol at a player in the Carolinas. Tit for tat!

There was still a frontier aspect to baseball.

Players died from weird diseases and in train wrecks. There were lots of suicides and mysterious, tragic endings. Between 1900 and 1910, Detroit pitcher Win Mercer killed himself by inhaling poison gas; Washington superstar Ed Delahanty stepped off a railroad bridge near Buffalo and was found, dead, below Niagara Falls; Boston manager Chick Stahl pressed a bottle of carbolic acid to his lips and died; and National League President Harry Clay Pulliam provided the decade's finale by shooting himself fatally through the temple.

To be fair, Ban Johnson made progress in his efforts to transform baseball—just not enough progress.

He began to professionalize the American League umpire corps, making it possible for the "men in blue" to become respected disciplinarians. No longer were umpires a collection of pickups and incompetents. They were career men, and their decisions were enforced. There's an old adage that every umpire should get down on his knees and thank Ban Johnson, and it's true. In both leagues, working stiffs in the crowd probably still equated the ump with the foreman at their jobs. But in the National League, they were more likely to make the ump a target for pent-up animosity and abuse.

The American League wasn't a Sunday school yet, but it began to feature a cleaner, nicer game than the National League as the decade wore on. And the fans responded. Attendance grew, particularly in the new league. "The fans weren't coming out to see violence," says historian Lloyd Johnson. "They were coming out to see *baseball.*" He elaborates: there were classic pennant races, the World Series caught on nationally, rowdyism was finally being cleaned up. "And just as this happens, who should appear on the scene but . . ."

Not the devil. But close.

Ty Cobb.

Cobb played baseball like the old Baltimore Orioles on amphetamines. His base running for the Detroit Tigers was "daring to the point of dementia." He slid like a Lamborghini and hit like a Mack truck. He likened his batting to "heavy artillery." He became the greatest player of his era, perhaps of any era, but wasn't even the most naturally gifted athlete. Like Pete Rose, only more extreme, Cobb achieved excellence through never-ending practice and a hormonally imbalanced competitive drive. Cobb would "dress out" the second baseman with his spikes, keep running, kick the ball out of the third baseman's glove, keep running, and flatten the catcher.

Tally one run for Detroit.

There was a wild look about him, something off-balance in his eyes that scared people. He beat the tar out of a lot of people, Cobb did. It didn't take much to jerk his string. Say the wrong word and Ty would pound your head into the concrete. He did it to teammates, and he did it to black guys in the street.

McGraw and Cobb were twin storm centers, one for each league. They defined the game.

As the decade wore on, macho ball grew in popularity. Ballplayers were gaining respect: no longer were they lumped with the guys who swallowed swords. The Giants drew close to a million fans in 1908, an astonishing number for the time. That year, McGraw invested in a pool hall with Arnold Rothstein, the upcoming socialite mobster, as his silent partner. McGraw was now running with a sophisticated crowd: theater people, business tycoons, politicians. There were moments when it appeared that he and the game were becoming gentrified. Then in 1909 the great concrete-and-steel ballparks began to open and the game became a spectacle. And yet . . . the fights continued.

As a finale to Ban Johnson's decade-long campaign to clean up baseball, consider the following episode:

It's August 4, 1909. Our old friend Timothy Hurst, who probably took part in more fights than any other ump in the game's early days, stands behind the plate at newly opened Shibe Park in Philadelphia. He is wearing his usual pair of spit-shined patent-leather shoes.

The batter is Philadelphia Athletics second baseman Eddie Collins, one of the cleanest players in the league. A Columbia graduate, Collins is a bit of an egghead. And a future Hall of Famer.

Here's the pitch.

Hurst calls, "Strike three!"

Collins protests and, in the course of their exchange, steps on Hurst's shoes.

That's too much for Timothy to handle. He lets fly a stream of tobacco juice into Collins's eye. The fans, being Philadelphians, riot.

The ump later tries to explain his way out of the mess: "I don't like college boys," he says.

But Hurst is history.

Ban Johnson fires him. And old Timothy, who began his baseball career twenty years earlier by firing his gun into the air to ward off a hostile crowd, moves on to new pastures. He becomes a boxing referee.

Strategy Changes

Tommy Tucker was the free spirit who fought John McGraw while the ballpark burned in Boston in 1894. He was a switch-hitter who specialized in fouling off pitches. A foul ball didn't count as a strike in those days, and Tucker would stand up there, leisurely poking at pitches, fouling off one after another without penalty until he nailed the one he wanted. This was an irritant to pitchers. One time Cy Young, going against Boston, announced that Tucker would only get three foul balls: "If you want a fourth," Young declared, "you can have it right between the eyes."

Young was heartened early in the new century when the major leagues finally decided to make a foul ball a strike. Suddenly the balance of power shifted from the hitters to the pitchers. Batting averages dipped markedly; .400 hitters almost vanished and "inside baseball" became more scientific than ever: bunt, steal, hit and run. Complex systems of signs between coaches and players came into use. And because the rubber-cored "dead balls" of the era didn't travel very far to begin with, there were lots of scrambling, one-run ball games and many violent collisions on the base paths. These were epitomized by Ty Cobb's maniacal, distracting baserunning techniques.

Pitchers gained even more of an upper hand with the legalization of the spitball in 1903. Think about it. Ban Johnson had decreed that this would be a *clean* game and then—NOT!—he lets pitchers load up the ball with saliva, hair tonic, mud, chewing gum, and licorice spittle?

This is not clean. This is not fair.

Why should a batter have to put wood on a heavy, loaded spitball whose trajectory was unpredictable because it had been surreptitiously cut on the pitcher's belt and was cuffed, bruised, and blackened from knocking around the rocky, rutted ball field all afternoon?

That was a difficult and dangerous task.

Batters now had to worry about the New York Highlanders' Jack

Chesbro, a mediocrity who nearly doubled his wins to forty-one in 1904 by throwing spitballs.

In 1907, Walter "Train" Johnson came up with the Washington Nationals and gave the hitters something different to worry about. Fearless Ty Cobb said Johnson's fastball "hissed with danger." In a fit of humility, Cobb admitted that "on a dark day" he couldn't even see the damn thing.

Between the spitballers' lead weights and the fastballers' bullets, it's a miracle that more batters weren't killed. Between 1909 and 1920, at least four minor leaguers were fatally beaned, according to the writer Bill James, whose endless research into the details of the game—and the larger meaning of those details—is unparalleled.

National Baseball Library

*Frank Chance,
Hall of Fame first
baseman for the
Chicago Cubs and
the Minnie Minoso
of his era.*

No one was killed in the major leagues. But beanings were common.

I nominate Frank Chance, first baseman and manager for the Chicago Cubs, as the leading beanball victim of the first decade of the twentieth century. Chance was hit at least thirteen times on his helmetless head, partly as a result of his tendency to crowd the plate. The beanings threw off his balance, made him walk funny, made him deaf. He suffered terrible headaches and eventually underwent brain surgery before dying at the age of forty-seven in 1924. But while he was alive and managing baseball teams, Chance expected his players to take the same risks he always had. He personified the dog-eat-dog approach to the game.

Batting helmets weren't available. And if they had been, no one would have worn one for fear of being labeled a milksop. Putting your life on the line was just part of baseball. That's why the National League almost repealed the hit-batsman rule—the one that awards first base to a batter when hit by a pitch. The rule was thought to be "sissifying" the game.

That was the mentality of the times.

Cobb 101

Ty Cobb was just eighteen when he played his first game with the Detroit Tigers in August 1905. Three weeks earlier, he had been notified of his father's death. William Herschel Cobb, a rural schoolteacher known as "the professor" in Royston, Georgia, had thought his wife was cheating on him. He crawled onto the porch roof outside their bedroom at night to check. Amanda Cobb, alone in bed, heard noises outside the window, picked up a shotgun, and shot her husband dead, thinking he was a prowler.

Thus, Tyrus Raymond Cobb was deprived of his only idol in life, a man who exhorted him to be a physician or scholar, who regarded ballplayers as riffraff—crude, rude and uneducated—and gave only belated and grudging consent to his son's career. Cobb, on the verge of success, never recovered from the loss: "My father," he said late in life, "was the greatest man I ever knew. He was a scholar, state senator, editor, and philosopher. I worshiped him. . . . He was the only man who ever made me do his bidding. . . . They blew his head off. . . . He never got to see me play. But I knew he was watching me and I never let him down."

In another sense, Cobb started his career off with a bang. The first headlines noted his hell-bent style of play. A year later, they reported Cobb's brutal beating of a teammate. Then they chronicled his annual attacks on black people—throttling the wife of the Detroit Tigers' groundskeeper, knocking a laborer down in the street, kicking a chambermaid down a flight of stairs—before concluding the decade with Citizen Cobb's controversial spiking of Philadelphia A's third baseman Frank Baker. The normally placid Connie Mack, Baker's manager, denounced Cobb as an undesirable and Philadelphia fans mailed him death threats, one of which stated: "I'll be on the roof of a house across the street from the ballpark with a rifle and in the third inning I'm going to put a bullet right through your heart!"

It didn't faze Cobb. He lapped up the hostility, found it nurturing.

Cobb thrived on the hatred of opposing fans and often came out of batting slumps on the road: "If there's anything that makes me work harder, it's for someone to bait me." On the base paths, he was demoralizing: "Hey, Kraut Head," he shouted to the great Pittsburgh Pirates shortstop Honus Wagner during the 1909 World Series, "I'm comin' down on the next pitch." Once in motion, Cobb wouldn't stop. He routinely raced from first to third, like a veritable kamikaze, on bunts and ground balls. At third, he would announce that he was about to steal home, then do it. Imagine the fear engendered by Cobb—six feet one inch tall and tremendously well-built, a much bigger man than most of his contemporaries—as he barreled toward home plate. His tactics helped make him the biggest gate attraction in baseball before Babe Ruth, even if the fans wanted to kill him, as in Philadelphia. But he antagonized opponents terribly.

It is often said that Cobb wouldn't have lasted a minute in today's sports world—no one would have put up with him—but that's irrelevant, because he was the product of another time and place. He was a white man from rural Georgia, born less than ten years after Reconstruction, who moved to a large Northern city where blacks didn't treat him with the deference to which he was accustomed. He was a Baptist whose teammates were largely Irish Catholic at a time when anti-Roman prejudices were fanned throughout Cobb's native South. These truths describe his cultural displacement in Detroit, but they don't explain his violence—certainly not his violence off the field. Not every white Southern racist would have kicked a black woman in the stomach and knocked her down the stairs, as Cobb did to the chambermaid, because she objected to being called "nigger."

Powerful theories have been put forth to explain Cobb's behavior—the need to vindicate his father's death being the best—but none quite seems to explain the hellfire that consumed him throughout life. There is a scene in Charles C. Alexander's *Ty Cobb* where the fifth-grade Cobb beats up a fat boy for misspelling a word in a spelling bee; the miscue made the girls' team victorious. While traveling with a country surgeon, the adolescent Cobb administered chloroform to a black who had been shot in the stomach by a white boy. Cobb plunged his hand into the victim's open abdomen, probing for the bullet, and "discovered that the sight of blood and exposed tissue hardly bothered him at all." With the Tigers, Cobb slept with a loaded pistol for fear that his teammates would kill him in his train berth. And as a dying old man, living alone in a Northern California mansion, he railed against perceived enemies past and present—it was *always* Cobb against the world—and continued to pack his Luger in bed.

His contemporaries felt a combination of animosity and pity toward him; he didn't have a friend in the world. As a ballplayer, he was frowned on for the pleasure he took in humiliating downtrodden opponents. In one "lopsided victory over Cleveland" in 1907, writes Alexander, ". . . he tripled to the scoreboard in left center to drive in teammate Sam Crawford and kept going around third as third baseman Bill Bradley relayed the throw home. Catcher Harry Bemis had the ball waiting, but Cobb, with a headfirst lunge, got a shoulder into Bemis, knocked him over, and made him drop the ball. Enraged, Bemis grabbed the ball and pounded the prostrate Cobb on the head with it until pulled away. . . . Subsequently Cobb beat out a bunt, doubled in another run, and stole third."

National Baseball Library

*When
Ty Cobb likened
baseball to war,
he wasn't kidding.*

Here Cobb rototills the ground as he slides into Philadelphia third baseman Frank "Home Run" Baker in a celebrated play in 1909.

Dust flies as Cobb slides under New York Highlander third baseman Jimmy Austin in 1909.

This was more than sixty years before Pete Rose crashed through catcher Ray Fosse at home plate to bring the 1970 All-Star game to its violent conclusion. At one level, Cobb, like Rose, simply played harder than most. At another level, Cobb was a "hot dog"—he made himself look good by rubbing salt in an opponent's wound. Hot-dogging was a serious crime in 1906, Cobb's first full season. The Chicago White Sox won the American League pennant that year—and hit a total of three home runs. Runs were *so* precious. They were achieved by scrambling, taking the extra base, and taking out infielders. Cobb did all of this and more—his .367 lifetime batting average, his 4,189 hits (for many years it was believed to be 4,191 hits, but that number was changed), his 892 stolen bases, all the familiar numbers, only hint at his mastery of the game. But by making a fool of his opponents, Cobb crossed a line and made more enemies than any other athlete of his era. For Americans believed in rough justice and retribution. Courts tended to act quickly and sternly against offenders, and this attitude carried over into the streets, onto the ball field, and straight through the doors of the clubhouse. If you had a problem with someone, you settled it personally. Cobb did this and so did his opponents.

His teammates did, too. They hated Cobb from the beginning.

During the 1906 season, they so unnerved Cobb that he apparently suffered a breakdown and took refuge in a sanitarium. Unnerving *Cobb*—that took some doing. Here he describes the events that pushed his buttons: "McIntyre and his roommate, Twilight Ed Killian, began by locking me out of the hotel bathroom the players shared. During Pullman rides a soggy wad of newspaper would fly down the aisle and smack me in the neck. At batting practice I'd be jostled aside and told, 'Get out to the infield, sandlotter.' I cherished the fine ash bats I had collected. I found them smashed. . . . I was harassed to the point of hating to show up at the park." These actions were cruel and, from Cobb's perspective, completely unprovoked: "I was a mild-mannered Sunday School boy. But those old-timers turned me into a snarling wildcat."

This was a blatant lie, of course. Cobb was always a bastard. Veterans typically hazed rookies; it was Cobb's attitude that forced the schoolboy hostilities to escalate. "His mind turned every little razzing into a life-or-death struggle," said teammate Sam Crawford in the classic *The Glory of Their Times*. "He always figured everybody was ganging up on him. He came up from the South, you know, and he was still fighting the Civil War. As far as he was concerned, we were all damn Yankees before he even met us."

When Cobb joined the Tigers, there were only eighteen members on a typical ball club. Then, and through the first two decades of the century, players were in intensely competitive circumstances with new leagues opening and folding and management exercising strict control of athletes' salaries and destinies. In this atmosphere, veterans viewed rookies as direct threats to their livelihoods. Rookies were *not* allowed around home plate in spring training for batting practice. They were *not* taken under some magnanimous veteran's wing. They were on their own, and it wasn't personal. It just *was*.

Cobb should have understood this state of affairs. He certainly knew that he could lose his job in a minute. He couldn't afford to perform poorly. Nor could he afford to miss a ball game. Stricken with a serious case of tonsillitis during a spring road trip, Cobb threw himself at the mercy of a hotel doctor in Toledo. The doctor put Cobb through three unanesthetized butcherings during which the young ballplayer nearly choked to death on his own blood. After the surgery, Cobb caught the first train to Columbus to play in an exhibition game. He learned later that the doctor wound up in an insane asylum.

In October 1906, Cobb started beating people up. The first fight was with Detroit pitcher Ed Siever.

Siever had the nerve to curse Cobb for failing to chase a fly ball. "Where I came from, men were killed for saying what he said," Cobb recalled a half century later, his blood still boiling at the insult. "I jumped up and stood over him. 'Get up! Get on your feet!'"

That night, in the middle of the hotel lobby, that time-honored location for so many baseball fights, he knocked Siever down with a series of fast, hard punches to the head. Then he kicked Siever in the face as the pitcher lay on the floor.

Rack one up for Cobb.

In 1907, Cobb had his altercation with the black groundskeeper at Bennett Park, where the Tigers played. Offended by the informality of the man's greetings one afternoon, Cobb slapped him. When the man's wife protested, Cobb fastened his hands around her neck and squeezed.

Rack two up for Cobb.

In 1908, Cobb had his run-in with the black laborer. Cobb was forced to appear in court "on a charge of assault and battery preferred by Fred Collins, a Negro whom Ty slugged on Saturday afternoon as he was leaving the hotel for the ballpark," the newspaper reported. "Tyrus claimed the Negro insulted him."

Oh, my. Rack three up for Cobb. No, four: this was also the year that Tyrus shoved the black chambermaid down the stairs for her uppity attitude.

All the blacks in Detroit seem to have been picking on Ty Cobb.

Here's another one.

In 1909, Cobb argued with a black elevator operator at the Hotel Euclid in Cleveland. He slapped the man—part of Cobb's cracker shtick—for being "insolent."

Then the hotel's night watchman, another black man named George Stansfield, appeared. He and Cobb started yelling at each other. Cobb pulled a silver penknife from his pocket and in the fracas, it seems, carved Stansfield about the head and shoulders.

But not to worry. Cobb weaseled out of the affair by paying a $100 fine.

Rack five up for Tyrus Raymond Cobb.

Yes, 1909 was a big year. In New Orleans, Cobb refereed a boxing match. And in this match he allowed one fighter to beat the other so savagely that the audience screamed for Ty to call the fight off. But Cobb wouldn't listen: you remember that the sight of exposed tissue didn't bother him. So he let the bloody battering continue until the police finally climbed through the ropes and stopped it.

In his defense, he was smart, pragmatic, and a shrewd investor. At the age of twenty, he bought stock in Coca-Cola; it eventually made him the first self-made millionaire in professional sports. At twenty-one, he held out for more money in spring contract negotiations; the team had offered only $3,000, a pittance. Cobb realized that the owners treated players like "damn slaves." His annual whining over salaries wasn't much different from that of Reggie

Jackson or Rickey Henderson in the modern game. But it had its effect. By the end of the decade, players were paid as much as $12,000 a year. By 1915, the salaries of Cobb and a handful of other superstars neared $20,000.

He took care of himself because he knew his worth. "Cobb fully understood that he was the biggest star in baseball and that he made a lot of money for his team and for others," Charles Alexander said in an interview. "He was an exceptionally intelligent young man . . . reflective and analytic. He really understood the way he affected the whole baseball picture and I think that explains why he was always willing to be the horse's ass that he was. He thought he was not only a better player, but a smarter person and a better person than anyone in baseball."

There you have it: Cobb was not only better than the blacks in the street, he thought, but better than his white teammates. He was not only a bigot, but a snob. Before the end of the decade, he met a future golfing partner: U.S. President William Howard Taft. Sure, Cobb played baseball. But he didn't need the company or the approval of others who played the game. After all, they were riffraff, like his daddy said, and Cobb held them in contempt. *He* played golf with the President.

Cobb 101

Hey, This Guy's a Rookie!

Cobb's opponents dissed Ty, too.

—In Cobb's second ball game, he "tried to steal second and went in headfirst against Kid Elberfeld, the tough little shortstop of the New York Highlanders," Cobb wrote in his autobiography. "He politely brought his knee down on the back of my neck and my forehead went smashing into the dirt, leaving most of the skin behind. . . . The very next time I went into second against Elberfeld, I slid feet first, caught him by surprise and knocked him sprawling. . . . The Kid patted me on the back and said, *'That's* the way to play, sonny boy.'"

—"Rowdy Jack" O'Connor, a hellion from the 1890s, was a grizzled thirty-seven-year-old catcher for the St. Louis Browns in '06. He greeted the mighty Cobb by holding his fingers behind the youngster's neck as a signal for St. Louis pitchers to throw the ball there.

—Jay "Nig" Clarke, Cleveland's Canadian-born catcher, tossed dirt on Cobb's shoes to distract him as a pitch was thrown. Later in life, Cobb refined this technique. While coaching a junior championship team, he taught his teenage catcher to grab some dirt as the pitcher went into his windup. Then, Ty told the boy, with the umpire focused on the pitch, you can toss the dirt *up* into the batter's eyes. There it is: advice straight from the Hall of Fame.

Macho Man: Charley "Boss" Schmidt

Charley "Boss" Schmidt was tougher than Ty Cobb, but just not as mean.

He was a well-buffed two-hundred-pounder from Coal Hill, Arkansas, who sparred with heavyweight champion Jack Johnson. After he joined the Tigers in 1906, his fame grew, and yours would, too, if you could do what the Boss Man did: he drove spikes into the floor of the Detroit clubhouse with his bare hands; he lay on the floor with his arms outstretched and lifted his teammates into the air, one in each big hand; he wrestled and pinned a live bear at a carnival while his teammates stood on and cheered. When Schmidt returned for an encore the next night, it's said, the bear cowered in the corner and refused to fight.

Schmidt was the Detroit catcher from 1906 to 1911, caught fourteen World Series games during the team's three-year pennant run from 1907 to 1909, refused to wear shin guards even though they came into vogue at this time, and broke his thumb and fingers twenty-three times in the line of action, the most impressive injury total among ballplayers outside of the eleven broken noses suffered by Al Rosen, the Cleveland Indians slugger of the 1940s and '50s.

Schmidt is probably most famous for beating up Cobb. He did it once on the ball field during spring training in 1906. He did it another time in the clubhouse. Schmidt lay on the floor, preparing to do his lifting trick. Cobb stepped on one of the Boss's hands with his spikes, and Schmidt, who didn't appreciate the joke, rose to his feet and knocked Cobb unconscious, it is said.

And after that they became fast friends. Because that's the kind of men they were.

Macho Man: Charley "Boss" Schmidt

Delahanty Falls

Ed Delahanty was one of the greatest players who ever lived, but the only thing most people remember about him is the way he died.

One of five brothers from Cleveland who made it to the majors, he came up with Philadelphia in 1888 and spent fourteen of his sixteen seasons there. Delahanty knocked in 146 runs in 1893, batting .368. He batted .407, .404, and .397 from 1894 to 1896. He peaked at .410 in 1899, collecting 238 hits. He once hit four homers in a game—this was in the *dead*-ball era—and supposedly broke a ball in half with one particularly savage cut. Delahanty was a slugger and a superstar, handsome and popular with the fans. His lifetime .346 batting average is the fourth-highest in baseball history.

But he was a gambler and a drunk, and the combination killed him.

His problems started in 1902 when the fledgling American League lured him away from the National League Phillies with a big salary increase. He hit .376 for the Washington Nationals, then signed an $8,000 contract—big bucks—with the New York Giants to return to the National League in 1903. The Giants gave him a $4,000 advance on his salary, which Delahanty promptly blew on horse races and bar bills. Then the American and National Leagues held a "peace conference" to put a stop to the escalating salary wars, and Delahanty was sent back to Washington. The Nationals reimbursed the $4,000 to the Giants, but Delahanty didn't have a dime to compensate his employer. So there he was, $4,000 in debt, and back playing with the same lousy team.

He was depressed.

Late in June 1903, Delahanty traveled with the Nationals to Cleveland for a series. He was continually drunk there, chased a teammate from his hotel room with a knife, and was put under informal surveillance by his friends on the club, who worried for him. Delahanty mailed a letter to his wife in Philadelphia insinuating that he expected to fall victim to some misfortune, and took out an accident insurance policy to benefit their daughter.

His drinking got worse, so Delahanty's mother and two of his brothers met him in Detroit for Washington's next series. The family tried to keep a watchful eye on him at the team's hotel, but Delahanty gave them the slip and boarded a Michigan Central train bound for Buffalo. There are two theories as to where he was headed. The first says his destination was Washington, where he planned to meet his wife and rejoin the team. The second says he was going to New York to negotiate his way back onto McGraw's Giants.

Whatever, he didn't get close to either city. Delahanty got roaring drunk on the train, throwing back five shots of whiskey. He threatened passengers with a razor and supposedly pulled men and women from their sleeping berths. And then the conductor threw him off the train in the middle of the night in Bridgeburg, Ontario, across the Niagara River from Buffalo. Delahanty, one of the highest-paid athletes of his day, stumbled by foot through the darkness without any luggage and decided to cross a railroad bridge to U.S. soil.

Ed Delahanty compiled the fifth highest lifetime batting average in baseball history . . . and drowned in Niagara Falls.

In the middle of the span he met a night watchman named Sam Kingston, and here the facts of the story fade to speculation. Delahanty may have fought with Kingston: the watchman, whose accounts of the incident varied, said there was a "wild look" in Delahanty's eyes. Or Delahanty may have simply evaded the guard and charged south toward Buffalo. He may have jumped, fallen, or been pushed. In any case, the drawbridge was open and the best hitter in baseball plunged into the river far below. His body, clad only in a necktie, shoes, and socks, was found six days later, miles downriver, below Niagara Falls.

Preview: Hal Chase

The saga of Hal Chase stretches from coast to coast and league to league for the better part of two decades. His arrival in New York in 1905 was as portentous, in its way, as Cobb's in Detroit that year. For while Cobb was the nastiest player ever to lace up cleats, Chase was the most corrupt. He was a borderline personality, entirely without morals, who gambled and threw baseball games without compunction, setting the tone for the rank corruption that led to baseball's greatest scandal in 1919.

And everybody loved him. Rookies, veterans, managers. Chase conned them all. He was a Fancy Dan first baseman, rated as the best ever by Babe Ruth and Walter Johnson, long after everyone knew that he was an outright crook. Off the field, he was a dashing figure who ran with a fast Manhattan crowd that included New York Highlanders co-owner Bill Devery, a big-time gambler and Tammany Hall operative.

There were suspicions about Chase almost from the time he put on pinstripes. In his first season with the Highlanders, Bill James has pointed out, the team's record fell off by twenty games. How might Chase have accomplished this sabotage if he was such a hotshot player? Well, maybe he didn't *quite* reach a hard-hit ground ball in a key situation. Or maybe he introduced a gambler to a Yankee pitcher before a ball game and took a cut when the pitcher threw the game. Or maybe . . . there were a thousand ways in which he might have undercut the team. After he left New York eight long years later, the team's record immediately improved by eleven games. In between, there were assorted rumors and scandals.

The dirty work may have begun in 1906, which is the year the Highlanders (soon to be renamed the Yankees) played almost unimaginably bad baseball down the pennant stretch, sending the anemic Chicago White Sox to represent the American League in the World Series. In 1908, the New York management floated a newspaper report that Chase was throwing ball games, so Chase bolted to California and played in an outlaw league. This set the pattern for coming years: accused of wrongdoing, Chase simply feigned outrage and moved elsewhere to sow more dissent. The Highlanders soon welcomed him back for his fielding prowess and gate appeal. And Chase said thank you by throwing more games, dodging responsibility, getting the manager fired, and persuading the owners to make *him* the new skipper. "God, what a way to run a ball club!" said his teammate Jimmy Austin.

Stay tuned. It gets worse—much worse—in the next decade.

Preview:
Hal Chase

Update: Mugsy McGraw

It's no surprise that John McGraw failed his tryout in the American League. Ban Johnson and he were selling different products. Johnson was selling clean. McGraw was selling dirty. Mac was a corrupting influence on St. Ban's noble experiment, and so he packed up and headed home to the National League to spread his masculine warrior's fire.

When McGraw joined the Giants in 1902, his playing days were nearly over—only occasionally would he insert himself into a ball game. But as manager he cloned himself, so what you saw on the field was essentially a group of nine McGraws. The Giants had a catcher named Frank Bowerman, big fella, six feet two inches tall, who had been a teammate of McGraw's on the old Orioles. Bowerman knew how to command respect from opponents. After the Giants lost an important game to the Pirates in 1903, he persuaded Pittsburgh player-manager Fred Clarke to visit the Giants' business office. Once inside, Bowerman closed the door and started swinging.

You can bet that there was a large, hostile crowd on hand the next time the Giants visited Pittsburgh. Which was the whole point. McGraw operated on the premise that the more unexpected excitement he provided the fans, the more they were going to buy his product. He routinely called ahead to a city to demand extra police protection, saying he had received threats and hate mail. It usually wasn't true. He did it just to stir things up. And once the newspapers got wind of his statements, things started to cook. McGraw would insult the city's mayor, its people, its weather, its cuisine, its whatever. It didn't matter. By game time, the park would be rocking and McGraw's Giants would have that fighting edge he so cherished. The we-they attitude made his team focus on the opposition. It made them winners. And more practically, it so enflamed the city's residents that McGraw's late-night drinkers thought twice about leaving the hotel at night in violation of the team's curfew.

He was the James Brown of baseball. You know the stories about Brown? How the Godfather of Soul fined the musicians in his crackerjack bands for playing wrong notes? McGraw was that kind of disciplinarian, enforcing his expectations with fines and sharp rebukes for sloppy play.

If you understood his agenda, though, if you played his brand of baseball, you were okay. You had McGraw's respect and you could join him in destroying your opponents' self-esteem. You could join in the fun as McGraw stood in the third base coaching box berating his rivals. If he heard a rumor that an opposing player was on the block, McGraw brayed, "You're for sale! You're for sale!" He kept it up throughout the game, twisting and twisting the knife until the player screwed up or started a fight—and then McGraw would start all over again with fresh insults.

"McGraw was the Little Rooster. Foul-mouthed: 'We're gonna get you guys,' " says former *New York Times* baseball writer Leonard Koppett. "He believed in overt antagonism as an asset, as opposed to a Connie Mack or a Branch Rickey, who came along a few years later. They thought overt antagonism was counterproductive and only served to awaken sleeping dogs."

Here are a couple instances from the annals of McGraw:

—In 1904, McGraw is arrested during spring training for hustling $2,300 in a gambling game at the hotel. A short while later, the team nearly mauls Tony Mullane, another old buddy of McGraw's from the Orioles of the '90s, who is now struggling to make it as an umpire. After the Giants win the pennant, McGraw refuses to play the American League champion Boston Pilgrims in the World Series—just to spite his nemesis, Ban Johnson. So there's no World Series, fans, thanks to McGraw.

—In 1905, McGraw curses out a reporter, grabs his nose, and *twists*. Then he threatens a rookie umpire named Bill Klem, who goes on to become the most revered officiator in the game, saying, "I can lick any umpire in baseball, you know. . . . I'm going to get your job, you busher."

—In Pittsburgh, thousands of fans swarm onto the field and encircle the Giants' bench after a particularly rowdy game; the Giants escape only after the police and the Pirates, armed with bats, clear a path through the throng. In Cincinnati, McGraw struts in from the center field clubhouse before a game and thumbs his nose at the crowd, effectively challenging everyone in the house to come on down and rumble. In Philadelphia, the Giants become such routine targets for street thugs that they take to stocking rocks in their horse-drawn wagon, hurling them at assailants.

And what's McGraw's comeuppance for all this? Why, the Giants win the pennant, trounce the Philadelphia Athletics in the World Series, and become the toast of Manhattan society.

It continues like this for the rest of the decade. McGraw is fined and suspended umpteen times for insulting umpires, for refusing to leave the field when ejected, or for sneaking back onto the field after being ejected. He locks the umpire out of the Polo Grounds one day for making poor calls the day before. National League president Harry Clay Pulliam denounces "McGrawism" and threatens to resign. But it doesn't stop McGraw, who throws water in umpire Klem's face, stomps about and brays some more, and works the Polo Grounds crowds into a lather that results in fights, riots, and forfeited games.

And that's when the Giants are on a roll. When the Giants are down, McGraw withdraws. He spends so much time at the racetrack that he barely makes it to the ballpark in time for games. He's too distracted by gambling, like Pete Rose years later, to be an effective manager. He invests in a couple of pool halls, once with the crooked Arnold Rothstein, a killer and future big-time mobster.

There are just so many smelly episodes surrounding the man. Minutes before the famous 1908 play-off game between New York and Chicago, Giants team physician Joseph M. Creamer tried handing Bill Klem an envelope filled with several thousand dollars in cash. The offended Klem later quoted Creamer as saying, "You know who is behind me and you needn't be afraid of anything."

Well, let's think. Who could have been behind Creamer? There was a league investigation into the bribe attempt, but they just couldn't get to the bottom of it. Maybe that's because the investigation was supervised by John T. Brush, who owned the Giants. Creamer was made the fall guy, booted out of baseball. And John McGraw slipped away without even a slap on the wrist.

Gobble Gobble Gobble: Mike Donlin

"Turkey Mike" Donlin's nickname fit. He was gloriously talented, but a showboat and a screw-up. In other words, he was cut from the same cloth as a lot of the characters who played under John McGraw. It seems that McGraw had the need to redeem these men. Or perhaps McGraw saw a piece of himself in them.

Donlin grew up poor in Erie, Pennsylvania, drifted to California, and wound up playing ball for the Santa Cruz Sandcrabs, a minor league club in what was then a fishing village. His play was so outstanding that the St. Louis Cardinals bought his contract, and it was with the Cardinals that Donlin met McGraw in 1900. Donlin hit .326 and followed McGraw to Baltimore in 1901. He raised his average that year to .340, but before the start of the next season, the turkey blew it. Alone with a bottle on the night of March 13, 1902, Donlin hit the streets of downtown Baltimore. Always enamored of the theatrical world, drunken Donlin stumbled by the Academy of Music, where a musical adaptation of *Ben Hur* had let out. He followed an actress from the cast, Mamie Fields, down the street, said something inappropriate, and was asked by her escort to "pass on." At which point Donlin belted the escort in the face. When Fields blurted out, "Please don't hit him," Donlin belted her, too.

Then he ran away. He hid in the nearby Diamond Café, a popular spot that was owned by McGraw and Orioles captain Wilbert "Uncle Robbie" Robinson. Donlin snuck out the back entrance and caught a train to Washington, D.C., where he was arrested a day or two later after getting into a fight on a D.C. trolley.

Ban Johnson didn't like this episode at all. Donlin was thrown out of the American League and spent much of 1902 in prison.

It was a minor setback. The National League wasn't as particular about a talented athlete's character, so Donlin joined the Cincinnati outfield and upped his batting average to .351 in 1903. Midway through 1904, McGraw brought Turkey Mike to New York City.

Playing in Manhattan made Donlin a celebrity. By night he was a playboy, the toast of the town. By day he was a member of the marauding Giants.

He had his career year in 1905, batting .356, collecting 216 hits, and scoring 124 runs. And then he blew it again.

Just prior to spring training in 1906, Donlin took a train to Troy, New York, where he was to play in an indoor baseball match. On the way upstate, Donlin got roaring drunk with his friends. They frightened a trainload of passengers and had some fun with the black porter on

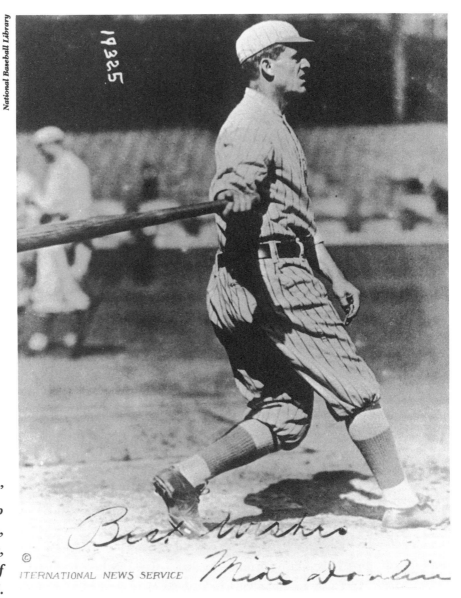

*"Turkey Mike"
Donlan beat up
one actress,
married another,
and drank himself
out of baseball.*

ITERNATIONAL NEWS SERVICE

board, a man named George. Someone pulled out a gun and told George to come "meet Mr. Gun." The porter later told police that Donlin brandished the gun in his face, and the Turkey spent the night in jail. Then he took a train to the Giants' training camp in Memphis, where McGraw suspended him for inveterate drunkenness.

Donlin didn't play much baseball that year. But he was courting a vaudeville headliner named Mabel Hite, and now they married. Mabel and Mike formed a popular song-and-dance team, and *Variety* reported that "Mike Donlin as a polite comedian is quite the most delightful vaudeville surprise you ever enjoyed." Entranced by the stage and encouraged by Hite in his new career, Donlin played baseball only sporadically over the next few years.

The Donlins were all about town: Mike would arrive at a theater in his $350 suit and diamond studs, his wife in a $500 bird-of-paradise hat. By all accounts they were a happy, attractive couple, and Donlin announced that he had given up drink to embrace the opportunities of his new life: "I've got a reserved seat on a crystal chariot and I'm not looking for a rain check either. Croton cocktails and cow juice is my limit."

But Mabel Hite, twenty-seven, died of intestinal cancer in 1912. Donlin, a widower at thirty-four, must have cut a pathetic figure about town. McGraw took pity and rehired him in 1914, but Donlin could no longer cut it in baseball, not even as a pinch hitter. He remarried, he had some bit parts in the talkies and on the stage, then moved to Hollywood where the Turkey's remarkable up-and-down career bounced into its last phase. The resilient Donlin produced over 20 films, some featuring John McGraw and other members of the New York Giants, before his death in 1933 at age 55.

Hot and Bothered:
Kid Elberfeld

The worst thing that shortstop Norman "the Tabasco Kid" Elberfeld ever did on a ball field was scoop up a large handful of mud and throw it into the mouth of an umpire. This followed a dubious call by the ump on a play at second base, and Elberfeld knew enough to walk off the field without waiting to be ejected. He sat out the next ten games. He thought it was the funniest thing he ever did in baseball.

At a time when John McGraw made important advances in the science of umpire abuse, Elberfeld conducted his own original research. He once said he would "walk through Hades" to win a game, a sentiment that must have appealed to McGraw, who wanted Elberfeld for the Giants but never got him. He came close in 1903, when Elberfeld signed contracts with both the National League Giants and the American League Tigers. In the interest of peace with Ban Johnson's new league, Giants owner John T. Brush gave up his rights to Mr. Tabasco and let him go to Detroit. Johnson then double-crossed Brush by arranging Elberfeld's transfer to the New York Highlanders, where he helped that club challenge Brush's Giants at the gate.

The Kid, a .271 career hitter, was called "the hardest man to manage in the world of baseball." A self-described "runt" at five feet seven inches, he poked umpire Timothy Hurst so many times in the gut that Hurst removed his mask and smashed it over Elberfeld's head. He was not infrequently escorted from the field by police. He was another little man who carried the concept of aggressive play to extremes: intentionally crowding the plate, he was hit three times in the head by pitches in a single game. He expressed the highest admiration for Cleveland's Napoleon Lajoie, whose spikes left a four-inch gash in Elberfeld's foot. After Ty Cobb spiked Philadelphia third baseman Frank Baker, igniting complaints in Philly about Tyrus's intentional cruelty, one Detroit columnist said "soft-fleshed darlings" like Baker would profit by learning to accept pain like the Tabasco Kid.

Elberfeld never played for a pennant winner, and maybe this is why he broke up restaurants, slamming bottles over waiters' heads and so on. He was frustrated.

The Highlanders included future Hall of Famers Willie Keeler, Jack Chesbro, and Clark Griffith, but the team "didn't have enough fight on it," Elberfeld analyzed. "We didn't have many . . . mean players who fought for everything, the way the old Orioles used to fight and the way the Giants then were fighting and scrapping in the National League. Jack Kleinow, our first-string catcher, would flare up once in a while, but the rest of the club was pretty quiet. Willie Keeler was a great player, but he didn't have the fight of the old Orioles. . . . Why, it used to burn me up, when we were hustling and fighting for games, to hear Willie singing to himself in the outfield."

For shame, Wee Willie.

Let's finish with this image of Norman Elberfeld:

Escorted from the field by police after heaping abuse on some helpless umpire in St. Louis, Elberfeld passed the press box and quietly asked a reporter to take a message to his parents in the grandstand: "Tell Pappy and Mammy it's all right," Elberfeld said. "I'll be up to the house for early dinner tonight."

National Baseball Library

Norman Elberfeld was called "the Tabasco Kid" because he was an inveterate hothead on and off the field.

Unforgettable

Is it necessary to review Fred Merkle's "bonehead" blunder that supposedly cost the New York Giants the 1908 pennant? Briefly, the Giants and Chicago Cubs were tussling toward the pennant when they met in New York on September 23. In the bottom of the ninth inning, with the score tied 1–1, in front of an anxious crowd, Merkle singled, advancing the Giants' Moose McCormick to third. Then Giants shortstop Al Bridwell lined a hit into center field, McCormick scampered home with what everyone thought was the winning run, the umpires walked off the field, and the Giants, including Merkle, ran triumphantly toward the center field clubhouse, leaping and screaming and embracing and trading high fives, or whatever it was they did in those days, to celebrate the 2–1 victory.

Unfortunately, Merkle had run off to celebrate without touching second base, a technical violation of the rule book. Noticing this, Chicago second baseman Johnny "the Crab" Evers, one of the biggest twerps of the decade, started screaming for his teammates to throw him the ball. He got it and stepped on second, while thousands of Giants fans milled about the diamond, still celebrating, but sensing that something was wrong. The umpires were brought back to the field to hear the Cubs' argument that Merkle was out. And in the stupidest, most egregious and anally correct application of the rule book in the history of the game, the umps agreed with the argument. They disqualified the Giants' winning run. And because the riot now taking place on the field precluded further play, they announced that the game would end as a tie.

It was a cheap way for the Cubs to avoid losing a critical game in the hottest pennant race ever. Two weeks later, New York and Chicago finished the season with identical records, necessitating a one-game playoff to decide the National League pennant. The Cubs won, of course, and nineteen-year-old Fred Merkle was labeled a "bonehead" for the rest of his career. Even though anyone could have made the same mistake. And even though the Giants could have put away the pennant in the final two weeks of the season after the alleged "blunder."

Isn't it remarkable how our view of history is distilled through time? The 1908 pennant race captured the nation like no other before it, and possibly since. Yet 86 years after the events, only the rookie Merkle's goof lives on in America's collective baseball memory. The drama that formed its background, that whirled around the key game and followed the teams until the end of the season—it's all lost.

The fact that the Chicago Cubs were as unpleasant and brutish as any of Billy Martin's championship teams in Oakland and New York during the 1970s—who remembers that? Who remembers that the Cubs' Heinie Zimmerman threw a bottle of acid at teammate Jimmy Sheckard's forehead in the Chicago clubhouse? And that the bottle smashed open, splashing ammonia over Sheckard's face and nearly blinding him? And that Cubs manager Frank Chance, the beanball king, went after Zimmerman with his teammates, knocked Heinie to the floor, and pounded the crap out of him so that he had to be hospitalized?

It happened in late July, ten weeks before the Cubs won the pennant. But who remembers?

Who remembers the immoral acts leading up to and surrounding the play-off on October 8? The allegation that the Giants—the victims in all of this, right?—tried unsuccessfully to bribe the Philadelphia Phillies with $40,000 to throw a five-game series in late September? As related earlier, the fact that the Giants' team physician Joseph M. Creamer, moments before the climactic playoff game with the Cubs began, offered umpire Bill Klem an envelope stuffed with thousands of dollars in cash? The fact that as Klem brushed Creamer aside, the crowd poured into the Polo

History's victim: Fred "Bonehead" Merkle of the 1908 Giants.

Grounds, breaking down fences, perching itself on rooftops and bluffs around the stadium, making a tremendous din? And that one fan fell to his death from his perch on a viaduct? And that the 30,000 fans jamming the park sent up a roar of profanity and abuse—"Oh, you robbers! You brigands!"—at the imperturbable Cubs as they loosened up on the field?

And that as all of this was happening, Giants pitcher Joe "Iron Man" McGinnity tried to provoke Frank Chance of the Cubs into a fight because the New Yorkers planned to beat up the Cubs' best player and eliminate him from the day's action? Do you remember that McGinnity—who either punched or jostled Chance, depending on who tells the story—retired from the majors after this very game? And that his shocking lack of ethics was later forgotten when he was voted into the Hall of Fame?

Pete Rose, take note.

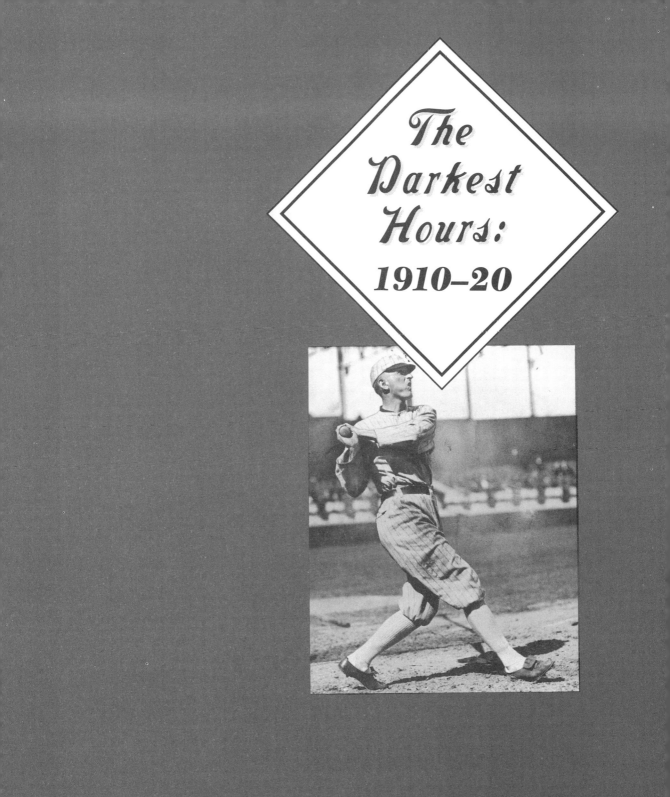

The Darkest Hours: 1910–20

132

The
Darkest
Hours:
1910–20

1910
- St. Louis Browns conspire to deny Ty Cobb the American League batting title.
- New York Yankees first baseman Hal Chase is accused by manager George Stallings of throwing ball games. Chase has Stallings fired—and replaces him as skipper.

1911
- Lively new cork-centered baseball is introduced; averages jump.
- The Polo Grounds burn in New York.
- American League owners collude to keep pitching great Walter Johnson from leaving the low-paying Washington Senators.
- Heckled by Brooklyn Dodgers and their fans, rookie umpire Ralph Frary ejects entire Dodger bench from game. Chased from field by bottle-throwing fans, Frary retires after season.
- Pitcher John Bender drops dead on mound during Western Canada League game in Edmonton, Alberta.
- Philadelphia Phillies outfielder Sherry Magee breaks umpire's jaw after called third strike. Fined and suspended, Magee later becomes National League umpire.

1912
- Ty Cobb attacks crippled fan in stands.
- Ex-Giants pitcher Bugs Raymond, drinker and burnout, is murdered with baseball bat at sandlot game in Chicago.
- Boston Red Sox beat up rookie pitcher Buck O'Brien after he loses sixth game of World Series to New York Giants by score of 2–1.

1913
- Hal Chase traded by Yankees to Chicago White Sox after New York manager Frank Chance accuses him of throwing games.
- Cobb attacked by street toughs outside Shibe Park in Philadelphia.

1914
- Babe Ruth signs with Boston Red Sox.
- First season of ill-fated Federal League. Salaries escalate as competing leagues bid for talent. Attendance collapses.
- Ty Cobb threatens butcher with gun; pistol-whips butcher's young black assistant.
- Philadelphia Athletics manager Connie Mack suspects team of throwing World Series against Boston Braves.

1915
- John McGraw pulls knife on fan in Boston.
- Rogers Hornsby, future gambler and Hall of Famer, plays first season with St. Louis Cardinals.
- Oscar Charleston, perhaps the greatest star of Negro Leagues, begins professional career.

133

1916
- Federal League has folded. Major league owners slash salaries across the board.
- Johnny Dodge fatally beaned by Shotgun Rogers in Southern Association game.
- John McGraw says New York Giants may have thrown games to Brooklyn.

1917
- Cobb spikes New York Giants second baseman Buck Herzog in exhibition game in Dallas. They punch it out in Cobb's room at Hotel Orient.
- In separate incidents, Cobb and McGraw both slug Bill "Lord" Byron, the singing umpire.

1918
- Racetracks closed to add horses to the war effort. Gamblers move from tracks to ballparks.
- Cincinnati Reds manager Christy Mathewson accuses his first baseman, Hal Chase, of throwing ball games. Three Reds support charges, but league investigation later clears Chase.

1919
- McGraw, who testified against Chase, hires Chase and Mathewson as New York Giants coaches.
- Mobster Arnold Rothstein helps arrange sale of New York Giants to millionaire gambler Charles Stoneham.
- Carl Mays throws baseball at spectator.

- Ty Cobb knees spectator in groin.
- John McGraw calls Cincinnati "home of the Huns," nearly setting off riot.
- Ruth hits twenty-nine home runs to revolutionize the game. Boston sells him to New York Yankees after the season.
- Chicago White Sox conspire with gamblers to throw World Series to the Cincinnati Reds.

The
Darkest
Hours:
1910–20

If you were a younger man, I would kill you.
—Ty Cobb, addressing John McGraw

This is the dawn of respectability. The big concrete-and-steel ballparks are up now, distancing the fans, both physically and psychologically, from the contest at hand. The game is becoming modern and impersonal, the historians tell us, a spectacle observed from afar. And not only have the increased distances made it that much harder for fans to taunt and attack their heroes, but the umpires are policing the action more carefully on the field. There are now two umpires present for each game. And, what's more, the arbiters of professional baseball are ready to pass new behavior codes to further reduce crude language and ruffianism on the part of the athletes.

It is a game reborn, we are told. At long last, there is something to cheer about.

Well, forget it.

This may have been baseball's filthiest decade. The tales of violence, greed, and corruption will make you gag; they are numerous and overwhelming. The All-American game was impure, immoral, and idolatrous—worshiping the holy dollar. Lawsuits abounded. Holdouts were common practice. Skinflinting management exacerbated the players' feeding frenzy. And the entire game was awash with gambling and its influences. The 1919 Black Sox scandal, which saw one of the greatest teams in the game's history intentionally lose the World Series, was no aberration. It was the culmination of years of corruption. And baseball's appointed, white-haired saint, Commissioner Kenesaw Mountain Landis, didn't really purify the game in the scandal's wake. He rooted out corruption selectively and instituted his own brand of hypocrisy. Later, he blocked baseball's racial integration for more than a decade.

Baseball, to quote the great Ty Cobb's immortal words, was "as respectable as a kick in the crotch." This was no soft game with soft heroes: baseball cards were packaged with cigarettes, not bubble gum. Catchers routinely played with jammed and broken thumbs—or much worse. When a base runner's spikes severed an artery above the knee of St. Louis Browns catcher Hank Severeid, he marched back to the clubhouse and calmly watched a doctor tie the two ends of the artery back together. He returned a week later.

The New York Giants had a madman for a team mascot. The Philadelphia A's had a hunchback. And every American Indian player in the majors was nicknamed "Chief." Ballplayers shot guns out of hotel windows for fun. Whoopee! And the Boston Red Sox beat up their own pitcher, a twenty-game-winning rookie named Buck O'Brien, after he lost the sixth game of the 1912 World Series by a score of 2–1. He never pitched effectively again.

The Red Sox managed to beat the New York Giants in the series, but Boston manager Jake Stahl was fired anyway. He was replaced by the team's catcher, Bill Carrigan, who insisted that his pitchers knock down opposing batters—and fined them when they didn't. His staff over the next several seasons included the young Babe Ruth and a sneering, submarine-style fastball pitcher named Carl Mays. It was Mays who threw the beanball a few years later in 1920 that killed Cleveland Indians shortstop Ray Chapman, one of the game's golden boys. Mays's Nixon-esque defense: "I am not a murderer."

This was a busy decade for beanballers.

The young, ornery Burleigh Grimes trained under manager Kid "I'm a Man" Elberfeld in Chattanooga before coming up with Pittsburgh; there Grimes uncorked his well-aimed fastballs and lousy disposition. Dolf Luque, whom everyone recognizes as the future mentor to Sal "the Barber" Maglie, emerged with Cincinnati to begin a twenty-year reign of brushback terror in the National League. And New York Giants pitcher Rube Marquard threw without compunction at the skulls of rookies. "In those days you handled the young fellows all the same way," he explained years later. "You threw a pitch at their heads to see if they could take it."

In this decade, the innocents were reborn as rogues. Shoeless Joe Jackson's transformation from the Natural to the Scoundrel can be taken as symbolic of changes in the game as a whole. He hit .408, whacking 233 hits, in his first full season in 1911, but today all anyone remembers is Joe walking down the courthouse steps in Chicago and the little boy saying, "Say it ain't so, Joe."

An apocryphal moment? Sure.

But the bad seeds in baseball were now bearing fruit.

All through the decade, first baseman Hal Chase planted bribes around the league like Johnny Appleseed. Was he the only crooked ballplayer? No, there were dozens. But he did his business so openly—and with such panache—that he became the exemplar for corruption. Chase was a virus, hard to treat. And no one even called the doctor. Every virus needs its host, and the general body politic of baseball only winked at Chase's behavior, content to let well enough alone as long as the stadium turnstiles kept revolving.

And then there were the Twin Peaks of Mean Baseball: John McGraw and Ty Cobb.

Sorry. We can't get rid of them.

Each, in these years, attacked one of the most obnoxious personalities in the game: umpire Bill "Lord" Byron, famous for standing behind the plate and breaking into song with lines like "You'll have to learn before you get older/You can't hit the ball with the bat on your shoulder." Cobb and McGraw, men without humor, slugged him.

Well, maybe he deserved it.

Still, McGraw's 1917 Giants were arguably the most violent ball club in the game's annals—after the old Baltimore Orioles and Cleveland Spiders. McGraw's famous confrontation with Cobb in a Dallas hotel lobby during spring training that year is the one in which Cobb more or less threatened to murder McGraw. This followed a game in which Cobb had a memorable base-path collision with McGraw's tough second baseman, Buck Herzog: Cobb slid into second, spikes high, ripping Herzog's trousers and cutting a gash along his thigh. Then Cobb ground Herzog's face in the dirt.

And the season hadn't even started yet.

This was Cobb's decade.

His unrelenting offensive excellence set standards that still hold today. In 1911, Cobb batted .420, racking up 248 hits and knocking in 127 runs. This was the year baseball experimented with a cork-centered ball, setting off some heavy hitting that foreshadowed the lively-ball era of the '20s. But when pitchers reestablished their dominance in 1913, Cobb still hit .390, and he barely tailed off through the rest of the decade. The man was awesome.

Managers were utilizing new strategies: the squeeze play, intentional walks, the use of pinch hitters. Runners were still stealing bases like crazy—everybody ran, and Cobb ran more than anybody else. If you came between him and the bag, you were at risk. He accelerated, only dropping into his slide at the last possible moment—a model for Rickey Henderson, a latter-day "problem child," as Cobb was dubbed. Cobb never chickened out on take-out plays at second base: if the shortstop or second baseman wanted to aim a bullet at his head, so be it. But usually, the fielder moved aside, not Cobb.

This was his decade.

It's the one in which he uttered the famous words: "I have observed that baseball is not unlike a war."

It's the one in which he threatened a butcher with a gun, beat up the butcher's black assistant, and, back at the ballpark, attacked a cripple in the stands.

The cripple had called Cobb a "coon" or "half-nigger"; reports differed. When Cobb was suspended for trying to address this insult, his teammates, who usually hated his guts, threatened a walkout. Out of this dispute, with Cobb assuming a leadership role, emerged a body called the Players Protective Association. This ultimately led to the establishment of the modern players' union and the end of the reserve clause. And so we see Cobb, who understood that players were exploited, accomplishing some good here, even though the whole chain of events started with his defending his white manhood.

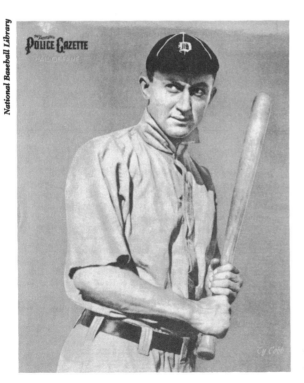

Cobb hit .420 in 1911, collecting 248 hits. In this decade he also attacked a crippled heckler and blacks in the street.

It fits the pattern: baseball strains toward respectability, but can't leave its rank origins behind.

There is good evidence that in the waning days of the 1919 season, Ty Cobb helped fix a ball game. The allegation didn't arise until 1926, when Cobb was managing the Detroit Tigers. No one ever proved it. Judge Landis said he didn't believe it. And yet both Cobb and Cleveland Indians manager Tris Speaker, the alleged co-fixer, were informally barred from ever managing in the big leagues again. Clearly, something fishy had gone down. And there you have it: the corruption in baseball during the second decade of the century was so insidious that it tainted even the great Ty Cobb, the fiercest competitor the game has known, an athlete whom people thought literally incapable of dishonesty.

How did baseball crash to such a low point?

Attendance dropped off at the start of the new decade after reaching an all-time high of 7.2 million in 1909. The result: most owners claimed to be financially constrained. In 1911, American League owners colluded to prohibit Walter Johnson, the league's best pitcher, from leaving the low-paying Washington Senators. The Detroit ownership shut down Ty Cobb two years later when Cobb held out for a pay raise along with his teammate Sam Crawford, the future Hall of Fame outfielder. Were the players greedy? Or was Detroit giving them the shaft? Five decades before the famous tandem holdout by Sandy Koufax and Don Drysdale against the Los Angeles Dodgers, the Cobb-Crawford affair was all over the newspapers and everyone had an opinion.

Mind you, Cobb had won five league batting championships in the previous six years. He now sought a raise to $15,000 from the $9,000 he had been paid three years running. Team owner Frank Navin's response: "You will play for Detroit or you won't play for anybody and you will take what I offer." Historian Harold Seymour writes in *Baseball: The Golden Age* that disgust with the Detroit club's arrogance extended to Capitol Hill. There an Illinois congressman named Thomas Gallagher called organized baseball a "predacious and mendacious trust" and asked for a congressional investigation. It didn't happen, of course.

And Cobb signed for $11,000.

Ballplayers felt beset by unfairness, and many—apparently including Cobb—reacted by throwing games as the decade moved on. Philadelphia A's owner and manager Connie Mack dismantled his club after the 1914 season, ostensibly because he could no longer afford the payroll. In fact, Mack thought the team had thrown the World Series against the Boston Braves.

Attendance collapsed in 1914. That year saw the launching of the rival Federal League and the outbreak of salary wars that were almost as ill-considered as those of the 1980s. The Federals planned to gut the majors and they literally threw money at defecting stars like Hal Chase, Mordecai "Three Finger" Brown, and Joe Tinker. In response, major league owners desperately escalated salaries to hold on to their best talent. As today, the media turned on the newly rich players. Sportswriter Francis Richter complained of their "mercenary spirit." And when New York Giants outfielder Benny Kauff flip-flopped between McGraw's crew and the Feds, he was excoriated. Sportswriter Sid Keener called him an example of "player insubordination, ingratitude, and disloyalty. . . . They forget their moral obligations completely."

But the money-grubbing players' day in the sun ended rather quickly.

The Federal League collapsed after the 1915 season, and major league owners immediately set about slashing salaries mercilessly. Try to imagine today's owners demanding 50 percent pay cuts from, say, Ozzie Smith and Kirby Puckett. This is what happened in 1916 to Honus Wagner and Tris Speaker, two of the most superb athletes of any era. The players were fed up, united in contempt for management. And they struck back. In 1916, John McGraw insinuated that his Giants had lain down against the pennant-winning Brooklyn club. In 1917, the owner of the St. Louis Browns accused two of his players of throwing games, and there were rumors that the Chicago White Sox were doing the same.

The Sox were now owned by Charles Comiskey, a key supporter of the renegade Players League more than 25 years earlier. Comiskey had long since gotten with the program, risen through management, and assembled a White Sox club that included Eddie Collins, Shoeless Joe Jackson, Eddie Cicotte. Superstars. One of the greatest teams ever assembled. And Comiskey, the former revolutionary, was one of the cheapest men ever to own a ball club. He made his men play in dirty uniforms to save on laundry bills.

World War I was raging. So was inflation, yet major league players' salaries were held in check. In 1918, racetracks were closed by the government to make more horses available for the war effort, and legions of gamblers moved from the tracks to the ballparks. Betting was wide open, with gamblers routinely seated behind the dugouts to take bets from players and spectators alike. "Place your bets," shouted a banner stretched across several houses outside Philadelphia's Shibe Park. Massive baseball betting pools operated around the country, with newspapers reporting the daily odds.

National League president John Heydler insisted that the "game's entire superstructure is founded upon absolute integrity."

But the game was a circus.

There was no leadership, no commissioner. The so-called National Commission, a no-teeth panel that ostensibly ruled baseball, was about to fall apart. The chaos at the top of the game reflected the chaos at the bottom, and all of it reflected the economic and labor chaos that engulfed the country.

Let's look quickly at the pandemonium of 1919.

Ty Cobb kneed a heckler in the groin. Was he punished? No.

Foul-tempered Carl Mays rifled a ball into the stands in Philadelphia, dazing a spectator. When the police issued a warrant for Mays's arrest, the Red Sox spirited him out of town, then dealt him to the Yankees. League president Ban Johnson tried unsuccessfully to block the deal because the Red Sox never effectively disciplined Mays for his unruly actions. By trading Mays to the Yankees, the best-paying club in the league, the Sox were rewarding him for his insubordination.

In 1919, the name of Manhattan mobster Arnold Rothstein circulated openly in baseball circles. Historian Seymour writes that Rothstein "bet on horses, ball games, elections, and prize fights. He was involved in a vast illegal drug trade and was a fence for expensive stolen goods as well as a banker for racketeers."

Now Rothstein helped arrange the sale of the New York Giants to an alcoholic millionaire named Charles Stoneham whose fortune had been made through gambling operations known as bucket shops. As the 1919 season waned, the Giants trailed in the standings and McGraw left the team under the care of his coaches. He went to Havana with Stoneham, and there they purchased a racetrack-casino complex from a suspected assassin.

Days before the opening of the World Series between the Chicago White Sox and Cincinnati Redlegs in September, rumors of a fix were reported on the front page of the *New York Times*.

And after a game or two of the series, White Sox owner Comiskey knew there was a fix. And American League president Ban Johnson knew there was a fix. But because the press as a whole wasn't buying it,

National Baseball Library

Shoeless Joe Jackson of the Chicago White Sox, admiring a shot off the bat in the days before his banishment.

and because the public didn't want to hear about it, and because blowing the lid off the fix would have damaged their prestige and hurt the game financially, Comiskey and Johnson did nothing. And it wasn't until the fall of 1920, when the guilt-ridden White Sox pitching ace Eddie Cicotte fessed up to the authorities and the cover-up started to collapse, that they volunteered any information. And still they didn't volunteer much. And as the good name of baseball was dragged through the dirt—"say it ain't so, Joe!"—each tried to use the game's misfortune to his advantage. Comiskey and Johnson, once close friends, tried to pin blame for the scandal on each other, each desperately hoping to hang on to his power. They fought like a couple of rats.

The owners hired Judge Landis, baseball's first commissioner, to clean house. The prosecutors in Chicago ignored the real power brokers, like Rothstein, who undoubtedly underwrote and arranged the fix. Instead they focused on the small-time hoods and the White Sox, indicting eight players who plotted with the gamblers or knew what was going down. And then the prosecutors' evidence was stolen, and the players were all tried and acquitted, and Landis threw the eight out of baseball anyway. He banished them forever to uphold the good name of the national pastime.

"FOR THE BASEBALL GAME IS SOARING," the *Sporting News* had rhapsodized shortly before the tainted World Series:

"HIGH ABOVE IT ALL, SERENE,
UNAFFECTED BY THE ROARING—
FOR THE GRAND OLD GAME IS CLEAN!"

Prince Hal

The New York Yankees who reported to spring training in
Bermuda in March 1913 were a bunch of sad sacks. They had
finished in last place the year before, posting a winning percentage of
.329 and losing 102 ball games. Standing amid the wreckage was Hal
Chase, the team's most popular and charismatic player. He was thirty, a
rock-hard, good-looking six-footer from California who, through eight
seasons, had proved to be a dangerous hitter, a league leader in stolen
bases, and the flashiest, most graceful and daring fielder at his position,
first base, that the game had seen. Chase was an artist, and one of the
biggest draws in the major leagues. But he didn't last the season. His
manager was convinced that he was "laying down" on defense,
intentionally losing games by blowing plays so deftly that the fans
would never suspect it. And so Chase, a superstar, was traded to the
Chicago White Sox—one more mark against the man whom historians
have uniformly labeled the single most corrupt player in the history of
the National Pastime.

"Something about him made wrong shine as if it were right and
evil smell like good," wrote baseball researcher Bill James, who defines
Chase's extraordinary achievement: that "one man could so alter the
ethics of the sport."

"Hal Chase proves that the devil doesn't walk around with cloven
hooves," says baseball researcher Bob Hoie, who has written
extensively on Chase. "This was not some furtive, corrupt-looking guy.
On the face of it, he was very congenial and well-spoken, a 'classy' kind
of guy. People gravitated to him. I spoke to some of his 1912
teammates when they were still alive, and their eyes lit up at the
mention of his name, as if Hal Chase was some kind of god. But he was
known in the baseball fraternity as someone who threw games—and
nothing ever happened to him. So over the years the other players
must've said, 'Hal gets away with it. Why not us?'"

Chase was in-your-face corrupt, almost certainly the only player in major league history to be accused by three managers of throwing ball games. Most amazingly, Prince Hal's corruption spanned fifteen years. Booted out of one league, he fled to California to fix games in the minors, then returned East and charmed his way back into the good graces of major league owners. Blacklisted after the 1919 season, he drifted to Arizona to manage a hard-scrabble mining town ball club, floated across the border, and is said to have nearly insinuated himself into the commissionership of the fledgling Mexican League—until the major league baseball hierarchy, tired of Hal, pulled some strings and killed the deal. His career has been likened by baseball historian Harold Seymour to a "squalid passage . . . bespattered by discord and dishonesty."

All the while, fans adored him. So did many teammates. In his Yankee years, Chase regaled the rookies nightly at Gallagher's steak

Prince Hal

Hal Chase was the most dishonest player ever to set foot on the diamond.

house in Manhattan. At the ballpark, they thought it great fun to watch Chase mimic manager Frank Chance behind his back. Chase "deliberately misinterpreted" the manager's orders, wrote author Frank Graham in his history of the New York Yankees, "and, taking advantage of the fact that Chance was deaf in one ear as a result of having been hit in the head so often by pitched balls in his playing days, sat on his deaf side in the dugout and slyly mocked him for the amusement of the other players."

It's easy to dump on Chase. But, in fairness, he may not have committed the greatest of his alleged crimes. For years, it was said that Chase was the agent who brought together the gamblers and crooked Chicago White Sox players who fixed the 1919 World Series. This notion is now dismissed by numerous historians. They say Chase, who played for the New York Giants in 1919, was more of an independent operator whose willingness to bet on and fix games over the course of his career was a key to the general corruption of the era. "Hey, Hal, what are the odds today?" opposing players are said to have asked Chase on the field. He apparently bribed opponents and teammates alike: "Until somebody worse can be found," Seymour once wrote, "he will serve as the archetype of all crooked ballplayers."

What drove Chase?

In the mid-1920s, S.L.A. Marshall was president of the so-called Copper League, a collection of rough-and-ready semipro teams in Arizona mining towns. Chase managed one, and Marshall remembered him years later as "completely and congenitally amoral. The man was born without any sense of right and wrong. . . . The deep pity of it is that the world thinks of him as a hoodlum rather than as a man who was mentally ill."

Unlike Pete Rose, whose 1990 conviction for income tax evasion arose from gambling activities, Chase was never convicted of a crime or formally condemned by baseball's hierarchy. Baseball historian Lloyd Johnson concedes that hard information on Chase's misdeeds is "elusive." Still Johnson is convinced that Rose's infractions "are nothing compared to Chase's."

What do we know definitively about Chase?

Born near San Jose, California, in 1883, he grew up on small-town sandlots, dropped out of high school, and wangled a baseball

The
Darkest
Hours:
1910–20

scholarship to Santa Clara College, where he starred briefly before joining the Los Angeles Angels of the Pacific Coast League in 1904.

In 1905, he joined the New York Highlanders, soon to be known as the Yankees. He held out for more money in 1907 and returned to the "outlaw" California League. When the major leagues threatened to banish anyone who jumped to the "outlaws," Chase played under the name of Schultz. The Highlanders took him back. But in 1908, Chase bolted again when the first story appeared in the press about his tendency to "lay down" on the diamond. Chase complained that the attack on his ethics was unfairly floated by the team's front office—ironic in that the club was co-owned by William "Big Bill" Deverey, a corrupt police commissioner, and Frank Farrell, one of the most famous gamblers in New York.

In 1910, New York manager George Stallings again complained about Chase's throwing games. But Chase was a star by now, and he managed to have Stallings fired—and replaced him as manager. American League president Ban Johnson accused Stallings of trying "to besmirch the character of a sterling player. Anybody who knows Hal Chase knows that he is not guilty of the accusations."

Right.

Chase lasted one season as manager. In 1913, the club was managed by Frank Chance, former star first baseman for the Chicago Cubs, who accused Chase of throwing games. Prince Hal was traded to Chicago: "That he can play first as it never was . . . is a well-known truth," wrote the *Sporting News*. "That he will is a different matter." Chase subsequently jumped to the Federal League, where more rumors of slack play followed him.

In 1916, after the Federal League folded, he was signed by the Cincinnati Reds—their manager was Christy Mathewson—and batted .339 to lead the National League.

In 1918, Mathewson accused Chase of throwing ball games. Three Reds players supported the charges, but a league investigation cleared Chase. One of the witnesses against Chase had been New York Giants manager John McGraw, a co-owner of a Manhattan pool hall that Chase frequented for years. McGraw now hired both Chase and Mathewson as coaches for the 1919 season—go figure it—and Chase finished the season without incident.

But the next spring, an old Cincinnati teammate named Lee Magee surfaced with new evidence of Chase's game-fixing. On the advice of the league president, the Giants quietly released him, and he was informally banished from the major leagues. Indicted by the grand jury investigating the Black Sox scandal, he eluded extradition from California, and nothing was ever proved against him.

By the mid-'20s, Chase was in Arizona, managing the Douglas Blues, whose roster included a number of former Black Sox, thrown out of the majors and recruited by Chase. In subsequent years, Chase wandered through Southwest desert towns, managing a laundry, drinking, hanging out in pool halls. He later moved to California's Sacramento Valley, where he suffered a stroke and heart attack and, before his death in 1947, gave an interview to a local reporter.

Chase, who was sixty-four, said he'd known about the World Series fix in 1919, but had played no role in arranging it and didn't make a nickel on the scheme. He said he'd made small bets—with a $100 limit—throughout his career, but never against his own team. He said his life had been "all wrong . . . and my best proof is that I am flat on my back, without a dime. . . . I wasn't satisfied with what the club owners paid me. Like others, I had to have a bet on the side and we used to bet with the other team and the gamblers who sat in the boxes. . . . Once the evil started, there was no stopping it and club owners were not strong enough to cope with the evil. . . .

"You note that I am not in the Hall of Fame," Chase lamented. "Some of the old-timers said I was one of the greatest fielding first basemen of all time. When I die, movie magnates will make no picture like *Pride of the Yankees,* which honored that great player Lou Gehrig. I guess that's the answer, isn't it? Gehrig had a good name; one of the best a man could have. I am an outcast, and I haven't a good name. I'm the loser, just like all gamblers are."

This was Cobb's decade. A fixture in Detroit, he was by far the best player and the biggest gate attraction in the major leagues. In fact, until Babe Ruth revolutionized the game by walloping twenty-nine homers in 1919, Cobb defined baseball. It was a "Cobbian" game. That's what the experts called it, just as they later called it a "Ruthian" game. In the ten-year period from 1910 to 1919, Cobb racked up nearly two hundred base hits and sixty stolen bases each season and won seven batting titles. Look at his batting averages for the decade: .383, .420, .410, .390, .368, .369, .371, .383, .382, .384.

Awesome.

But Ty Cobb was the most unpleasant, vile, and thoroughly debased individual to ever play the game of baseball. And more than that, he was self-obsessed.

We hold to the idea that large egos are an affliction of modern players. But Cobb's ego looms supreme. As his career took wing, he combined the unbridled arrogance of a Reggie Jackson with the pouting moodiness of a Rickey Henderson. A perennial late show to spring training because he couldn't stand the lousy food and accommodations, Cobb was also a frequent holdout whose antics irritated management, teammates, and fans alike. His public demands to be traded by Detroit were suspiciously followed by poor performances in the field. But once Cobb stopped sulking, he railed against teammates whose performances struck him as substandard. Sometimes he refused to play alongside them.

Ty Cobb looked after Ty Cobb.

Let's take a tour down memory lane with the immortal Ty Cobb, sampling a few shining moments from this, his very own decade.

1910

With two days left in the season, Cobb was hitting .383—.008 ahead of Cleveland's Napoleon Lajoie, his closest contender for the American

League batting title. Convinced that he was a shoo-in to win his fourth straight title, Cobb skipped the Tigers' last two games to take a short trip with his wife. There was a gift that came with winning the batting championship—a luxury Chalmers automobile—and the Cobbs looked forward to driving it about Detroit.

His teammates didn't want him to win it.

Nor did his opponents.

On the final day of the season, the St. Louis Browns played a doubleheader against the Cleveland Indians. St. Louis manager Jack O'Connor positioned his third baseman—a rookie named Red Corriden—far back on the outfield grass every time Lajoie came to bat. The manager explained to the naive Corriden that he might otherwise be injured by one of Lajoie's wicked line drives. (Lajoie had broken a third baseman's leg with a line shot earlier in the season.) So what happened? Lajoie laid one lazy bunt after another down the third base line. Corriden had no chance to field them in time, so Lajoie tallied six hits. Over the course of the afternoon, he went eight for nine, and lifted his average to .384 to edge Cobb by .001 and win the batting title.

After the game, Cobb's Detroit teammates sent Lajoie a telegram offering their congratulations.

1912

Outfielder Cobb began one more season as a source of dissension on the club, boasting that he could pitch and play first base better than the Detroit regulars. Teammates thought him "swell-headed," the press reported, and were "in open rebellion against his domineering attitude." But Cobb turned this situation around. He managed to secure his teammates' support in a novel way—by attacking a crippled fan.

This event, one of the most infamous in Cobb's twenty-four-year career, happened on May 15 in the fourth inning of a game in New York. The fan, Claude Lueker, who was well known for verbally abusing athletes and city officials, had traded insults with Cobb earlier. Now he miscalculated by calling Cobb a "coon" or "half-nigger." Cobb quickly jumped the guardrail in front of the grandstand, climbed twelve rows to Lueker's seat, and launched the attack.

Lueker was a former pressman who had lost eight of his ten fingers in a workplace accident the year before; he now made a pathetic sight, holding his arms in front of his face for protection as Cobb punched and kicked him. "He cut me with his spikes, tore a big hole behind my ear, and cut my face in several places," Lueker reported. When neighboring spectators screamed that Lueker had no hands, Cobb responded with the memorable line, "I don't care if he has no feet."

1914

After a game against Washington late in the spring, Cobb learned that a butcher had sold his wife 20 cents' worth of spoiled fish earlier in the day. Cobb went straight to the shop to demand an apology, pointing a gun at the butcher's head. The butcher complied. But his assistant, a twenty-year-old black man named Harold Harding, argued. Cobb pistol-whipped Harding and spent a night in jail.

1915

Cobb feuded all year with the pitching staff of the Boston Red Sox, whose manager, Bill Carrigan, promoted the beanball. During a game in May, Boston's Dutch Leonard came at Cobb with a series of pitches, and finally hit the Tiger. In his next at bat, Cobb drag-bunted between the pitcher's mound and first base. Leonard took the throw at first for the out and ran straight into the coach's box, seeking a zone of safety. But the hell-bent Cobb sprinted out of the base line in pursuit and lunged, feet first, into the coach's box, tearing his spikes through Leonard's pants leg. Cobb said Leonard never threw at him again.

1918

Stirred by President Woodrow Wilson's call to service in World War I, Cobb enlisted in the military. Typically, he headed straight for the thick of things by obtaining a commission in the Chemical Warfare Service. During a gas mask drill, he and fellow officer Christy Mathewson were accidentally exposed to poison gas. Mathewson never quite recovered his health and died of tuberculosis seven years later. But Cobb, strong as a bull, returned to baseball.

1919

Cobb exchanged words one fall afternoon with a loud-mouthed fan who sat behind the Detroit dugout. Afterward, when the fan went onto the field to get in Cobb's face, Cobb kneed him in the groin. Later, when a group of the man's friends waited for Cobb outside the ballpark, Cobb challenged them to fight, one by one. And one by one, they slunk away, chastened by the glowering Mr. Cobb.

Cobb vs. McGraw

During a spring training game in Dallas in 1917 before ten thousand people, McGraw's Giants taunted Cobb. Their pitchers whistled a few pitches past his head and glanced one off his shoulder.

National Baseball Library

"You talkin' to me?" McGraw (pictured here) and Cobb nearly had it out in 1917 . . .

Cobb took first base and threatened pitcher Jeff Tesreau: "I'll take care of you the next time I go up there."

Tesreau answered, "You try any funny business with me and I'll knock your brains out."

The next batter came up. On the second pitch, Cobb took off toward second base. He should have been out by a mile—the Giants had pitched out, anticipating the steal. But as Giants second baseman Buck Herzog waited for him, Cobb shifted into his rocket mode. He accelerated and leaped toward Herzog, feet first—Cobb's "I-will-now-end-your-career" routine—and branded and bloodied the second baseman with his spikes.

A wild brawl followed, with police taking the field to pry Cobb and Herzog apart.

That night, Cobb and McGraw crossed paths in the lobby of the Hotel Orient.

We pick up the narrative with this excerpt from author Frank Graham's history of the New York Giants:

McGraw's eyes flamed and his neck swelled. Thrusting his face close to Ty's, he called him every name he could think of—and there were few, if any, that he omitted. For once, as they were ringed quickly by the crowd in the lobby, Ty kept a check on his temper.

"That will be enough," he said, coldly. "If you were a younger man, I'd kill you."

"I'm young enough!" McGraw shouted. "Start killing, you yellow xxxx! You white-livered xxxx!"

Cobb, now shaking with rage, walked away from him.

"You tramp!" McGraw yelled after him. "You yellow xxx! I wouldn't have you on my ball club if you were the last ballplayer in the world!"

In the dining room a short time later, Herzog went to Cobb's table.

"What's the number of your room?" he asked.

Cobb told him.

"I'll be up there at ten o'clock," Herzog said. "I'll bring one player with me and you can have one of your players there. You can have [Tigers trainer] Harry Tuttle there, too, to act as referee."

At ten o'clock Herzog and [teammate] Heine Zimmerman entered Cobb's room. Tuttle was there—and, in addition to Cobb, eight other Detroit players.

"Take your shirt off," Herzog said to Cobb.

They stripped to the waist and started punching. It wasn't much of a fight. Herzog knocked Cobb to his knees with the first punch. But Cobb got up and beat him unmercifully until Tuttle stepped in.

"They fought like a couple of washerwomen," Tuttle said later.

Both, however, were satisfied. Herzog considered that he had avenged himself for the spiking by knocking Cobb down. Cobb figured he had squared accounts by blacking Herzog's eyes, bloodying his nose, and pounding him into a state of helplessness.

155

Cobb vs. McGraw

. . . but it was the Giants' Buck Herzog who knocked Cobb to the floor with one punch in the legendary hotel fight in Dallas.

Tale of the Killer Grapefruit

Wilbert "Uncle Robbie" Robinson tracked plenty of high pops during his seventeen-year career as a major league catcher. And so in the summer of 1915, while managing Brooklyn, he bet his players that he could catch a baseball dropped four hundred feet from an airplane.

The next day, Robinson and his team trooped to the beach where the great catch was to be made. Standing in the crowd was Casey Stengel, Brooklyn's twenty-six-year-old outfielder and resident joker. Team trainer Frank Kelly boarded the airplane hired for the occasion. He had volunteered to drop the baseball from the plane, only he wasn't carrying a baseball. Kelly was toting a large pink grapefruit, and, according to most tellings of this story, the man who handed it to him was Stengel.

The plane took off. The sphere was dropped. And Robinson tried to get a bead on it, turning in circles in the sand as the sphere hurtled down, twisting, curving, and finally accelerating through Robinson's expectant fingers. The grapefruit smashed into the stunned manager's chest, knocked him down, and splattered him with its ruby-red flesh.

"Jesus!" Robinson screamed, writhing in the sand. "Jesus! I'm killed! It's broke open my chest! I'm covered with blood! Jesus! Somebody help me!"

But nobody helped. Everybody laughed.

National Baseball Library

**Brooklyn manager Wilbert Robinson
thought he had been killed by a
falling grapefruit.**

Yuck!

The move to ban the spitball began at mid-decade. It wasn't strongly prompted by concerns about safety: that wildly veering spitters were being thrown at batters' heads. Or by the fact that the spitter at times demoralized hitters, making the game actionless and boring. No, the move to ban the spitball came about largely because the spitball was *disgusting*.

Who wanted to touch a baseball loaded with spit and phlegm? You think infielders wanted to pick that mess up? The amazing thing is that it took so long for the players to protest. Apparently they had grown so used to handling the gross, loaded baseballs that it didn't dawn on them to complain.

By 1915, players were complaining a lot about the health hazards involved. Newspapers editorialized against the use of unsanitary loaded baseballs. The pitcher Ad Brennan missed the 1916 and 1917 seasons when he became ill with diphtheria; his sickness was widely blamed on the use of unsanitary balls.

A worldwide flu epidemic broke out toward the end of World War I, killing thousands. It sealed the spitball's fate. After the 1919 season, the first restrictions on the spitball were passed. These limited the number of spitballers per team to two. The pitch was too ingrained in the game to eliminate it at once; too many pitchers would have lost their livelihoods. But this was a start.

The campaign against the spitter and the throwing of all dirty, scuffed, and doctored baseballs continued in 1920. The impetus: the fatal beaning of Cleveland Indians shortstop Ray Chapman.

Preview: Carl Mays

In 1915, his rookie season, Boston Red Sox pitcher Carl Mays threw a series of fastballs past Ty Cobb's head. This initiated a feud in the course of which Cobb threatened to shatter one of May's kneecaps with a line drive.

Mays kept throwing them past Cobb's head.

Sometime later, when Cobb drag-bunted toward first base and Mays covered the bag, Tyrus left an imprint with his spikes on the back of the pitcher's leg. Mays fell to the ground, bleeding profusely.

"Next time I'll take the skin off the other one," Cobb warned him.

But Mays kept throwing them past Cobb's head.

They detested each other.

Yet they were so alike, these two pit bulls.

Like Cobb, Mays was highly intelligent—to the point of being scornful of his colleagues. He was a good family man, didn't drink or carouse, and, like Cobb again, displayed an admirable work ethic. But like Cobb, too, he didn't get along with people and didn't understand why he provoked their hostility. More than Cobb, he was introspective about this failing: "I always have wondered why I have encountered this antipathy from so many people wherever I have been," he once said sadly. "And I have never been able to explain it, even to myself."

Well, the mystery was not so profound. Like Cobb, Mays was antisocial. He never participated in clubhouse banter; it was beneath him. At least this was the attitude he projected. He was a scowler: one teammate said he had the disposition of someone with a permanent toothache. He was ungracious, like Cobb, carrying on if teammates were less than perfect in the field; he screamed at them if they made errors.

In his book on Mays and the 1920 pennant race, *The Pitch That Killed,* author Mike Sowell chronicled the many cruelties that Mays suffered—and may have brought upon himself—both on and off the field.

In 1919, during spring training, his new custom-built house in Mansfield, Missouri, burned to the ground. Mays was convinced that it was arson; several of his mules had been shot a short time before.

His mitt was stolen from the Boston clubhouse; when Mays asked if any of his teammates would lend him a glove, there was silence in the dugout.

Throughout all of this, Mays remained a highly effective pitcher. He was one of the best hurlers of his time, winning over two hundred ball games. And he was one of the most unusual: he used an extreme sidearm delivery, his knuckles often scraping the ground as he corkscrewed toward his release. His pitches rose as they hurtled toward the batter. And if a right-handed hitter crowded the plate, they often wound up in the vicinity of his head.

159
Preview:
Carl Mays

Mays was known to have unusually good control, which puts a dark cast on the fact that he hit batters more frequently than almost any other pitcher in the league. He became known as a beanballer. And just as Cobb denied intentionally spiking opponents, Mays denied intentionally throwing at hitters—in fact, he acted affronted if it was suggested that he did. And yet, like Cobb again, Mays realized that his reputation gave him an advantage. He played off the fear that was in the minds of the batters who faced him. His primary concern was winning ball games; this was more important than being popular.

Like Bob Gibson in the 1960s and '70s, Carl Mays was an intimidator who didn't go out of his way to be friendly to people.

Like Rob Dibble in the 1980s and '90s, Mays didn't object if people thought him a little bit crazy.

But unlike Gibson and Dibble, Mays eventually killed one of his opponents. In the history of major league baseball, he stands alone.

Read more about it in the next chapter.

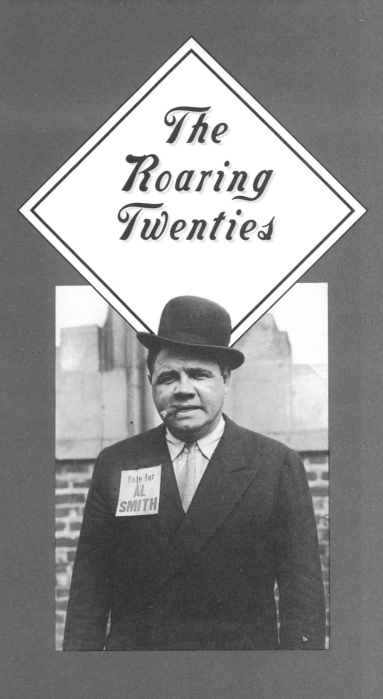

162

*The
Roaring
Twenties*

1920
- Rube Foster founds the first Negro National League.
- Yankee infielder Chick Fewster is beaned in spring exhibition game.
- Babe Ruth hits fifty-four home runs during season. One fan dies of excitement watching the Bambino loft one out.
- In August: Yankee pitcher Carl Mays fatally beans Cleveland shortstop Ray Chapman.
- September: Black Sox scandal breaks. Eight White Sox indicted in Chicago.
- November: Judge Kenesaw Mountain Landis is hired as game's first commissioner.

1921
- Ty Cobb becomes manager of Detroit Tigers.
- Cobb slams head of umpire Billy Evans into concrete during fight under grandstand in Washington, D.C.
- Former Giants catcher Larry McLean is shot and killed in barroom brawl.
- All eight White Sox are acquitted by jury of conspiring to fix the 1919 World Series. Landis, convinced of their guilt, banishes them from the game.

1922
- Unsuccessful attempt to start players' union.
- Ruth is suspended five times for altercations with umpires.
- Yankee outfielder Whitey Witt is hit in head by bottle thrown in St. Louis.
- Giants spitballer Phil Douglas is banned from baseball. He secretly offered to desert Giants during pennant race if St. Louis rivals paid him.

1923
- St. Louis Cardinals slugger Rogers Hornsby punches out his manager, Branch Rickey.

- Cincinnati pitcher Dolf Luque leaves the mound and rages, fists flying, into New York Giant dugout after razzing about Latin heritage. Thrown out of game, Luque returns, brandishing bat.
- New York Giants court Jewish fans by hiring outfielder Moses H. Solomon in the fall. "The Rabbi of Swat," who hit forty-nine homers in the minors earlier in the year, bombs.

1924
- Giants utility player Jimmy O'Connell offers $500 to Phillies shortstop Heine Sand to go easy in crucial game. O'Connell is banished from baseball.
- Brooklyn fans batter down gate with telephone pole to gain entrance to Ebbets Field.

1925
- Ruth collapses from his famous "bellyache." Many suspect he suffers from syphilis.
- Christy Mathewson dies of tuberculosis.
- St. Louis Browns slugger Ken Williams is hitting .331, with twenty-five homers and 105 RBIs, when he suffers a near-fatal beaning. Williams misses last third of the season and is noticeably gun-shy for the rest of his career.
- Umpire Richard Nallin is caught in pop-bottle shower in Detroit.

1926
- Cobb and Tris Speaker are accused of having fixed a game in 1919. They are forced to give up managing jobs with Detroit and Cleveland, respectively. But each continues to play.
- Cardinals win the World Series. Two people die in rioting in St. Louis.

1927
- Baseball gambling pool in Albany, New York, grosses over $4 million.
- Ban Johnson resigns as American League president after more than a quarter century.

1928
- Ty Cobb plays his final season.
- Leo Durocher plays his first.
- Billy Martin is born in Berkeley, California.

- Chicago White Sox first baseman Art "the Great" Shires beats up manager Lena Blackburn three times. Shires goes on a successful boxing tour.
- "Pop-bottle riot" erupts over unpopular call by umpire during game in Cleveland. One fan, struck in the head, dies.

*The
Roaring
Twenties*

National Baseball Library

Ruth reigns . . .

I tried to kick the big bastard's eyes out with my spikes. I about lost my mind.
—Umpire Lee Ballanfant

These were baseball's golden years.

Green grass and Babe Ruth.

Can't you just see the Sultan swatting those long arching home runs, hot-dogging it around the bases with that fool grin on his face, as the adoring crowd cheers?

Big bang baseball had arrived with Ruth. Sports fans were sick of the old, tight-ass "scientific" game. Enough with the science. It was time to party with the Babe. And once George Herman Ruth started socking those home runs over the wall, all the other players realized that, why, they could do it, too. And they did: Rogers Hornsby, Lou Gehrig, Hack Wilson. Boom! Boom! Boom! Offenses went crazy. Batting averages and run production soared. So did attendance. Gate receipts zoomed, and the focus of the sports world was fixed on New York City. The Yankee dynasty was established for the next forty years. Ruth reigned.

He brought the game prosperity and wider acceptance. His persona was larger than baseball itself: "Ruth-o-mania" swept the country.

But there's a lot missing from this picture.

These were schizoid times: the optimism and prosperity that Ruth helped bring to baseball were balanced against a looming sense of doom and gloom.

As Ruth slugged his way toward a .376 batting average and fifty-four home runs in the 1920 season, tragedy struck. On August 16, with Babe looking on from his position in left field, Yankee pitcher Carl Mays unleashed the fastball that struck Cleveland Indians shortstop Ray Chapman on the side of the head. Chapman dropped to the ground instantly, blood streaming from his left ear. He died early the next morning.

Mays haters around the league—and there were a lot of them—insisted that he had beaned Chapman on purpose. Mays remonstrated that no decent white man would intentionally kill another. The pitch had simply slipped, he said, and Chapman, crowding the plate, had trouble picking up the dirty-gray baseball as it shot toward his head.

But the major leagues were gripped with fear that more fatal accidents might occur. And this fear generated far-reaching changes in the game: tighter restrictions on spitballs and an outright ban on trick pitches that relied on scuffing or dirtying the baseball.

The spitball phaseout continued as the leagues drew up a new short list of veteran spitballers who could finish their careers without penalty. These included Burleigh Grimes of the Dodgers, who once knocked a clubhouse boy around for failing to clean his socks properly. Outside this group, the spitball was now illegal. Moreover, from this time on, no one on the field was allowed to rub up the ball with tobacco juice, licorice juice, mud, grease, or anything else. And umpires, for the first time, were ordered to keep fresh balls on hand and in play. The dirty, stained, waterlogged, and otherwise abused baseball—long an emblem of the game—was history.

The repercussions were enormous. It's always been said that the owners introduced a lively new "rabbit" ball at this time to encourage heavy hitting. More likely, the new insistence on clean baseballs—combined with the example of Ruth's free-swinging success, and the availability of whiplike bats with thin handles—tipped the balance of power toward the batters. All of this spurred the wave of heavy hitting that characterized the decade.

Baseball's big guns excited the press and public, to be sure, pulling in hundreds of thousands of new fans. But while they proved a distraction, nothing could cover up the news that broke on September 28, 1920, little more than a month after the Chapman beaning. It was announced that day that eight members of the Chicago White Sox had been indicted for throwing the 1919 World Series to Cincinnati. Chicago owner Charles Comiskey proclaimed that he would run the men out of baseball if the allegations proved true.

Of course, Comiskey had known about the fix for nearly a year. He had hoped that his little secret wouldn't go public and, in a remarkable display of upside-down morality, had even awarded salary raises to the crooked players at the start of the 1920 season.

But with the indictments came panic. And with the panic came a radical restructuring of baseball's hierarchy. The changes were established in November when Comiskey and the fifteen other club owners agreed to centralize power in the office of an independent baseball commissioner. The man they chose to wield that power was federal judge Kenesaw Mountain Landis. Desperate to restore baseball to respectability, the owners granted him wide-ranging investigative and punitive powers to shine up its image. Landis declared, "If I catch any crook in baseball, the rest of his life is going to be a hot one."

But if truth be told, the stony-faced Landis—he carried himself as if he belonged on Mount Rushmore—had a tendency to nail the little fish and let the big ones swim away.

Like Comiskey and an array of moralists through the years—Branch Rickey and Peter Ueberroth come to mind—Landis knew how to project just the right public image. He appeared fixed on making the game pure for God and country. But he also served the almighty dollar.

For too long, the judge has been portrayed as an Old Testament prophet, come to banish iniquity and prepare the Kingdom of Baseball for a millennium of glorious peace.

Give us a break.

Landis had a history of showmanship.

A high school dropout, he finished his degree at night, and never went to college. He enrolled in a YMCA law

National Baseball Library

White Sox owner Charles Comiskey. He knew his team threw the 1919 World Series, but engaged in a coverup.

school in Cincinnati and was on his way. Exercising family connections, he eventually secured a federal judgeship and became notorious for his courtroom theatrics, his vengefulness, and his circumventing of legal protocol. His decisions were constantly thrown out on appeal. But they were dramatic. He imposed a $29.4 million fine on Standard Oil in a famous trust-busting decision that was later dismissed. A foe of organized labor, he imposed incredibly heavy fines and prison sentences on a group of Wobblies, who were handcuffed during court proceedings and berated by the judge for being unpatriotic.

He knew how to frame issues, simply and starkly, in the strongest moral terms. And so the major league club owners made him their savior.

Landis became the Big Baseball Cleaner-Upper. When the eight Black Sox were acquitted in court of conspiring to throw the World Series, Landis banished them from baseball anyway. As long as the judge had the broom out of the closet, he was going to sweep.

Now, you can argue that Landis had to banish the Black Sox. Their prosecution was probably mishandled, a number of them had confessed before the trial, and, besides, Landis had to make an example of someone if baseball was going to bounce back from the moral pit into which it had fallen.

Of course, the campaign needed to be tempered with practicality: Landis conceded privately that if he went after every player who threw games before 1920, the ranks of major league baseball would be decimated. It's not hard to see that there was an arbitrariness to the way he meted out punishment.

In 1921, New York Giant outfielder Benny Kauff was acquitted in court of the charge that he stole an automobile on Manhattan's East Side. Landis called the acquittal "one of the worst miscarriages of justice that ever came under my observation" and banned him from the game.

That same year, Giants owner Charles Stoneham was indicted for using the mails to defraud investors. Stoneham had been tied in with a complicated financial scandal that drained innocent people of millions of dollars. While under indictment, the Giants owner was elected to the National League's board of directors.

Landis did nothing.

And when Stoneham was acquitted, the judge did nothing again—except let out a sigh of relief.

In 1924, Frankie Frisch, George Kelly, and Ross Youngs of the Giants were implicated in an attempted bribe of Philadelphia shortstop Heinie Sand. Landis barely looked into the matter. He asked the three future Hall of Famers if it was true, they said it wasn't, and the judge dropped the case right there. Yet he banished the naive twenty-three-year-old Giant outfielder Jimmy O'Connell, who admitted offering the money to Sand—and said Frisch, Kelly and Youngs knew all about it. O'Connell wasn't a star.

Judge Kenesaw Mountain Landis became baseball's first commissioner in the wake of the Black Sox scandal.

Money drives the game now, and it drove it then.

In the early '20s, the New York Yankees sucked the Boston Red Sox dry. Taking advantage of Red Sox owner Harry Frazee, a Broadway theater entrepreneur who was always short of cash, the Yankees had already bought Ruth from Boston for $125,000. Now they bought pitchers Carl Mays, Waite Hoyt, and Herb Pennock and the outstanding defensive catcher Wally Schang. By 1923, the twenty-four members of the World Champion Yankees included eleven ex-Bostonites. The Red Sox became known as the Dead Sox.

And that's how the Yankee dynasty got started.

There was a lot of money around.

Ruth made a ton, peaking at $80,000 one year.

But first baseman Bill Terry, a future Hall of Famer who batted in the .370s through most of the mid to late '20s, couldn't buy a two-year contract from the New York Giants. Shortstop Dick Bartell, one of the hardest-working young players in either league, fought with Pittsburgh Pirates owner Barney Dreyfuss over the cost of a lobster dinner on the road. Dreyfuss deducted $2.40 from his shortstop's paycheck.

Through the decades, we've come to think of the Roaring Twenties as an idyllic time for baseball. But there's so much missing from that notion.

—The effects of segregation are missing.

The first Negro National League was founded in 1920 by a retired pitching star named Rube Foster, a pipe-smoking strategic genius. The Kansas City Monarchs and Chicago American Giants—these were among the black teams that could take on the major leaguers, no sweat. But most Americans never even heard of black stars like Oscar Charleston (*the* greatest ballplayer of the era, said John McGraw) and Willie "the Devil" Wells (so dangerous a hitter that he was later forced to wear a mining helmet to protect himself from beanballs).

These fellows played hard and mean—and when they competed against white major leaguers on informal barnstorming tours, they usually won. But they played to little popular acclaim, their skills largely unrecognized outside their segregated communities.

—Alcohol is missing.

Drinking was endemic in baseball. In the minors, the Quebec-Ontario-Vermont League was nothing more than a cover to smuggle hooch into the United States. In the majors, the legion of alcoholic superstars included shortstop Rabbit Maranville and pitcher Grover Cleveland Alexander, who was drunk as a skunk after he shut down the Yankees during the 1926 World Series. Bill Veeck remembered watching the arrival of pitcher Vic Aldridge at the Chicago Cubs training camp in the mid-'20s. Aldridge carried "one huge suitcase, so heavy that it took two redcaps to lug it to his room. . . . In his bag was a toothbrush and maybe 100 bottles of Pinaud's hair tonic."

Ballplayers didn't live in a vacuum. This was the Jazz Age. Prohibition fostered the alcoholic haze of the times: there were thirty-two thousand speakeasies in New York City. When Babe Ruth & Co. arrived in the South for spring training, they brought their habits with them. One headline of the era tells the whole story: "Yankees Training on Scotch."

—Violence is missing.

The fans were, as always, crackbrained: a bottle thrown from the grandstand flayed the head of Yankee outfielder Whitey Witt during the 1922 pennant race.

Stadium security guards were crackbrained: in Brooklyn and Manhattan, they had a habit of beating up spectators who tried to pocket foul balls.

Ty Cobb was as crackbrained as ever: "I fight only one way, and that's to kill," he informed umpire Billy Evans before flattening Evans under the grandstand in Washington, D.C., in 1921. Ty slammed the ump's head, up and down, into the concrete, while digging his fingers into Evans's throat.

Violence was woven into the very execution of the game. This was a heyday of the brushback pitch, which was the physical expression of this attitude: "I'm gonna knock you on your ass."

The model for 1920s-style intimidation was pitcher Burleigh Grimes: "He made Bob Gibson and Don Drysdale look like the angels of mercy," said shortstop Dick Bartell, who played with Grimes on the Pirates in the late '20s.

For ten years, Grimes threw at Frankie Frisch every time they met. The switch-hitting Frisch, who played for the Giants and the St. Louis Cardinals, was a great low-ball hitter from the left side, and he

The
Roaring
Twenties

Long before
Maglie, Drysdale,
or Gibson,
there was the
intimidating
Burleigh Grimes.

could handle Burleigh's sinking spitter without much problem. "It annoyed the hell out of Burleigh, so he started throwing at Frank," said St. Louis sportswriter Bob Broeg, explaining how the feud got started. "But Frisch could move so goddamn fast that Burleigh had a hard time hitting him.

"One day, Frisch drag-bunted down the first base line and accidentally spiked Grimes as they raced to the bag; he almost severed one of the tendons in Burleigh's ankles, which would have ruined his career. So sometime later, Frisch, before a game, said, 'Jesus Christ, Burleigh, I never meant to do that to you.' But the next time Frankie came up, Burleigh hit 'im, and the war was on again. On the way down to first base, Frisch yells, 'Jesus Christ, Burleigh, I apologized.' And Burleigh says, 'Yes, but you didn't *smile.*' "

The stubble-bearded Grimes won 270 games with this unvarnished approach. It didn't make him unique; the '20s were filled with stars who fumed their way to glory. Another was Hack Wilson of the Chicago Cubs, who once beat a fan over the head with a bat.

One of Hack's trademarks was the way he walked to home plate looking like he had just stepped out of a coal mine. He owned the dirtiest uniform in baseball. Hack would reach down in the batter's box, scoop up some dirt, and bathe his arms in it, luxuriating in the dirt as it flew all over his jersey.

Then he would hit a home run.

Cubs slugger Hack Wilson hit even more bottles than home runs.

Wilson was one of the most devastating sluggers in the game. His roommate, Pat Malone, is sometimes remembered as the number one headhunting pitcher of all time. Both men loved to drink. Their friendship, wrote Bill Veeck, was "bonded in bourbon and bottled in rye."

In 1929, they helped lead the Cubs to the National League pennant.

One day, after finishing a series against the Reds in Cincinnati, Wilson and Malone were racing through the train station to catch the team train after dallying to have a few drinks in a local bar. And who should approach them from the opposite direction? None other than Cincinnati pitcher Ray Kolp, who had spent that afternoon riding Wilson from the Reds' dugout.

"Have we got a minute?" Wilson asked Malone.

His friend "squinted at his watch," Veeck recounted, "and decided they might be able to spare one minute but precious little more. Hack skidded to a stop, dropped his bag, and belted Kolp out with a right hook. Pat, who had nothing against anybody particularly, dropped his own bag and belted out Kolp's roommate just to show whose side he was on. They then presumably sang two choruses of 'Friendship' and shuffled off to catch the train."

These are the eight members of the Chicago White Sox who were banished from baseball for their alleged roles in fixing the 1919 World Series.

Eddie Cicotte—The first of the eight to confess prior to trial in 1921: "I've lived a thousand years in the last year. . . . I got $10,000 for being a crook."

One of the best pitchers of his time, Cicotte finished his career with 208 victories and a 2.38 ERA.

Happy Felsch—"This time it looks like the joke's on us," the Black Sox center fielder philosophized.

Chick Gandil—Said to be the ringleader. In 1955, the old first baseman said, "I don't believe we would have ever been caught if Cicotte hadn't gabbed."

Joe Jackson—Though he apparently had attended planning sessions for the fix and said he received $5,000 for his role in the conspiracy, Jackson hit .375 in the Black Sox Series and knocked in six runs.

Shoeless Joe was among the most gifted hitters of any era, batting .356 in thirteen seasons. He hit .408 in 1911.

Fred McMullin—The second-string infielder said he was willing to help with the conspiracy if he could see some action during the Series. He pinch-hit twice and got one hit.

The infamous 1919 "Black Sox"

Swede Risberg—The shortstop batted .080 in the Series, with two hits in twenty-five at bats. Risberg supposedly threatened to "bump off" Jackson when the Shoeless one considered making a confession.

Buck Weaver—The third baseman backed out of the plot and played well in the Series. But he was banished for his guilty knowledge of the fix; he didn't squeal.

Lefty Williams—His 0–3 record and 6.61 ERA during the Black Sox Series tells all.

The Bambino

Ty Cobb is a prick.
—Babe Ruth

And so was the Babe.

Okay, he liked kids. And he was a charmer, the big lug, even though he was funny-looking, with that pie-shaped face and porcine nose. He was exuberant, brimming with energy, and so appealing as he drove around town in his big, shiny Packard, with his camel's-hair cap tilted rakishly to the side, and the ever-present fat cigar stuck in his mouth. He looked even better on the ball field in his New York Yankee pinstripes, executing the double steal on his spindly legs, and, most of all, swatting those enormous home runs—at will, it seemed. He hit fifty-four of them in 1920, nearly twice as many as the year before. And his free-swinging success turned the game on its head, brought a new attitude to baseball, as hitters unleashed an offensive explosion in both leagues. Ruth's domination of the game was total—nothing like it had ever been seen before in any sport. And the cult of personality that emerged around him was new not just to sports, but to American popular culture. He seemed to embody the free-living spirit, the optimism, of the Roaring Twenties. And the public responded by flocking to ballparks in record numbers, more than five million in 1920, more than ten million a decade later.

It's all true.

You've heard it all before.

But we are looking at baseball through a different lens.

Red Smith once wrote that "many players are physical animals with a layer of muscle enclosing the intellect." That describes Babe Ruth to a T. He was a man-child, egocentric and out of control: the very prototype for the modern athlete, drunk on headlines, who can't get enough money, enough drink or drugs, enough women. These characters had been in the game all along, but Ruth truly delivered the whole ball of wax. He set the standard. And though we tend to look back at his era as a golden one, it set the stage for the emergence of today's celebrity athletes—irresponsible, spoiled men.

In his first week of spring training with the Yankees in Florida in 1920, the Babe, drunk out of his mind, ran into a palm tree in the outfield and was knocked unconscious.

He gave his manager, Miller Huggins, heartache.

Were he playing today, Ruth would be in and out of alcohol rehabilitation programs. Babe used to down fifths of Old Grand-Dad while playing hearts on the team train. The young Leo Durocher, who turned out to be a far bigger bastard than Ruth, once looked on aghast as the Babe hung Huggins from the window of a speeding train. That was Babe's idea of a joke.

Arriving in the next town, Babe ran a meat market at the hotel; young women were always there to meet him. Babe chose two or three and took them upstairs. Maybe his wife was traveling with him; maybe she wasn't. His teammates covered for him.

The next morning, as usual, he drank whiskey for breakfast. At batting practice, he ate three hot dogs and washed them down with bicarbonate of soda.

He belched a lot.

And in the spring of 1925, he collapsed from the effects of a horrible "bellyache"; most of the people who knew him assumed the Babe was suffering from syphilis. Ruth missed almost half the season and was fined $5,000 for failure to manage his personal life.

The Babe was incensed: "Why, I know of guys killing people . . . and even bootleggers, who don't get that tough a

National Baseball Library

*Babe Ruth was out of control.
The very prototype for the modern athlete.*

fine. It ain't right!" he shouted, red-faced, to sportswriters. "I'll never play for that xxxx Huggins again."

The fine was largely inspired by his behavior off the field.

On the field, he punched umpires in the nose. He threw dirt in their faces. He chased hecklers through the stands. He called his manager, the diminutive Huggins, "little boy." He was suspended five times in one season, 1922, for his shenanigans.

Apparently Ruth's behavior caught on with his Yankee teammates. The sportswriter Grantland Rice wrote that Huggins's "constant struggle to take and keep charge of the greatest collection of high-priced primadonnas the game has ever seen wore him down and, eventually, killed him."

Once Ruth got good and drunk and drove a car full of passengers into a ditch in a Philadelphia suburb at 3 A.M., flipping it on its side. No one was hurt. But the press was filled with complaints about how this nitwit was earning a lot of money and it was about time he acted responsibly.

Still, Ruth wasn't always the bad boy.

Sometimes he was a victim of the racist bench jockeying that went on in the game. The Babe was said to have stereotypically Negroid characteristics: big lips, a swarthy complexion, the physique of an ape. His own teammates called him "you big ape." Going back to his school days in Baltimore, Ruth had been nicknamed "Nigger Lips." This moniker was known throughout the big leagues, and there was speculation around the country that Ruth was indeed part black.

In the 1922 World Series between the Yankees and the Giants, John McGraw assigned his little second-string second baseman, Johnny Rawlings, to sit in the dugout and harass the Babe. That was Rawlings's sole job: to scream at, insult, and distract Ruth. Babe was particularly sensitive to the racial insinuations, and so he ambled over to the Giants' dugout before one of the games to discuss the matter.

"Hey, you guys," he said, "I don't mind if you call me cocksucker or motherfucker or sonofabitch—but lay off the personal stuff, will ya?"

With the ascendance of Babe Ruth, big lumbering white men took over the major league game of baseball. It became a less subtle game, in which strategies developed over decades became somewhat marginal. Mostly, everyone sat around and waited for one of the hulks to belt the ball out of the park with a couple of men on board. Over and out.

But as praise and attention was lavished on the titans of the white game, the practitioners of speed-dominated black baseball toiled in the shadows, unrecognized by most of mainstream society. The Kansas City Monarchs swept a doubleheader from the Babe Ruth All-Stars during a barnstorming tour in 1922, but then they returned to the segregated world of Negro baseball. Salaries were dismal. Teams often played more than two hundred games a year, bedding down in Jim Crow rooming houses around the country. The magnificent shortstop John Henry Lloyd, who became a professional in 1905 and was among the most famous black ballplayers for the next twenty-five years, did not retire to comfort or acclaim. He became a janitor in Atlantic City, New Jersey.

By ignoring stars like Lloyd, society at large didn't just accede to segregation—it missed a spectacle.

In black ballparks, fans were as unruly as in the majors, possibly more so. Bottles were thrown like crazy. Spectators jumped over fences to attack players and umpires. Police charged in on horseback to break it up. During one melee, the cops clubbed third baseman Jud "Boojum" Wilson over the head. Wilson, who came up with the Baltimore Black Sox in 1922, wasn't even hurt. One of the legendary desperados of the game, he was a crude fielder who blocked ground balls with his body and showed off his bruises afterward. A fearless fellow with a massive torso, Wilson assaulted pistol-toting umpires with his bat, chasing them around the bases. "The minute he saw an umpire, he became a maniac," said shortstop Jake Stephens, who later became

182

*The
Roaring
Twenties*

*Jud
"Boojum"
Wilson.
"I'll break
every bone
in your
body, boy."*

his best friend and roommate. One night, Stephens returned late to their hotel room in Chicago and disturbed Wilson, who "grabbed a hold of my leg and held me out the window sixteen stories above the street," Stephens recalled. "He said, 'You goddamn midget.' I said, 'Oh please, Willie, don't drop me.' "

Was this typical?

Boojum's behavior was certainly extreme.

After all, in black baseball the moonshiners and barroom miscreants played alongside church deacons and middle class college graduates. Not everyone behaved like Boojum Wilson. But we can recognize, and maybe admire a little, the pure malice on the hoof that Wilson represented as he intimidated his opponents with his Herculean frame. We can try to imagine how the scrappy outfielder Charles "Chino" Smith felt when he lost his senses and slid a little too hard into Boojum at third base one day and found himself lifted into the air by Wilson and thrown a distance of twenty feet.

"I'll break every bone in your body," Wilson muttered. "You better go about your business, boy."

Rogers Hornsby

Rogers Hornsby was the greatest right-handed batter in the history of baseball, but nobody liked him and few wanted him in their club.

He hit .358 over twenty-three years, the highest lifetime average after Ty Cobb. In the years 1921–25, Hornsby averaged an astounding .402. In 1926, he upped his credentials by moving full-time into management. That year, as player/manager of the St. Louis Cardinals, he led his team to a tense, seven-game World Series victory over the New York Yankees of Ruth and Gehrig. It was one of the most celebrated series ever played. Celebratory riots followed in St. Louis. And Hornsby was declared a baseball genius.

His career was at its peak.

But the next season, St. Louis sold him to the New York Giants.

And the season after that, the Giants traded him to the Boston Braves.

And the season after that, the Braves sold him to the Chicago Cubs.

Nobody wanted him.

Why? He wasn't violent. He wasn't dishonest. In fact, he was too honest. He was utterly tactless.

The Rajah, as he was known, was also a compulsive horseplayer whose gambling addiction embarrassed the game's moral arbiters in the post-Black Sox era.

There has always been a close association between baseball and gambling. Ballplayers to this day bet on the horses or go to the dog races.

But Hornsby became a devoted gambler almost immediately after the 1919 Black Sox scandal, when there was such great sensitivity in baseball to gambling. This, of course, was perfectly in character for the obstinate Hornsby, who didn't care what anyone thought of him. While Judge Landis railed about rooting out gambling from the game,

Hornsby became a racetrack regular and habitually telephoned bets to out-of-state tracks.

Baseball historian Charles C. Alexander has written that when Cardinals president Sam Breadon questioned his star's betting habits, Hornsby snapped, "Nobody's damn business."

But Commissioner Landis thought differently.

He called Hornsby to his Chicago office some time after the stock market crashed in 1929. It was common knowledge that Landis had dipped into the commissioner's reserve fund to purchase stock in a company known as Kelsey Wheel before the crash. This money had been lost, of course. And now, when Landis told Hornsby that his betting was a problem, the Rajah answered, "It is my recreation and it is gambling. Playing the horses is no different from playing Kelsey Wheel, except that I use my own money."

Touché.

But Hornsby didn't just insult Landis. He insulted teammates with his criticisms of their playing abilities. He insulted managers with his critiques of their decision-making abilities.

In the early '20s, when Branch Rickey managed the Cardinals, Hornsby showed his boredom and contempt by yawning during Rickey's blackboard lectures in the clubhouse.

Hornsby was so universally disliked that he was cheated out of the National League's Most Valuable Player award in 1924. That was the year he batted .424, the second-highest average in this century. But Jack Ryder, a member of the committee that selected the award winner, left Hornsby off his list of ten nominees. "Hornsby is a most valuable player to himself," Ryder said, "not to his club."

So the award went to Brooklyn's Dazzy Vance.

Ryder's criticism wasn't really true: Hornsby was devoted to his team and to the game to a fault. He skipped his mother's funeral in Texas after St. Louis clinched the pennant in 1926, even though the World Series against New York didn't start until the next week: "I've got a job to do here," he explained, "getting this club primed for our games with the Yankees. Mother would have understood."

Hornsby grew up near the stockyards district of Fort Worth, Texas. But he carried himself as a Victorian. His strict code of behavior made people uncomfortable and self-conscious.

He refused to go to movies or the theater during the season for fear of damaging his vision and batting ability.

He didn't bowl, for fear of hurting his arm.

He didn't smoke. He didn't drink liquor or even coffee.

He didn't do much of anything. He rarely even smiled.

One of the baseball directories asked him to name his favorite activities and Hornsby listed "lobby sitting."

Seriously.

But the man could gamble.

Hornsby was constantly in debt, sometimes for tens of thousands of dollars. While managing the Chicago Cubs, he borrowed money from some of his players. When team owner Bill Veeck, Sr., questioned whether this was a prudent course of action, Hornsby mouthed off and got himself fired.

But he didn't bet on baseball. Just on the horses.

He was never charged with a felony. He was never in any trouble with the law. There is no evidence that he moved in big-time gambling circles or with shady associates. He was happy with his bookmaker and handicapper and just wanted to be left alone to sit in the hotel lobby with his *Racing Form* stuffed into his back pocket.

"Never—get that—never has my wagering in any way interfered with my affairs on the diamond," Hornsby growled. "A ball game always is a fight to me and nothing else enters into it."

The Roaring Twenties

Macho Man: Umpire Lee Ballanfant

Lee Ballanfant, National League umpire from 1936 to 1957, talks about a 1926 incident in the minor leagues:

"I remember an incident in Corsicana, my first year in the Texas Association. I called a guy safe at the plate on a close play, and Bill Speer, a great big 215-pounder, who was on deck, said, 'You ain't got no guts.' I said, 'Hey, brother, when the ball game is over, we will see who has the guts.' I weighed only about 130 pounds, but as soon as the game was over, I tapped him on the shoulder and said, "What was that you said about having no guts?" He turned around, and goddamn, I parted his hair with my mask. He started bleeding like a stuck hog, and as I drew back to hit him again, the catcher, [Adolph] Dutch Krauss, grabbed the mask from me. Well, I jumped on his back just like I was climbing a telephone pole and started banging him on the jaw. Finally, a policeman pulled me off, but in the process I tried to kick the big bastard's eyes out with my spikes. I about lost my mind." (From *The Men in Blue,* by Larry R. Gerlach.)

Death on the Diamond

During a Florida exhibition game between the Yankees and Dodgers in the spring of 1920, Brooklyn pitcher Jeff Pfeffer threw a fastball that beaned New York second baseman Chick Fewster. Fewster dropped with a thud while his friend Yankee pitcher Carl Mays looked on. The twenty-four-year-old Fewster looked lifeless on the ground. He suffered a fractured skull and a brain concussion. A silver plate was inserted in his skull, and he was hospitalized for weeks. "Chick has everything," Yankee manager Miller Huggins had once said, anticipating that Fewster's career would rival that of the legendary second baseman Eddie Collins. Now this was in doubt.

Mays had long had a reputation for throwing at people, and his friend's misfortune seemed to bring home the sobering truth that Mays was placing his opponents in jeopardy. More than a month into the 1920 season, he sat in the bullpen, afraid to throw the ball at the inside corner of the plate. But as the weeks wore on, Mays regained his confidence and his place in the starting rotation.

On August 16, the Cleveland Indians were in town for a game at the Polo Grounds. Mays was on the mound, and Cleveland's shortstop, Ray Chapman, led off the fifth inning. Mays went into his corkscrew delivery and delivered his first pitch—a sidearm fastball that shot up and in. Was Chapman crowding the plate? Yankee catcher Muddy Ruel later insisted that the pitch was in the strike zone. But Chapman seemed to freeze. The ball struck him flush on the left side of the head, fracturing his skull and knocking him to the ground. As members of both clubs tried to attend to the injured batter, Mays, by some accounts, accused Chapman of feigning his injury. But within hours, Chapman was dead.

Cleveland's team doctor said Mays should be "strung up." Players around the league threatened to boycott Mays and the Yankees if the pitcher wasn't disciplined or even thrown out of baseball. Mays

*Carl Mays of
the Yankees.
His fastball killed
the Indians'
Ray Chapman
in 1920.*

received death threats and was provided a police bodyguard. He
seemed amazed by the accusation that he had intentionally beaned
Chapman: "When any man, however ignorant, illiterate, or malicious,
even hints that a white man in his normal mind would stand out there
on the field of sport and try to kill another, the man making that
assertion is inhuman, uncivilized, bestial."

He experienced some wildness in his starts after the beaning. Yet
he managed to win four in a row and finished the season with
twenty-six wins and eleven losses and a remarkable 2.10 ERA.

His statistics the next year were even more impressive:
twenty-seven wins against nine losses.

190

Ray Chapman,
the unlucky
shortstop
for the
Cleveland
Indians.

But Mays was a peculiar man whose accomplishments on the field were undercut by the fundamental doubts others held about his character.

Miller Huggins detested him. He was convinced that Mays intentionally lost ball games in the 1921 and 1922 World Series against the Giants. He held the same suspicions about Yankee pitcher Joe Wood.

These were the only two men he ever managed whom he would refuse to help in time of need, Huggins said: "If they were in the gutter, I'd kick them."

In November 1922, the Yankees placed Mays on waivers, but there was virtually no interest in him among the other clubs.

In *The Pitch That Killed: Carl Mays, Ray Chapman, and the Pennant Race of 1920,* author Mike Sowell quotes a newspaper account of New York's efforts to dump Mays: "His fits of temper, his outbursts of rage, his petty fault finding, made life a rather miserable proposition for Miller Huggins. The conduct of Mays came about as close to cracking the morale of the team as any human agency could. Mays is . . . one of the most fervently hated men in diamond annals. It wouldn't require the use of many fingers to count up his total of baseball friends."

Huggins tried to ruin Mays's career by benching him without explanation for almost the entire 1923 season.

In 1924, the Yankees sold Mays to the Cincinnati Reds for a pittance, and he enjoyed two more outstanding seasons before retiring in 1929. But the Chapman beaning branded him for life. Mays was acutely aware of this. He won 207 games in his career, lost only 126, and posted a lifetime 2.92 earned run average. But as the years passed, Carl Mays was never seriously considered for the Hall of Fame. And this made him bitter: "Just because I killed a man in an accident," he complained, "they keep passing me up."

A Sad Day for Baseball:
Durocher's Arrival

What a shock it must have been to meet the twenty-two-year-old Leo Durocher in his rookie season as a shortstop with the New York Yankees. Most rookies were button-lipped, respectful of their elders. Leo the Lip, from the moment of his arrival in the Bronx in 1928, was braying and abrasive.

He told manager Miller Huggins to bench the slumping Babe Ruth.

He believed in overt antagonism as the path to victory.

Why?

He had his teachers.

"Pat Malone of the Cubs used to get insulted if a hitter like me just took a good swing at the ball," Durocher wrote. "He'd come halfway down to the plate snarling, 'You're swinging *pretty good* for a humpty-dumpty. I think I'd just better knock your cap off.' The next pitch would come at my head and—boom—down I'd go. 'Throw at me again, you dumb Irishman,' I'd bray."

Nothing fazed him.

Durocher's earliest warfare instructor in the majors was the quiet, pipe-smoking Yankee manager Miller Huggins—another little man with a complex. Huggins looked at Durocher as a spark plug, a motivator to the Yankees, an irritant to everyone else.

He wanted Leo to sit in the dugout and "supply the old razzle-dazzle,"

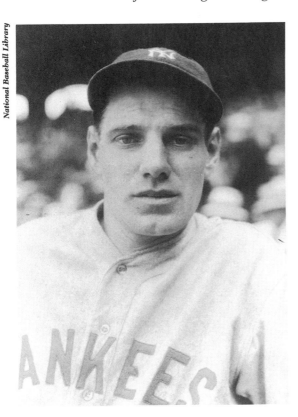

Meet insufferable rookie Leo Durocher.

Durocher said. "I get under his skin, but I know he likes to have me yipping on the bench."

When the Detroit Tigers came to town, Leo had a special name for Bob "Fatty" Fothergill, their jumbo outfielder: "Taxi."

When Leo learned that Ty Cobb was known as a cheapskate, he started calling him "pennypincher."

Durocher was the most offensive—and effective—bench jockey of the next several decades. He transformed the crude insult into high art. Leo would say anything—*anything*—to an opponent in his effort to break the man's concentration. He knew how to find the raw spot and stick in the knife. The sportswriter Dick Young once said that Durocher "devoted his life to making people hate him."

Throughout his playing career and decades managing the Dodgers, Giants, and, later, the Cubs, Durocher was baseball's bad boy. He dropped $100 bills inside the lockers of pitchers who threw at opponents' heads. He said he would trip his mother if she tried to get by him on the base paths, and no one doubted it. He whored around, got married, slept with other women within days of his wedding ceremony, got remarried, dressed like a sharpie, hustled pool, hung out with the Sinatra crowd, ran high-stakes card games in the clubhouse, and fell out of step with the times in the 1960s when he publicly humiliated his players with his brutal criticisms, referring to some of them as "wop" and "kike."

You will be hearing a great deal more about Durocher.

193

*A
Sad
Day for
Baseball:
Durocher's
Arrival*

Art the Great

His batting skills were compared to Ruth's and Cobb's.

His mouth was compared to Durocher's.

For a brief moment in the late '20s, Art Shires dominated national headlines with his braggadocio, his fistfights in the clubhouse, his boxing tours of urban arenas.

He called himself Art "the Great" Shires.

His teammates snickered and called him Art "What-a-Man" Shires.

What-a-Man wore a derby hat and spats and carried a walking stick. Like Bat Masterson. "I'm going to make $250,000 out of baseball before I'm through," he boasted. The press ate it up.

Shires was born in Italy, Texas, in 1907. While playing for the Waco team in the Texas League in 1928, he deliberately threw a ball into the stands. It hit a black man named Walter Lawson in the head and either killed or severely injured him; news accounts of the time differ. Shires went unpunished.

In fact, he was rewarded. Later that year, the White Sox brought him to the big leagues. In his first game, Shires tripled and hit three singles in five at bats. He batted .341 for the remainder of the season, a sensation, and was named team captain the following year.

But Shires was a swellhead and a drinker. During spring training in 1929, manager Lena Blackburn admonished him for cutting up during team exercises. Shires responded with a left hook, blackening one of Blackburn's eyes.

After the season began, Shires belted Blackburn a second time. And on the road in Philadelphia, when Blackburn tried to stop the drunken Shires from turning his hotel room into rubble, Shires punched out the manager again. Hotel detectives tried to intervene, but Shires chased the cops away by heaving liquor bottles at them.

He was suspended for the remainder of the season.

Shires was hurting financially now. The White Sox had fined him more than $3,000, so he sought out a famous Chicago prizefight manager named Nessie Blumenthal and suggested they stage a series of bouts. Blumenthal thought this was a terrific idea—Shires was a big name—and directed him to Jack Blackburn, Joe Louis's old trainer.

Shires's first match was in December 1929 in Chicago in front of a sold-out house of five thousand fans. His opponent was "Mysterious Dan Daly," a novice pulled off a construction site where he had been seen mixing concrete.

What-a-Man won. Fight number two was against the Chicago Bears' big center, George Trafton. They looked like two klutzes, but Trafton pounded Shires a few times and won the decision.

Then the Great One took his show on the road. He was packing them in, and winning. But when he returned to Chicago to fight Hack

*Art "the Great" Shires
beat up his manager
three times in 1929, then
went into boxing.*

Wilson, his bulky crosstown rival with the Cubs, Judge Kenesaw Mountain Landis decided that this circus had traveled far enough.

"Art," he said, "I'm the commissioner of baseball. You can either play baseball or fight. But you can't do both."

Shires reluctantly returned to the White Sox. But the pizzazz had gone out of his game, and he was traded to the Washington Senators. Soon he faded from sight, played some semipro ball, wrestled professionally, and opened a tavern in Dallas.

In 1948, he was charged with murdering W. H. Erwin, an old friend and former minor league ballplayer. "He hit me across the face with a telephone receiver," Shires explained, "and I knocked him down without thinking. I had to rough him up a good deal because he grabbed a knife and started whittling on my legs."

Erwin suffered internal injuries in the fight, an autopsy showed, but Shires was exonerated. It was determined that Erwin's death was due to natural causes; he had suffered from pneumonia and cirrhosis of the liver.

What-a-Man returned to his tavern, and died in 1967 at age fifty-nine.

The
1930s

198

*The
1930s*

1930
- The Year of the Hitter: National League batters collectively hit .303.
- Major league attendance tops ten million.

1931
- Lefty Grove, on his way to 31–4 season, wrecks his own Philadelphia A's locker room after losing ball game 1–0. It would have been his seventeenth consecutive win, a record. Grove loses when a young, inexperienced outfielder drops fly ball.
- Commissioner Landis is upset: Cubs catcher Gabby Hartnett has been chatting at the ballpark with Al Capone.

1932
- St. Louis Cardinals shortstop Charlie Gelbert shoots himself in the leg while hunting rabbits.
- Red Sox pitcher Ed Morris is fatally stabbed at Florida fish fry held in his honor.
- Umpire George Moriarty challenges entire Chicago White Sox team to fight at Memorial Day doubleheader in Cleveland. Several accept invitation.
- Bill Dickey breaks Carl Reynolds's jaw in Yankees-Senators brawl on Fourth of July.

1933
- Fans riot, players brawl during Yankees-Senators rematch in April.

1934
- John McGraw dies.
- Clyde "Pea Ridge" Day, ex-Brooklyn pitcher and hog caller, kills himself.

1935
- Brooklyn outfielder Len Koenecke is beaten to death with fire extinguisher by small-plane pilot in midflight.

- Chicago Cubs taunt and Jew-bait Detroit Tigers first baseman Hank Greenberg in World Series. Tigers win.

1936
- Umpiring team attacked with bottles in Savannah, Georgia. One ump is badly beaten; the other's skull is cracked by missile.
- Minor leaguer George Tkach is killed by pitch.
- Yankees trade ornery Ben Chapman to Senators for ornery Jake Powell.
- Detroit Tigers catcher Mickey Cochrane's career is ended by beanball thrown by Yankees' Bump Hadley.
- Umpire Bill Summers is hit in groin by bottle during barrage in Chicago.

1937
- Reds pitcher Lee Grissom, who won a total of two ball games in 1935 and 1936, holds out for more money.

1938
- Joe DiMaggio is fried by the public and press for contract dispute. The Yankee Clipper is booed everywhere. Receives death threats.
- Jake Powell of the Yankees and Joe Cronin of the Red Sox instigate big brawl before overflow crowd at Yankee Stadium on Memorial Day.
- Chicago White Sox pitcher Monty Stratton, an All-Star in '37, shoots himself in the leg while hunting rabbits. Leg is amputated.
- Deranged Brooklyn fan, Robert Joyce, kills bartender and patron after argument about the Bums.

1939
- Lou Gehrig retires.
- Billy Jurges and umpire George Magerkurth fight at Polo Grounds; each spits in the other's face.
- Leo Durocher becomes manager of Brooklyn Dodgers.
- Charlie Keller of Yankees knocks out Reds catcher Ernie Lombardi at home plate to win World Series.

I've been mobbed, cussed, booed, kicked in the ass, punched in the face, hit with mud balls and whiskey bottles, and had everything from shoes to fruits and vegetables thrown at me. I've been hospitalized with a concussion and broken ribs. I've been spit on and soaked with lime and water. I've probably experienced more violence than any other umpire who ever lived.
—*American League umpire Joe Rue*

As the 1934 World Series between the Detroit Tigers and St. Louis Cardinals moved toward its seventh and last game in Detroit, sportswriters proudly called it a throwback to the rabid contests of the 1890s. Spikings and fistfights punctuated the first six, hard-fought games. But game seven was a blowout. Dizzy Dean, who had toured Detroit in the back of a convertible earlier in the week, shouting at pedestrians as he strangled an inflatable rubber tiger, was on the mound for St. Louis. He did more than shut down the Tigers. Dean doubled and singled in the third inning as St. Louis batted around the order and scored seven runs. The 41,000 Detroit fans were disconsolate when, in the top of the sixth inning, St. Louis's ornery slugger Joe Medwick lofted a triple off the right-field wall and arrived at third base in a dust cloud. He slammed into third baseman Marv Owen with his left foot raised as if to spike Owen in the chest. A fight broke out, but umpire Bill Klem stepped in and restored the peace.

Not for long. As Medwick trotted out to his position in left field in the bottom of the inning, the seventeen thousand fans packed into the wooden bleachers began to catcall and shout. The noise grew sharp and menacing; it sounded like a prison break, one reporter wrote. The spectators began pelting Medwick with apples, oranges, tomatoes, cabbages—a fusillade of fruits and vegetables. This forced Medwick to retreat to the infield while the umpires called time to confer and a squad of laborers picked up the debris. Medwick returned to left field, but this time the noise doubled, along with the barrage. He retreated

*Opposite:
Riot in Detroit
during the
seventh game
of the 1934
World Series
against St. Louis.*

again. There was literally a riot going on in the bleachers now, with thousands of livid fans screaming and hurling fruit. The stadium police were helpless. There were only two narrow entrances to the bleachers, one at each end, and the cops could not begin to penetrate the mob. All they could do was line up along the chicken-wire fence outside the bleachers and stand there, while the fans hurled more fruit over their heads. Two more times, Medwick tried to go back to the outfield. The public address announcer pleaded with the crowd to stop and let the game continue. But the reaction only grew louder and more violent.

Finally baseball commissioner Landis, seated along the first base line, called Medwick, Owen, and their managers to his box. He suggested that Medwick and Owen shake hands to pacify the crowd. Medwick declined. Figuring that the game would never continue if he remained in the game—and that the outfielder risked being killed by the artillery attack—Landis removed Medwick from the contest, which the Cardinals went on to win 11–0.

The anarchy at the ballpark was not a one-time event. All through

**The
1930s**

**Security
at Ebbets Field.**

the decade there were grudge matches and riots at major league stadiums. Yankees versus Red Sox. Yankees versus Senators. Reds versus Giants. And everyone versus the St. Louis Cardinals, the "Gas House Gang" of Dean, Medwick, Durocher, and Frisch, men who viewed argumentation and fisticuffs as sport. Often as not, the biggest fights in baseball took place on Memorial Day or on the Fourth of July or during the World Series, when stadiums were packed. There was something in the air; fans were pining for violent communal experiences. The Depression was on. People were broke. Around the country, headlines carried news of labor strikes and violence. Not surprisingly, the pent-up hostility of the times was released on the field and in the stands. There was an epidemic of fans hurling not just fruit and vegetables but glass bottles at players and umpires. As National League umpire Beans Reardon later put it: "They should never have let fans have bottles—it was like putting weapons in the hands of imbeciles."

All this flies in the face of standard dissertations on baseball in the 1930s, which say these were peaceful, conservative years. After all, Babe Ruth retired in 1935, leaving the game to less flamboyant stars like Lou Gehrig, Joe DiMaggio, Hank Greenberg, and, a little later, the young Ted Williams. As the game passed from Ruth's hedonism to DiMaggio's classy professionalism, historians conclude, it grew into a new sense of maturity. The iconoclastic "gentlemen owners" of the clubs were retiring and handing on their franchises to a new breed of businessmen, the forerunners of today's numbers crunchers. In St. Louis, Branch Rickey was pioneering the first minor league farm system; he viewed ballplayers as crops to be grown, owned, and exploited. Landis negotiated the sale of radio rights to broadcast major league games. The public began to see the game for what it was: a business venture. And this was not necessarily a bad thing. For while attendance in 1930 topped ten million, it plummeted in the next few years as the Depression took hold. A few teams, including the Yankees and the Tigers, were flush. But both St. Louis clubs struggled, and creative business minds were needed to keep ventures like these afloat. Rickey's Cardinals drew only 325,000 fans during the team's 1934 championship season. More than once, the rival Browns pulled in fewer than 100,000 fans in a year. The poorer teams proposed a profit-sharing system among the sixteen big league clubs to eliminate the disparities. But, as today, the idea was killed by the wealthier franchises.

On the field, National League hitters collectively battled .303 in 1930, which came to be known as "the year of the hitter." Bill Terry hit .401. Hack Wilson knocked in 190 runs. The offenses had been goosed by a league decision to flatten the seams on the baseball, which made it hard for pitchers to throw curve balls and other breaking pitches. In 1931, the seams were raised back up and the offenses were tamed, but only a bit. Through the decade, baseball settled further into its big-gun, home-run-oriented style of play. The running game was dropping out of sight; the New York Giants didn't even have a steal sign at mid-decade. The dissertations say correctly that everyone sat and waited for the big inning, while the DiMaggios of the game cruised the outfield, effortlessly pulling in long fly balls hit to the far corners of the various parks. But the dissertations generalize falsely: they say this style of graceful play represented all of baseball in the 1930s, and that the fans sat blissed-out in the stands, ever appreciative of the peace and poetry on the diamond.

A gentle game?

Eddie Joost throws his head back and laughs deeply.

Joost, a retired All-Star shortstop who came up with the Cincinnati Reds in 1936, remembers getting knocked down in his first at bat.

"The pitcher was Charlie Root of the Chicago Cubs, and Gabby Hartnett was catching. So Gabby says to me, 'Where are you from, kid?'

"I said I was from the Coast League.

"He said, 'You are? What'd you do out there this year?'

"I said, '.290.'

" 'Not good enough for up here.'

"I looked up just in time to see Root fire it: *Zip!* Down I went.

"Gabby said, 'It's kind of tough, isn't it?'

"He says, 'Let's try that one more time.'

"I dust myself off. Root fires another one. *Zip!* Down I go again! Into the dirt. And that was my introduction to major league baseball."

Thinking back on his seventeen years in the game, Joost is struck by the unfeigned hatred that fueled the rivalries between clubs. He remembers when Billy Jurges, a shortstop with the Chicago Cubs and New York Giants and possibly the toughest player of the 1930s, slid into him with the force of a fast mail train going downgrade: "He kicked me and broke my wrist right there. Bang! He was out. I held on to the ball. I flipped over. My wrist is bleeding and I got up and I'm screaming! He just walked on, didn't say another word. He got me. I was out the whole season. A lot of guys would hate you. Really hate you. Didn't know you, but they'd hate you anyway. It was part of baseball."

Jurges was a bad apple whose personal life was as controversial as his life on the field. In 1932, he was shot twice in his hotel room by a twenty-one-year-old divorcée and former chorus girl named Violet Popovich Vallee, whom he had spurned. But Violet was a poor shot. Jurges's wounds were superficial and he was back in uniform two weeks later, executing his waist-high takeouts at second base. And fighting. Newspaper morgues are filled with single-paragraph accounts of his fights, which became routine, year in, year out. He became a target for beanballs—and one of them nearly wrecked his career.

Billy Jurges of the Cubs barrels into rival Dick "Rowdy Richard" Bartell of the Giants.

Why was there so much anger in the game?

Salaries were slashed during the Depression. By the end of the '30s, team payrolls were lower than they had been ten years earlier. There was no players' union, no security. There were only eight teams in each league, squads were cut from 25 to 23 players, and there was always some young guy nipping at your heels, fighting to take your job away. Athletes in the '30s didn't have as many options as they do today. Football was gaining in popularity. But baseball and boxing were still the only sports to which most young blue-collar athletes looked for employment. It all added up to this: low pay for a job that you could lose at any moment. And as the Depression wore on and attendance dropped, the situation deteriorated further. Connie Mack broke up the Philadelphia A's after the 1932 season, unloading his best hitter, Al Simmons, to save money.

Wouldn't you be angry?

And so Detroit pitcher Dizzy Trout jerked a heckler over the guardrail onto the field and beat on him until the police pried him off. Dick Bartell, a cocky, noisy little shortstop who was known as "Rowdy Richard," made a habit of tromping with his spikes on the feet of big men who tried to intimidate him. When the Cardinals' six-foot-two-inch outfielder Harry Walker barreled into Bartell at second base, the shortstop stepped intentionally on the big guy's hand: "I was kinda sorry 'cause the groundskeeper had just sharpened my spikes that day," Bartell recalls, "but, boy, he never came close to me again."

In the Negro Leagues, shortstop Willie "the Devil" Wells remembered the routineness of beanball intimidation: "They threw at me so much, just like I was a rat or something." In the field, Wells stuffed the fingers of his mitt with river rocks so he could lay on the tag extra-hard at second base. He faced some extra-rough opponents. Outfielder Ted Page carried a gun in his jockstrap. Third baseman Oliver "Ghost" Marcelle is said to have retired after second baseman Frank Warfield bit his nose off during a fight while on tour in Cuba.

It was a hard-bitten game, to be sure.

On July 4, 1932, the Yankees and Senators met before a full house at Griffith Stadium in Washington, D.C. On a close play at home plate, with Yankee catcher Bill Dickey blocking the dish, Senators outfielder

Carl Reynolds scored. He headed back to the Senators dugout, then reversed directions, intending to go back and stamp his foot on the plate a second time, for good measure. Dickey heard Reynolds's footsteps behind him and, fearing an attack after their collision, whirled and landed a knockout-quality right hook to Reynolds's head. The Senator collapsed over home plate, his jaw broken, and one of the most outlandish brawls of the decade ensued, with spectators climbing out of the stands to join in. Dickey was suspended thirty days and fined $1,000, and the bad blood brewed for the rest of the season.

The following April, the two teams met in Washington again. The Senators' Buddy Myer, a tough Mississippi Jew, spiked Yankee first baseman Lou Gehrig, baseball's number one symbol of the Protestant work ethic, on a play at first base early in the game. So Yankee manager Joe McCarthy called a team meeting to promote this message: "Get Myer." Breaking up a double-play ball later in the game, Yankee outfielder Ben Chapman slid ferociously into Myer, who tagged Chapman and then kicked the Yankee as he lay on the ground. The two mixed it up for a minute, but the umpire settled things down, and kicked both men from the game. Then Chapman, a charmer who liked to give Nazi salutes to umpires and taunting fans, headed back to the Yankee clubhouse. On his way, he passed Senators pitcher Earl Whitehill, another legendary sorehead, who taunted Chapman. About a second later, Chapman belted Whitehill. Both benches cleared, hundreds of fans and a couple dozen cops poured onto the field, and the mob duked it out. Yankee manager McCarthy was slugged and knocked down by a respectable fellow wearing a monocle.

American League president William Harridge was aghast. He suspended Myer, Chapman, and Whitehill. Stating that baseball was not meant to be played like football, Harridge announced that he intended to implement penalties for "unnecessary roughness."

Obviously his message resounded strong and clear throughout the game.

Straight through to the 1934 World Series, when Medwick creamed Owen.

Straight through to the 1935 season, when Washington Senators outfielder Jake Powell, a self-proclaimed bigot, ran through Detroit Tigers first baseman Hank Greenberg on a routine toss-out at first base. Greenberg, dubbed the "Hebrew first baseman" and the "big Jewish boy" by the liberal press, broke his wrist but recovered in time to play in the World Series against the Chicago Cubs. In that series, the Cubs pushed the bench-jockeying envelope by Jew-baiting Greenberg through all six games, trying to unnerve him. Greenberg was a "Christ killer," a "Jew bastard." It went on like this, unabated anti-Semitic yapping from the dugout, until umpire George Moriarty had heard enough. He sent several of the Cubs to the showers and threatened to clear the bench if the verbal attacks were renewed. And do you know what Judge Landis did when he heard about it? He fined each of the offending Cubs $200—*and* he fined Moriarty the same.

Justice marches on.

Let's march through the rest of the decade.

In July 1936, the Yankees swept a doubleheader from the White Sox at Comiskey Field in front of fifty thousand frustrated fans. During the second game, the crowd uncorked "an exhibition of pop-bottle throwing almost unparalleled for intensity," the *New York Times* said the next day. In the course of the attack, umpire Bill Summers was felled by a bottle to the groin, which left him writhing on the ground. Judge Landis, seated as always in his box to witness the latest catastrophe, authorized the announcement of a $5,000 reward for information leading to the arrest of whoever threw the bottle. But years later, umpire George Pipgras recalled going to court with Summers to witness the judgment against the culprit. The guy who threw the bottle turned out to be the son of the city water commissioner and the judge fined him $25. "There's your politics," Pipgras said.

Ball clubs had been tinkering with bleacher design ever since the '34 World Series, trying to get a handle on how to control large, excitable crowds. They weren't making a great deal of progress. Toward the end of the decade, both leagues briefly tried to diffuse the heckling problem by barring players from *ever* speaking to spectators. This didn't work. Heckling continued, and so did bottle attacks. Fans in Florida even developed a new artillery technique. During a game in the South Atlantic League, they showered the field with bottles. And when the bottles ran out, they grabbed the big wooden cases that the bottles were packed in and threw *those* on the field. A first baseman

named Roy Zimmerman was caught in the barrage and knocked unconscious.

That was in August.

Let's finish with an October knockout.

You may remember the conclusion to the 1939 World Series between the Yankees and Cincinnati Reds. The final game was tied 4–4 going into the top of the tenth inning.

The Yankees came to bat.

They got a walk and a hit, and the Reds made a couple of errors.

And then Yankee outfielder Charlie "King Kong" Keller came charging around third base toward home plate, where the massive catcher Ernie "Schnozz" Lombardi was waiting for him. Keller slid hard, and his knee came up and slammed Lombardi in the jaw. Big Ernie was knocked out cold. The Schnozz was snoozing for a good twenty seconds, lying in the dirt with his eyes closed, as one, two, and then three Yankee runners scored.

The World Series was over.

And so was a very brutal decade.

DiMaggio scores after Charlie "King Kong" Keller ko'd Ernie Lombardi (No. 4 of the Reds).

The Gas House Gang

Branch Rickey was a Bible-reading catcher who promised his mother never to play ball on Sundays. He became the game's biggest empire builder and always held to his strict Methodist values, quoting from Scripture, never taking a drink. The paradox was that Rickey's clubs were some of the most debauched, loudest-braying and most pugnacious teams in baseball. In the '40s and '50s, he ran the Brooklyn Dodgers. In the '30s, his protégés were the St. Louis Cardinals—the Gas House Gang. Obnoxious to opponents, they also fought each other on the bench, in the clubhouse, in the headlines. Like the Yanks of the '70s or the Oakland A's of the '80s, the Cardinals provided the most disturbing, if entertaining, sideshow in baseball.

The Cardinals of 1934: Dean, Durocher, Orsatti, Delancey, Collins, Medwick, Frisch, Rothrock, Martin.

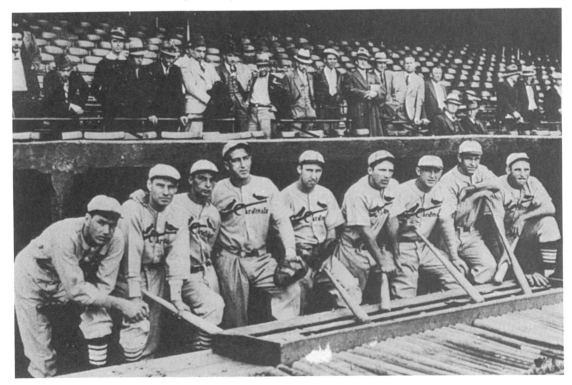

Dizzy Dean—Diz was the Babe Ruth of the Cardinals, boastful and free-living, breaking curfews and demanding—and receiving—special treatment from the front office. He called National League president Ford Frick a "crook" in one highly publicized feud, and made Frick back off from demands for an apology. Rickey admitted that he treated Dean with kid gloves. And Dean came through by winning 120 ball games from 1932 to 1936, thirty of them in the 1934 championship season when Diz was only twenty-three. Dean gleefully intimidated batters, intentionally hitting seven Giants in a row in one spring exhibition game; New York couldn't touch him the rest of the year.

"That's right, pardner," Dean liked to shout at hitters, "dig in a little deeper, so I can bury you."

Joe Medwick—"Ducky" Medwick was among the premier players in baseball, peaking in 1937 when he hit .374, collected 237 hits, and drove in 154 runs. He exemplified win-at-all-costs baseball—the same philosophy that, say, drove Pete Rose to bulldoze through Ray Fosse in the 1970 All-Star game. For Medwick, the defining moment came in the final game of the '34 Series when he bulldozed Marv Owen of the Tigers at third base. "The only way to the base was through him," Medwick later explained.

But he fought constantly with teammates. When Cardinal pitcher Ed Heusser accused him of failing to hustle after a fly ball, Medwick knocked him unconscious in the dugout. When pitcher Tex Carleton took too many swings in the batting cage, Medwick decked him. Durocher called Medwick a "one-man rampage." Management got tired of it. By the end of the '30s, Medwick was acting like a Reggie Jackson–ish prima donna, spouting off and throwing tantrums at the slightest criticism. He was traded to Brooklyn.

Pepper Martin—The outfielder and third baseman was a lifetime .298 hitter whose nickname, "the wild horse of the Osage," was a tip-off to his playing style. Martin was always unshaved, his uniform a filthy mess from his dust-clearing Comanche slides (performed, to the amazement of his teammates, without wearing a jock strap). These became a trademark of the Gang. But Martin's defining moment came years later when, at age forty-two, he managed a minor league team in Miami. Upset at an umpire's call during a game in Havana, Martin grabbed him by the throat and bounced his head up and down on home plate like a Ping-Pong ball.

He was called for a hearing before baseball commissioner Happy Chandler, who wanted to give Martin the benefit of the doubt.

"You were just overexcited. You didn't mean anything, did you?" Chandler asked him.

"I sure did," Martin responded. "Mr. Commissioner, I was trying to kill that man. I would have if they let me."

Frank Frisch and Leo Durocher—The team's manager–second baseman and shortstop argued over every pitch called by the umpire; their petulance helped bring about the rule against

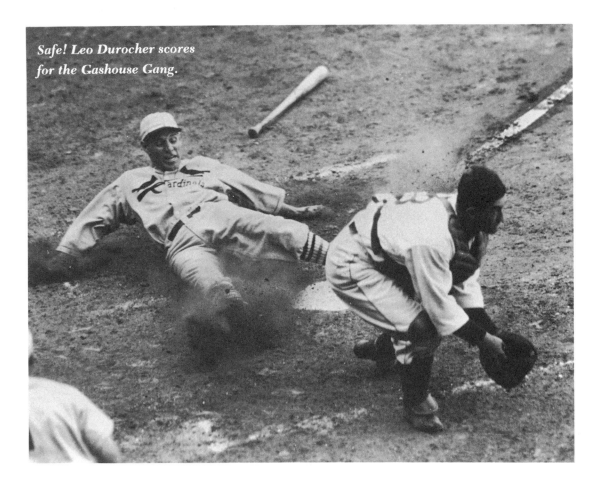

Safe! Leo Durocher scores for the Gashouse Gang.

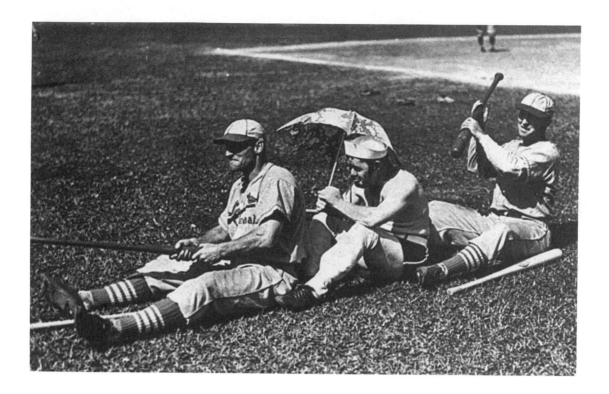

arguing over balls and strikes. Frisch, a middle-class boy from Fordham
University, liked to play the tough guy. But while he yakked plenty, he
was not one to start fights.

Durocher did both. A player of limited abilities, he became a
winner by playing for every conceivable advantage, psychological and
physical. The rude remark, the fistfight, the extra hustle on the
basepaths—all these were part of his formula for winning. As manager
of the Dodgers and Giants, he later instilled this approach in players
like Eddie Stanky, another small man with limited skills and a very
large attitude.

The Unholy Alliance

Negro League baseball in the big Eastern cities in the 1930s was run by gangsters: numbers barons whose "unholy alliance," as it was once described, sustained the game through the Depression. To learn that black franchises were owned by racketeers shouldn't come as too great a shock; white teams had a rich tradition of ownership by law-breaking politicians, gamblers, and shady financial marketeers. The Negro League owners weren't violent criminals; in fact, they tended to be beneficent supporters of black businesses and cultural events. Still, virtually every dime they earned was illegal. The owners included Harlem's Alex Pompez, who belonged to the Dutch Schultz mob and ran the New York Cuban Stars; Ed "Soldier Boy" Semler of the New York Black Yankees; Tom Wilson of the Baltimore Elite Giants; Abe Manley of the Newark Eagles; and Ed Bolden of the Philadelphia Stars. Racketeers all.

The situation was similar in Pittsburgh, the center of Negro League baseball in the 1930s. The legendary Homestead Grays, who boasted the talents at one time or another of Oscar Charleston, Cool Papa Bell, and Buck Leonard, was founded by a non-racketeer named Cumberland Posey, Jr., the son of a wealthy local businessman. but even Posey was eventually forced to turn to the barons for financing, recruiting numbers banker Rufus "Sonnyman" Jackson as his partner.

The impetus for this move came from across town. There Gus Greenlee, "Mr. Big" of the North Side numbers operation, bought the Pittsburgh Crawfords in the early '30s. "Big Red" Greenlee stole Bell from Posey and further stocked the Crawfords with Charleston, Satchel Paige, Josh Gibson, and Judy Johnson, all headed for the Hall of Fame. It was Greenlee who reinvigorated the Negro National League in 1933, initiated the popular East-West All-Star Game between black players, and built his own stadium, Greenlee Field. An entrepreneur and political power, he bootlegged liquor, owned a stable of boxers, and dispensed patronage from his Crawford Grill, a celebrated jazz spot.

But the Crawfords were the centerpiece of his empire. They dominated the league until 1937, when General Trujillo, dictator of the Dominican Republic, lured away the Crawfords' stars to play for his national team. One story had it that Greenlee, not long after, couldn't come up with the cash to pay off a big numbers hit. He folded the team before the decade was out, demolished the stadium, and cashed out of the baseball business.

Old Macho Men:
Mike Donlin, Joe Tinker, Johnny Evers
Passing the time in 1930

DONLIN: It's different in baseball nowadays, John. I was up to the Polo Grounds a few times last summer and the players on the two clubs were talking together as nice as you please.

TINKER: Next year they'll probably be kissing each other.

DONLIN: Yeah, they're a lot of sissies now.

TINKER: Remember that fight I had with McGraw?

DONLIN: Which one?

TINKER: The time at the Polo Grounds when he called me a xxxx.

DONLIN: Sure, I remember. But do you remember the day of the playoff in 1908, when everybody was trying to pick a fight with somebody on the other club, hoping to get him put off the field?

EVERS: That was the day McGinnity belted Chance in the ribs, hoping Frank would take a punch at him. But Frank was too smart.

DONLIN: You weren't so dumb yourself that day, John. Remember when I got to second base once I got hold of your ear and kept pulling it to get you sore so you would smack me and get put out?

EVERS: And what did I do?

DONLIN: What did you do? You grabbed my hand so I couldn't let go of your ear and hollered to the umpire, "Look what he's doing to me! Are you going to let him get away with that? Put him out!"

TINKER: Those were great old days.

Hog-Calling Boy:
Clyde "Pea Ridge" Day

Clyde Day hailed from Pea Ridge, Arkansas, where he pumped gas, tended strawberries, and performed hog calls. When "Pea Ridge" Day, as he came to be known, arrived in Brooklyn in 1931, he brought a little bit of the farm with him. Every time the screwball specialist struck out a batter, he broke out in a hog call. Every minute he sat on the bench, he performed hog calls, which was an irritant not just to the opposition but to his own teammates.

Day was famous for boasting that he was the strongest man in baseball, and he tried proving it with this act: borrowing a belt from a teammate, he would fasten it around his chest, breath deeply to expand his lungs, and break the buckle. The team grew tired of the routine and challenged Day to perform the trick once more, this time substituting a horse harness for a belt. Pea Ridge accepted, fastened on the harness, took a deep breath—and broke half his ribs.

Pea Ridge Day bombed out in Brooklyn. He returned home to Arkansas, bounced around the minor leagues and semipro circuit, and had expensive surgery performed on his arm when it lost its power. The surgery didn't work, and Day slit his throat with a hunting knife in 1934, five weeks after the birth of his first child.

Casey's Pearls

When Casey Stengel began his rookie season as manager of the Brooklyn Dodgers in 1934, one of his charges was the blimpish Hack Wilson, well past his prime and fitfully preparing for his final season. Standing outside on the playing field that spring in Florida, Stengel watched a large tanker truck drive past. "There's Hack Wilson," Casey said, "reporting at last."

Chapman and Powell

Midway through the 1936 season, the New York Yankees and Washington Senators arranged the trade from hell: Ben Chapman for Jake Powell. These were two hustling outfielders who numbered among the best second-line players in the game—the type of players that franchises are built on. But they were two miserable men.

Chapman, a lifetime .302 hitter, came up with the Yankees in 1930, when he was probably the fastest man in baseball. Known for his temper, he stood in front of the stands to deliver anti-Semitic diatribes against fans who disturbed him and charged over the guardrail to punish those who truly offended him. It was Chapman who set off the famous Yankee-Senator riot of 1933 after he veered out of the base path to erase Washington second baseman Buddy Myer, a Jew, from the field. "Back then you could do just about everything," Chapman mused years later, relishing the memory.

Always in trouble for spouting off, he signed with New York for only $10,000 in 1936, with a $2,000 bonus for hustling and keeping his mouth shut. Manager Joe McCarthy told him he had the skills to earn $30,000: "God and nature intended you to be the greatest player in the American League, but you won't let them make good for you. Your temperament runs amuck." This was the year that Chapman's estranged wife, Elizabeth, back home in Birmingham, Alabama, testified that he had left her with $2.87 and refused to give her a dime more. But Ben was on the road with Washington by this time, calling umpire Ernie Stewart, who thought he was Chapman's friend, a "pretty boy son of a bitch" for calling Ben out on strikes. The Senators dumped him. The Red Sox released him after he hit .340 in 1938. "You're the number one Bolshevist in baseball," owner Tom Yawkey told him. "That's why we're trading you."

The resilient Chapman managed to recycle himself as a manager and emerged as the number one tormenter of Jackie Robinson a decade later.

Jake Powell, another hothead from the South, started his career with Washington in 1930. He didn't possess the same offensive skills as Chapman, but played with as much fire, maybe more. Like Chapman, he wasn't fond of Jews—as was made clear in the gratuitous collision with Hank Greenberg recounted earlier.

Despite warning signs like that one, McCarthy was relieved to obtain the hustling Powell in 1936. But predictably, Jake caused trouble. When the Yankees traveled to Washington, the fans habitually threw bottles at Powell, who calmly picked them up and fired them back into the stands. He initiated a 1938 Memorial Day riot at Yankee Stadium in front of more than 83,000 spectators by charging the mound against Red Sox pitcher Archie McKain. That year, in a radio interview, Powell announced that he derived "pleasure" from "beating niggers over the head" in his off-season job as a cop in Dayton, Ohio. He was suspended and didn't see much playing time for the rest of his career.

The Joyce Murders: 1938

On the night of July 12 there was the usual group of neighborhood customers in Pat Diamond's bar and grill at Ninth Street and Seventh Avenue in Brooklyn. The Dodgers had lost to the Giants that day, and they were talking about the ball game. One of them, Robert Joyce, stared gloomily at his beer.

"The Dodgers!" William Diamond said.

William, son of the proprietor, and a Dodger fan, of course, was having fun with Joyce, who took the Dodgers' ball games, and particularly their defeats, with dreadful seriousness. Sometimes, even if you were a Dodger fan, it was fun to tease Joyce when the team lost.

"The Dodgers!" young Diamond said again. "Whoever first called them bums was right. Don't you think so, Frank?"

He turned to Frank Krug, whose home was in Albany but who was spending his vacation with relatives in the neighborhood. Frank was a Giant fan.

"Certainly," Krug said. "It takes the Giants to show them up as bums, too. Ha-ha! What our guys did to them today! Why don't you get wise to yourself, Bob? Why don't you root for a real team?"

The bartender grinned. Joyce was a nice young fellow, but nobody should get hipped on a ball club, not even the Dodgers, like he was. It would do him good to take a little kidding about them. Some of the others joined in the fun.

Suddenly Joyce straightened up, his eyes blazing.

"Shut up!" he screamed. "Shut up, you xxxx! You lay off the Dodgers, you xxxx!"

They laughed.

"Why Bob!" Diamond said. "You don't mean to say you're mad at us boys, do you?"

And Krug grinned at Joyce and said:

"Don't be a jerk."

"A jerk!" Joyce was hysterical now. "I'll show you who's a jerk!"

He rushed from the saloon, and the crowd along the bar laughed.

"Jesus," the bartender said. "He's got it bad, ain't he?"

Three minutes later Joyce was back, a gun in his hand.

"A jerk," he said. "A jerk, hey?"

Suddenly frightened, they stared at him. He shot Krug through the head, then turned his gun on young Diamond and shot him in the stomach. Krug had sprawled across the brass rail, falling with a crash, his head, with its gaping wound, striking the floor. Young Diamond sagged slowly to the floor and sat there looking up at Joyce, his hands clawing at his stomach, blood welling from his mouth.

"Jesus, Bob," he said. "Looka what you done to Willie!"

(From *The Brooklyn Dodgers: An Informal History,* by Frank Graham.)

The

1940s

224

*The
1940s*

1940
- Crybaby Indians lose pennant to Tigers. Frustrated Cleveland fan drops tomato crate from upper deck onto head of Detroit's Birdie Tebbetts.
- Rumors fanned by press that poor-hitting Yankees have been infected by the dying Lou Gehrig.
- Parolee attacks umpire George Magerkurth at Ebbets Field. *Brooklyn Eagle* hails assailant for upholding Brooklyn's honor.
- Dodgers acquire Joe Medwick from Cardinals. Six days later, Medwick is beaned by St. Louis pitcher Bob Bowman. Brooklyn D.A. investigates.
- Yankee fans hurl bottles at umpire Joe Rue to protest home run call.
- Cincinnati Reds catcher Willard Hershberger kills himself in hotel room.

1941
- Dodgers experiment with first major league batting helmets.
- Anti-Semitic overtones to press coverage of Hank Greenberg's draft dilemma.
- Ted Williams hits .406
- Joe DiMaggio hits in fifty-six consecutive games.
- Pete Reiser beaned twice. Runs into center field wall in Ebbets Field chasing fly ball by Enos Slaughter.
- DiMaggio charges after Whitlow Wyatt of Dodgers ("the meanest guy I ever saw") for throwing at him in World Series.
- Lou Gehrig dies.

1942
- Commissioner Landis blocks major league discussion of racial integration.
- Ted Williams is dazed by controversy over his draft status.
- Pete Reiser runs into center field wall in St. Louis chasing another fly ball by Slaughter.
- Branch Rickey leaves Cardinals after season to replace Larry MacPhail as Dodger general manager.

1943
- Landis blocks Bill Veeck's plan to buy and integrate Philadelphia Phillies.
- Chicago White Sox outfielder Moose Solters hit in head by tossed ball in pregame practice. Knocked unconscious, he gradually goes blind.
- Stan Musial charges the mound at Brooklyn beanballer Les Webber.

1944
- Judge Landis dies at age seventy-eight, removing barrier to integration.
- St. Louis Browns win first and only pennant.

1945
- Rickey announces signing of Jackie Robinson by Dodger organization.
- Happy Chandler named new baseball commissioner.

1946
- Opening Day riot in Philadelphia in Negro National League: players attack umpire; mounted police clear crowd from field.
- Jackie Robinson joins Montreal Royals.
- Evangeline League scandal: five minor leaguers expelled for allegedly fixing play-off games.
- Bob Feller's fastball clocked at 98.6 miles per hour.
- Nine members of Western International League's Spokane team killed when bus veers off mountain in Washington state.
- American Baseball Guild formed; forerunner of modern Major League Players Association.
- Mexican League lures major leaguers with high salaries. Chandler blacklists jumpers, including Sal "the Barber" Maglie.
- Durocher acquitted of blackjack assault on heckler John Christian.

1947
- Jackie Robinson debuts with Brooklyn Dodgers.
- Durocher suspended for season for associating with gamblers.
- Pete Reiser crashes into concrete center field wall at Ebbets Field. Administered last rites in clubhouse. Returns to action.

1947
- Minor league outfielder James "Storm" Davis, forty, is fatally beaned.
- Dodgers win pennant.

1948
- Babe Ruth dies of throat cancer at fifty-three.
- Ex-Yankee Jake Powell kills himself in Washington, D.C., police station.
- Roy Campanella joins Dodgers.
- Major league attendance peaks at 21.3 million.
- Negro National League folds.

1949
- Chicago Cubs first baseman Eddie Waitkus is shot in hotel by nineteen-year-old female "fan."
- Beanball wars against black minor leaguers.
- Federal court rules there is merit to $300,000 lawsuit filed against major leagues by Danny Gardella, Mexican League jumper who was banned by Chandler. Fearing attack on reserve clause, owners agree to settle with Gardella out of court.

Give me some scratching, diving, hungry ballplayers who
come to kill.
   —Leo Durocher

Whitlow Wyatt was a no-talent pitcher for ten years before Leo Durocher got hold of him in Brooklyn and made him mean. After a game in which Wyatt buzzed a few fastballs at his opponents' heads, manager Durocher dropped a couple $100 bills in his pitcher's locker. Wyatt got the message. He became the ace of the Dodger staff, which was Durocher's breeding ground for borderline personalities. It included Kirby Higbe, who built up his arm as a child in South Carolina by throwing rocks at Negroes. It included Hugh Casey, the first bullet-firing relief specialist, who would just as soon throw the ball right between your eyes as over the edge of the plate. Casey was a silent but formidable man with a healthy paunch who retired to his room at night with comic books and straight whiskey, and reemerged the next afternoon, as Red Barber once said, "a killer in a ball game." In 1941, Casey got pissed off and threw four consecutive fastballs behind the head of Pirates catcher Al Lopez—a wicked move, for the batter's inclination is always to fall away away from the plate. Once, when umpire George Magerkurth called a balk on Casey, he threw three straight pitches past the ump's head. This was an unprecedented attempt at intimidation, inasmuch as Magerkurth was another legendary bulldog who tangled with fans and players, spat in their faces, and had sixty-seven professional boxing matches to his credit before becoming an umpire. But he didn't frighten the glowering Casey, who once threw a man through a plate-glass window after a night of saloon-hopping on Flatbush Avenue. "He could drink till it was coming out of his ears," an admiring friend said of Casey, "and then he'd bottle it and drink it again."

Mind you, these men were in their prime in 1941, which has been depicted in recent baseball histories as a summer of splendor. True, the artful DiMaggio was in the midst of setting his record for hitting in fifty-six consecutive ball games. And Ted Williams, who should have worn a laboratory smock in the batter's box, was refining the science of hitting, methodically slashing his way toward a .406 season, the last year in which any hitter broke the .400 barrier. These men were surely images of perfection, and the season in which they achieved their feats has come to be known as a baseball dream time, a final reverie before the realities of World War II hit home for the baseball public and America.

But the truth is that, on the field and off, this was the war decade. And Durocher was the baseball general—a new little Napoleon, like McGraw—who defined the era. He had been a dirty, unscrupulous

Leo "the Lip" Durocher squares off with the ump.

ballplayer and he was a dirty, unscrupulous manager. He upped the ante in baseball; if you played his Dodgers, you literally had to watch out for your life. He would deny it in later years, but from the time Durocher took over the club in '39, he taught his pitchers to throw at enemy heads, and to keep doing it until the enemy either folded or started throwing at Dodger heads. Durocher enjoyed the escalation. In 1942, he had a pitcher on the staff named Les Webber who tried to hit all the batters in the St. Louis Cardinal lineup one day, including the young Stan Musial. When Webber did it again the next year, Musial charged him—perhaps the only time the impassive Musial got down to Durocher's level. Leo was pleased: "Hit 'em on the 6!" he shouted to his pitchers, urging them to plant fastballs on Musial's back. It was just one of Durocher's war cries. "Christ, in those days all you heard was 'Stick it in his ear,' " said Dodger outfielder Pete Reiser. " 'Drill him.' 'Flip him.' If you got hit, you got hit," reasoned Reiser, who said, "There were times I thought we should've got combat pay, playing for Leo."

229

But Reiser didn't resent the loss of pay. Why, he enjoyed the combat. He ran full-speed into concrete outfield walls, again and again, while pursuing fly balls. He absorbed one beanball after another, full-force into his felt baseball cap. He broke his neck, his skull, suffered three days of paralysis and a blood clot on the brain, and was administered the last rites in the clubhouse before pulling through and returning to uniform. Reiser hit .343 in 1941, his first full season. He might have been as great as Willie Mays. But his all-out playing style knew no moderation. He was Durocher's soldier to the hilt. And by the late '40s, wrote Red Smith, he "had literally broken his magnificent body to bits." Even then, there were no complaints from Reiser, who became the consummate war veteran.

War imagery dominated the decade.

It started with Durocher's beanball wars and multiple feuds: the Dodgers versus the Cardinals, the Dodgers versus the Giants, the Dodgers versus the Cubs. It proceeded with constant reminders that the war was on in Europe, as major league teams were stocked with draft rejects who played a dismal brand of baseball. The Cincinnati Reds had two epileptic infielders. The St. Louis Browns won their first and only pennant in 1944 with eighteen 4-F ball players, and in 1945 fielded a celebrated one-armed outfielder named Pete Gray. Then when all the able-bodied players returned from military service for the 1946 season, there were new wars to be fought. It was a time of violent labor unrest in the country, of expanding unionism and the rise of organized pressure groups, and there was labor discontent in the baseball world, too. Baseball management was chilled by the founding of the American Baseball Guild, forerunner of the modern Major League Players Association, which talked about salary arbitration and fought to wrest concessions from the corporate types and syndicates who were taking over the game. Older, more traditional owners complained of having endured Depression hardships; the Cardinals' Sam Breadon tried to put a $14,000 salary cap on all his players, including superstar Musial. When Yankee shortstop Phil Rizzuto had his felt cap swiped by some exuberant fans, New York general manager Ed Barrow made him pay for a new one. Ballplayers were ready to revolt, and a rejuvenated Mexican League almost managed to lure away a band of major league stars before the owners got together and stomped the threat out.

But much more visible and ugly than these labor-management battles was the racial war that was being fought in baseball in the second half of the 1940s. Around the country, racial discrimination in the military, in the defense industry, and in college sports was finally becoming a source for debate and anxiety. And as race became an issue in baseball, the tough, boozing war veterans, many of them southern, who returned to the game after World War II couldn't deal with the changes on the field. An old-timer named Billy Werber warned that baseball is a contact sport and "spikes sometimes cut deeply." Sure enough, when Jackie Robinson suited up in his Dodger uniform in 1947, he became a pincushion for spikings by opponents all over the National League. Beanball wars intensified, because they were now fueled by an added racial dimension, and Robinson was flattened again and again—more times in the first half of 1947 than any other National Leaguer in the entire 1946 season. Teammate Dixie Walker, who had objected to Robinson's black presence, said he "never saw anyone who could get that forearm up as fast to keep the pitch from hitting his head." Bench jockeying grew viler and far crueler, because when screaming ballplayers called Robinson "monkey" or "gator bait" they spoke out of deep hate. All this took its psychological and physical toll on black athletes. Outfielder Willard Brown of the St. Louis Browns joked about carrying a mattress to the plate for protection, he was thrown at so much. The decade was ending on a violent exclamation point.

It had begun with a bang.

In July 1940, more than 68,000 people at Yankee Stadium witnessed what was called "the worst outbreak of rowdyism" in the park's history. Umpire Joe Rue was showered with pop bottles when he ruled that what appeared to be a Yankee home run was in fact a foul ball. In September, a fan in Cleveland dropped a basket of tomatoes from the upper deck onto the head of the

September 1940. Big George Magerkurth, the toughest ump in the game, is pummeled by an irate fan at Ebbets Field.

unsuspecting Tiger catcher, Birdie Tebbetts, who was sitting in the Detroit bullpen. Tebbetts was knocked out cold. This was one year before White Sox outfielder Julius "Moose" Solters paused during pregame warm-ups at Griffith Stadium in Washington, D.C., to wave to his brothers-in-law in the stands. In one of the freakiest accidents in the game's history, Solters was hit in the head by a ball thrown by a teammate. It knocked him unconscious and eventually deprived Solters of his eyesight, making him the only player ever to be blinded in action.

Solters was a six-footer who could pound the ball, and it was his type of ballplayer that the fans turned out to see. For the third straight decade, baseball was a game for bruisers who hit lots of home runs, struck out like mad, but still hit for high averages, while hardly ever stealing a base. In 1945, the major leagues set a new attendance record when 10.8 million fans turned out at the ballpark. In 1946, 18.5 million euphoric postwar fans turned out. And in 1948, the number jumped to a remarkable 21.3 million spectators as night baseball caught on and the expanding leisure economy took hold. These folks sat back in their seats, munching peanuts and ripping open boxes of Cracker Jack, as eighteen angry men fought it out on the field below.

None was angrier than Ted Williams of the Boston Red Sox. Tightly coiled like Cobb, he was prone to verbal explosion and expectoration rather than to physical violence. But like Cobb, Williams was single-mindedly focused on the task at hand—hammering the baseball. To do this, Williams needed to keep himself on an emotional edge. To achieve that edge, he fought with the press. Williams was a thoroughly modern athlete who defined himself through newspaper wars and public image. It was a long, ongoing process: from the time he arrived in Boston in 1939, the press battered Williams. When he received a draft deferment so that he could continue to support his mother—she rang bells for the Salvation Army in San Diego—the newspapers went wild: "There is suspicion. There is contempt. There is hatred," wrote Harold Kaese of the *Boston Globe*.

And Ted struck back. "I'm always nice enough in the spring until I read what those shitheads write about me," he remarked. His standard reply to interview requests was "Go fuck off." If a writer approached his locker anyway, he would boom, "Hey, what stinks? Something stinks? Oh, no wonder—you. That shit you wrote last night." Williams once lifted tiny Hy Hurwitz of the *Globe* into the air by the necktie and held him there, releasing the startled writer by cutting the tie below the knot with a pair of scissors. None of this was entirely random; Williams orchestrated his anger to improve his game. In *Ted Williams: A Baseball Life*, biographer Michael Seidel quotes this refrain from Williams: "I hit better when I'm mad. I'm sharper. My reactions are quicker. My sensibilities keener." Williams offered the same explanation when asked "how he managed to navigate his fiery and shell-racked jet fighter back to base after a mission during the Korean War. 'I fly better mad.' Williams had a shrewd sense of what focused him and excited his energies."

There was no such sense of control in the National League, where General Durocher marshaled his troops with war whoops and calls to tumult: Let the Wild Rumpus Start!

What a crew the Dodgers were.

Durocher was a philandering gambler who didn't drink. Brooklyn general manager Larry MacPhail was a raving alcoholic: "When he was sober, he was one of the best baseball men I ever saw," said Happy Chandler, who became baseball commissioner in 1945. "When he drank too much whiskey, he'd push little ducks in the pond and hit little girls."

Look at the team Durocher and MacPhail assembled. There was Casey, who knocked out Ernest Hemingway in a Havana boxing match during spring training one year. There was Dolph Camilli, a former professional boxer who dropped teammate Joe Medwick with one punch for picking on Pee Wee Reese.

The Dodgers had picked up Medwick from St. Louis in June 1940. He was a superstar whose acquisition legitimized Brooklyn as a contender. Six days after they got him, Brooklyn played St. Louis. Medwick stepped up to the plate. Cardinal pitcher Bob Bowman threw a fastball. Bam! Right in Medwick's head. He was plate-shy for the rest of his career.

This was just one of the beanings of '40. A couple weeks earlier, rookie shortstop Pee Wee Reese was hit. A couple weeks later, shortstop Billy Jurges of the Giants got hit. National League commissioner Ford Frick called for an end to it, said the beanings left a "mean taste" in the public's mouth.

But baseball grew no kinder. Durocher's Dodgers became legendary for breaking the will of opposing ballplayers by constant

Transcendental Graphics

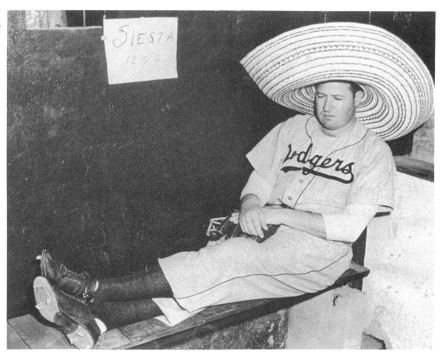

Brooklyn's Hugh Casey relaxes in Havana where he once ko'd Ernest Hemingway in the author's living room.

verbal pounding. One of the St. Louis pitchers had a retarded son, so Durocher shouted at him, "Hey, how's your syphilitic boy?" (Leo was insensitive to the fact that one of his own pitchers, Carl Erskine, had a retarded child.) The Cardinals kept throwing at Dodger heads: Reiser, Camilli, Mickey Owen. And the Dodgers kept striking back. Down the '41 pennant stretch, Brooklyn's Fat Freddie Fitzsimmons, a seventeen-year veteran who could barely lift his arm, mustered all his strength to buzz one behind the ear of St. Louis slugger Johnny Mize. "Get ready, Picklehead," Fat Freddy screamed, then threw another at the same spot. "Right at that thick picklehead skull of yours," he shouted, and did it again. And finally, on a three-two count, Fitzsimmons flipped a lazy curve ball toward Mize, who was so wobbly by this time that he practically fell over as he swung and missed for a third strike. "You picklehead!" stormed Fitzsimmons. "You never could hit me!"

This is the way the Dodgers won the pennant.

After the 1942 season, Branch Rickey took over from MacPhail as general manager. But Rickey's arrival, despite his religiosity, did not transform the Dodgers. If anything, even as he bickered with Durocher over his cursing, cardplaying, and womanizing, Rickey became Leo's great defender in times of crisis. And together, they built an even more lawless ball club.

In 1944, they acquired second baseman Eddie Stanky from the Cubs. Off the field, Stanky was the nicest guy, a role model to neighborhood kids, a strict Catholic family man at home. On the field, it was a different story. As a boy in Philadelphia, Stanky was once knocked out by a pitch. His mother saw it. "Just throw a bucket of water on him. He'll be all right," she said. He became a tough little guy. He was like Durocher: short, with limited skills. He didn't even look like an athlete. But "the little SOB would do anything to win," said umpire Lee Ballanfant. Stanky would wiggle and fidget and call constant time-outs at the plate, throwing off the pitcher's timing and drawing a walk. At first base, Stanky would reach down and pick up a handful of dirt. Then he would race to second base, slide, and flip the dirt into the shortstop's eyes. Safe at second, Stanky would take his lead, screaming and jumping up and down, waving his hands in the air to distract the pitcher. Spiked on top of the head one day, "Stinky"

235

Stinky Stanky.
The most
annoying player
in baseball.

Stanky bled like crazy, but checked out of the hospital and played the next afternoon. He was nuts. Durocher loved him.

Leo had problems in 1945. A two-hundred-pound heckler named John Christian claimed that a stadium cop took him underneath the stands and that the cop and Durocher beat him with a blackjack. Durocher was charged with assault. But a sympathetic judge saw to his acquittal in 1946, a packed courtroom cheered, and Leo went back to business. That year, Cincinnati Reds coach Jimmie Wilson complained that Dodger beanballers were serious threats to the well-being of his players: a ballplayer "doesn't like to think that his very life is in jeopardy because of beanball tendencies by the opposition."

But Durocher didn't understand Wilson's concerns.

"What's all the yammer about?" he asked. "What's wrong with loosening up the hitter?"

This was baseball's big macho year.

The war was over. Hard-charging veterans returned to the diamond in 1946 to prove that they hadn't lost anything while in the military.

This is the year that there were a record number of assaults on umpires in the minor leagues. This is the year that Williams and Musial hit like thunder gods. It's the year that Bob Feller's fastball was clocked at 98.6 miles per hour. And it's the year that the Cardinals' Enos Slaughter won the World Series by scoring from first base on a gentle hit over Boston shortstop Johnny Pesky's head.

Hormones were flowing.

But 1946 was also a year of racial violence. There were at least thirty lynchings of blacks in the United States. There was antiblack rioting by whites in Tennessee.

It was the year that Jackie Robinson suited up with the Montreal Royals, a Dodger farm team. His manager, the Mississippi-bred Clay Hopper, reportedly asked Branch Rickey, "Mr. Rickey, do you really think a nigger's a human being?"

Off we go. The integration of the game was about to begin.

How did it come about?

For one thing, Commissioner Landis died in 1944.

His death cleared the way for integration, because Landis had singlehandedly blocked it for years. A master of double-speak, he said there was no rule preventing the game's integration. Yet he blocked league discussion of the matter. He ignored the diplomatic admonitions of Paul Robeson to reconsider his opposition. He blocked Bill Veeck's plan to purchase the financially shaky Philadelphia Phillies and stock the team with black players. And he scolded Durocher—who for once was behaving like a hero—for saying he'd like to have some black ballplayers on his team in Brooklyn.

For seventy years, major league baseball had supported segregation. And the general public had never so much as questioned why black people were banned from the national pastime. By signing

Robinson to a contract with the Dodger organization, Branch Rickey was now punching a fist through that apathy. But as the game integrated, the threat of violence loomed.

In the minors, pitchers suddenly couldn't find the plate: Jackie went *down*. Again and again. Members of the Syracuse team threw a black cat on the field when Robinson kneeled in the on-deck circle: "Hey, Jackie, there's your cousin." Then Robinson doubled.

Major league owners and general managers almost unanimously opposed black participation. Larry MacPhail, formerly of the Dodgers and now running the Yankees, chaired a 1946 policy committee that secretly codified its continued support for baseball apartheid: "The use of Negro players," the committee's report stated, "would hazard all the physical properties of baseball."

What made Rickey stick his neck out and sign Robinson?

His motivations were mixed.

Rickey was the shrewdest trader in baseball and a pennypincher. "He'd go to the safe to get you a nickel change," said Enos Slaughter, who played in St. Louis when Rickey ran the Cardinals. The press dubbed him "El Cheapo." Rickey honored his Methodist mother's wishes by never setting foot in a ballpark on a Sunday, but he always phoned in to find out the attendance. He paid himself handsomely, but his players stingily. He always believed that the best player was a hungry player: "Mr. Rickey came to kill you," said Durocher, sensing a kindred spirit.

Major league baseball had always been a Northern operation. Before World War II, the majority of black Americans lived in the South. But the black migration North quickened

The threat of violence hung over baseball with Branch Rickey's decision to hire Jackie Robinson to a major league contract.

National Baseball Library

in the 1940s; this was the heyday of the Negro Leagues. There was clearly a market to be exploited, and Rickey saw that. He raided the Negro League teams to sign Robinson, Roy Campanella, Don Newcombe. He didn't purchase their contracts from the Negro League owners. Rickey was under no obligation to do so; the old contracts were often sloppily written. But by taking advantage of these loopholes, he cheated the Negro League teams of compensation for losing their stars and hastened their demise. There was a ruthless aspect to Rickey's integration campaign.

But what if he hadn't acted at all? Baseball apartheid would have stood undisturbed. Through the 1940s, MacPhail insisted that the Yankees could not find a single black ballplayer who had enough talent to play in New York. "There is not a single Negro player with major league possibilities," the *Sporting News* editorialized. Bob Feller of the Cleveland Indians, a future Hall of Famer who had competed against the rich array of Negro League talent during numerous barnstorming tours, made similar disingenuous judgments. Feller had this to say about Robinson: "If he were a white man, I doubt if they would consider him big league material."

The nerve of it.

Robinson was an intellect, strong-willed, decent. And here he was, forced to listen to these attacks. The criticisms were a joke. Robinson was probably the best athlete in the major leagues. He starred in baseball, football, basketball, and track at UCLA. National sportswriters called him the best basketball player and top gridiron ball carrier in the United States. "He tried his hand at golf and won the Pacific Coast intercollegiate golf championship; he won swimming championships at UCLA; in tennis he reached the semifinals of the national Negro tournament," writes historian Jules Tygiel in *Baseball's Great Experiment: Jackie Robinson and His Legacy.* Tygiel concludes, "It is probable that no other athlete, including Jim Thorpe, has ever competed as effectively in as broad a range of sports."

And now Robinson had to swallow hard and listen to people like Feller.

The story of Robinson's 1947 season is well-worn by now. How Robinson had to abide by Rickey's admonitions to hold his tongue and set higher standards for behavior than the white men who taunted him.

How he had to sit silently while his Brooklyn teammate Dixie Walker circulated a petition to keep him off the field. How he had to endure boycott threats by the St. Louis Cardinals, and then slurs and spikings by Slaughter, Joe Garagiola—that's right—and Medwick, who had rejoined St. Louis. And how, worst of all, he had to endure the absolutely vicious bench jockeying of manager Ben Chapman and the Philadelphia Phillies. Chapman had his men screaming about niggers and monkeys and Robinson's thick lips and extra-thick black skull and how Robinson was going to infect the Dodgers with venereal disease and ought to go back to picking cotton. He had a dugout full of laughing Phillies aim their bats at Robinson when he came to the plate and make rat-a-tat machine-gun noises.

"I felt tortured and I tried just to play ball and ignore the insults," Robinson said. "But it was really getting to me. . . . What was I doing here turning the other cheek as though I weren't a man?"

He didn't kowtow. Robinson had so many kinds of slides that his

The most aggressive base runner of his time: Jackie Robinson in mid-flight.

opponents didn't know where he was coming from. Robinson was a menace; screaming at the pitcher, dancing off third base, threatening to steal home. You've seen the old newsreels. He shook up the opposition badly, always an aggressive, disconcerting presence. In 1947, he led the league in stolen bases and batted .297. In 1948, he hit .296. In 1949, he came into his own, jumped his average to .342, won the league's Most Valuable Player award, and led the Dodgers to the World Series against the Yankees.

Rickey and Robinson had decided by now that it was time for Jackie to take off the wraps. He didn't have to hold his tongue any longer. A pitcher named Herm Wehmeier knocked him down a couple times, and Robinson jumped up shouting, "You white motherfucker!"

Wehmeier didn't do that again.

Robinson was ready to rumble his way into the 1950s and seize his place in the national game.

CryBaby Indians

On September 27, 1940, Detroit Tigers catcher Birdie Tebbetts was sitting in the bullpen at Cleveland Stadium when a crate of tomatoes landed on his head. Indian fans had been pelting the Tigers with fruit, vegetables, and eggs throughout the game, but this was the *coup de grâce*. Dropped from the upper deck of the left field pavilion, it knocked the catcher out. "I thought Tebbetts was dead," said umpire George Pipgras, who witnessed the attack. "I thought they had killed him."

The tomato crate was thrown by a young man named Armen Guerra, who must have sensed the Indians' pennant chances slipping away that afternoon. Cleveland had blown a five-and-a-half-game lead down the pennant stretch; it was a classic choke, abetted by the infantile, sometimes violent, outbursts of fans all over the American League. For in 1940, the Indians were targets of fans in almost every park. This wasn't because the Cleveland roster included an aging sorehead, Ben Chapman; or an up-and-coming slugger with a bad attitude, Jeff Heath; or one of the least attractive personalities of the last decade, a knockdown pitcher named Johnny Allen who gave children the cold stare when they asked for his autograph.

No, everyone hated the Indians because they were a bunch of babies.

They became the "Crybaby Indians" in June, when a group of players got together and asked team president Alva Bradley to fire the manager. The Indians' skipper was Ossie Vitt, a sour old guy who had played third base for the Tigers years earlier. Vitt didn't know how to groom the new breed of player. He reamed his men out in the privacy of the clubhouse, and he reamed them out in public. Even pitcher Bob Feller, on his way to a 27–11 season, had his wings clipped: "I'm supposed to win with him?" Vitt would remark sarcastically if Feller had an off day. And so the players, led by Feller, Heath, and a forgotten slugger named Hal Trosky, took their complaints to president Bradley, who promised to rein in the ornery Vitt.

Word got out about the insurrection, and the Indians were reborn as "the Crybabies."

The *Sporting News* campaigned in 1940 for "elimination of the deadly pop bottle" from ballparks. But in the American League that season, fans were throwing something different at the Indians: baby bottles. The fans brought megaphones to the parks and chanted, "Crybaby! Crybaby!" The Indians were unnerved, and as the publicity grew, they started to fold. When Cleveland arrived in Detroit for a September 19 ball game, the two teams were tied for first place. The nervous Indians were met at the railroad station by Detroit fans who pelted them with eggs and tomatoes; the team was led to safety by police escorts, who snuck them through the baggage room and into an alley. At the hotel, the Indians were kept awake all night by boisterous Detroit fans who played musical instruments on the sidewalk. And at the ballpark the next day, the Indian dugout was decorated with diapers—and the fans wheeled baby carriages atop the dugout roof during the game.

Detroit took two out of three and moved into first place.

Back in Cleveland on September 27, Indian fans prepared to retaliate. They arrived at the stadium with baskets filled with fruit and vegetables. It was Ladies' Day and the left field seats were jammed with fifteen thousand women and their families, who barraged the Tigers with fresh produce before the game. In the bottom of the first inning, Detroit's Hank Greenberg was hit with a ripe tomato as he ran after a fly ball. He caught the ball, but umpire Bill Summers got on the public address system and threatened to forfeit the game to Detroit. The fruit assault continued, however, and police fanned out through the park to catch offenders. It was at this point that Armen Guerra decided to destroy all evidence by heaving his tomato crate out of the upper deck and onto Birdie Tebbett's head. But clever Guerra, wearing a brightly striped sweater, was quickly nabbed by police, who brought him to the Detroit clubhouse. There he was introduced to the revived Tebbetts, who was apparently allowed to knock Guerra around a bit. And can you believe it? Guerra, who had nearly killed the catcher, turned around and charged him with criminal assault.

But Tebbetts won twice.
He was acquitted of the charge.
And the Tigers won the pennant.
Waaah! Waaah! Waaah!

*CryBaby
Indians*

Ultimate Macho Man: Pete Reiser

As good as Mantle. As good as Mays. As good as Cobb. Brooklyn's Pistol Pete Reiser could have been as good as anyone; he might have been the most superb ballplayer who ever suited up; but he just kept running into concrete walls. This was before the days of warning tracks and foam padding. Such things would have meant little to Reiser, who performed every one of his ballplaying duties with maximum commitment. He stood his ground at the plate and took fastballs in the head. He crashed into fences and fielders. He gashed his butt on an exit gate, and when the blood started to soak his uniform, he asked the trainer to put a metal clamp on the wound, then played on. He slid into second base and broke his ankle during the 1947 World Series against the Yankees. And when the doctors wanted to put a cast on his leg, Reiser asked, "Can't you just tape it up?"

He pinch-hit the next afternoon.

In a book called *Once They Heard the Cheers,* author Bill Heinz tabulates the injuries Reiser suffered in his short, memorable career with the Dodgers. He was carried off the field eleven times. Nine times he regained consciousness in the clubhouse or a hospital. He broke his right elbow and taught himself to throw lefty; Pistol was ambidextrous. He crashed into walls nine times; on seven of those occasions, he broke his collarbone or dislocated a shoulder. He was hit in the head twice, and was once operated on for a blood clot on the brain.

This fails to mention the paralysis.

"Willie Mays had everything," Leo Durocher wrote in his autobiography. "Pete Reiser had everything but luck."

It started in 1941, Reiser's first full season with the Dodgers. How he accomplished what he did amid the injuries is difficult to figure out, but Reiser led the league with thirty-nine doubles, batted .343, and became the first rookie to win the National League batting title.

He was also hit in the face with a pitch by Phillie right-hander Ike Pearson at Ebbets Field. The sound of ball striking bone was audible around the park, and Reiser woke up in Peck Memorial Hospital that night around midnight, still in uniform. The doctor advised him to take the week off; Pete was back on the bench the next day. With the bases loaded and the score tied 7–7 in the eighth inning, and Pearson coming in to relieve for Philadelphia, Durocher said, "Pistol, get that bat."

Boom! Over the fence to win the game.

Reiser's nemesis, the center field wall in Ebbets Field, was "a cement-hard sloping monster," the historian Gerald Green wrote in an essay about Reiser. "For Reiser, it did not exist, or if it did, it was an enemy that had to be defied. Like Ahab's white whale, or Mallory's Everest, it had to be challenged, because it *existed.* As did all ballpark walls. Or a beanballing pitcher. Or a catcher blocking the plate. They used to say of Bobby Layne, the potbellied quarterback, he never lost a game—he just ran out of *time.* In Reiser's case, one could argue that he never muffed a ball—he just ran out of *space.*"

Well, Reiser did muff a ball. Once.

It happened in St. Louis in July 1942. He was batting .380, with nineteen hits in his previous twenty-one at bats, when the Dodgers' Whitlow Wyatt took the mound. With the score tied in the thirteenth inning, the Cardinals' Enos Slaughter tied into one of Wyatt's pitches and sent it hurtling toward Reiser.

"It's a line drive directly over my head," Reiser remembered, "and my first thought was that it can be caught. Which is pretty much the way I felt about any ball that was hit. I'm a firm believer in positive thinking. I used to stand out there in center field and say to myself, 'Hit it to me, hit it to me.' Every pitch, I wanted that ball.

"Well, if this ball isn't caught, it's a cinch triple, and Wyatt can get beat, and above all the Dodgers. I caught it, going at top speed. I just missed the flagpole in center field, but I hit the wall, hard.

"I dropped the ball, picked it up, relayed it to Pee Wee Reese—how I did that, I'll never know—but we just missed getting Slaughter at the plate. Inside-the-park home run. Wyatt's beat, one–nothing. And I'm out cold in center field. It was like a hand grenade had gone off inside my head."

He suffered a severe concussion and fractured his skull. The doctor at the hospital told him to take the rest of the season off. But Reiser was back on the bench two days later for a game against the

Pirates. In the fourteenth inning, Durocher asked him to pinch-hit, and Reiser lined one over second base to drive in the winning runs. When he reached first base, Pistol collapsed. He woke up in the hospital and Durocher told him: "You're better with one leg and one eye than anybody else I've got."

The next three years, Reiser took it easy. He was in the military, played for an Army team, dove after a ball and broke his right elbow. That's when he learned to throw lefty.

Then he returned to Brooklyn.

Red Smith once did the tabulations for Reiser's '46 season: "Pete was knocked out making a diving catch, ripped the muscles in his left leg running out an infield hit, broke a leg sliding, broke his collarbone, dislocated a shoulder, and led the league with thirty-four stolen bases."

Time for last rites? Brooklyn's Pistol Pete Reiser is carried off the field . . . again.

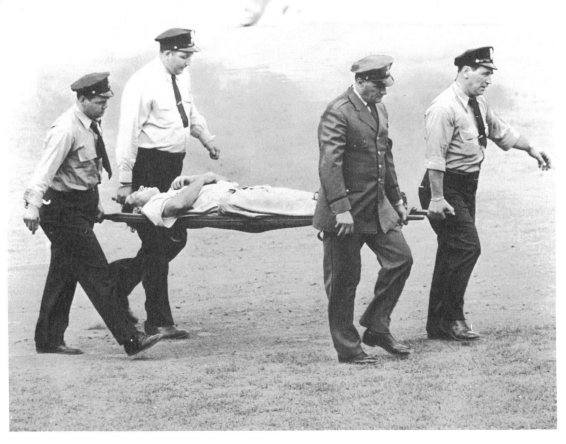

Smith continued:

"At an exhibition game in Springfield, Missouri, a radio announcer was asking the Dodgers where they thought they would finish that year. 'First place,' said Pee Wee Reese. So did Hugh Casey and Dixie Walker.

" 'Here comes Pistol Pete Reiser,' the announcer said. 'Where do you think you'll finish the season, Pete?'

" 'In Peck Memorial Hospital,' Pete said."

So he had a sense of humor about the injuries, but still no sense of caution. He hit .309 in 1947, the year he ran into Moby Dick with such force, and was knocked out so completely, that a priest administered the last rites in the clubhouse. Paralyzed for three days, Reiser was back a week later. Working out before a ball game in Pittsburgh, he bumped heads with a teammate, raising a lump that turned out to be a blood clot on the brain. It almost killed him. He underwent surgery, came back, suffered another concussion making a diving catch, and broke his leg in the World Series.

All in one year.

His body savaged, he never played effectively again. He didn't regret it. "It was my style of playing," he explained, matter-of-factly. "I didn't know any other way to play ball." Had he not played the way he did, he reasoned, he might never have reached the major leagues to begin with. So once he got there, he just kept right on going. "You slow up a half step, and it's the beginning of your last ball game. . . . Hell, any ballplayer worth his salt has run into a wall. I'm the guy who got hurt doing it, that's all."

Willie Wells Is Walloped

In the Negro National League, shortstop Willie Wells was intentionally beaned one afternoon by a spitball pitcher on the Baltimore Elite Giants named Bill Byrd. Wells was carried unconscious from the field on a stretcher. And when he got back in uniform a few days later, just in time for a rematch with Byrd, he wore a modified construction hat for protection. Another time, Wells donned a miner's helmet while hitting against a pitcher named Edsel Walker. What did Walker do? He hit Wells in the ribs with a fastball and said, "That hat didn't do you any good now, did it, Willie?"

1947: Durocher's Suspension

There was one thing missing from Jackie Robinson's first year with the Dodgers: Leo Durocher.

Just before opening day, baseball commissioner Happy Chandler announced that Durocher was suspended for the season. Chandler cited an "accumulation of unpleasant incidents" in Durocher's recent past that were "detrimental to baseball" and required his removal. There were no specifics given, but everyone knew what Chandler was referring to. Durocher was an old friend of the actor George Raft, who used Leo's Manhattan apartment one night in 1945 for a dice game and allegedly fleeced a man of $18,000 by using loaded dice. Durocher wasn't there. But Chandler didn't like hearing about Durocher's friendship with Raft, just as he didn't like reading unproven newspaper reports that Durocher knew the mobster Bugsy Siegel. Chandler didn't like it when Durocher was indicted for the blackjack beating of a heckler, for which Leo was acquitted. And he didn't like it when Durocher's off-season neighbor in Los Angeles, a man named Ray Hendricks, accused Leo in December 1946 of being a "love pirate" who had an affair with Hendricks's wife, the actress Laraine Day. Chandler didn't like it when Durocher and Day got married. And he really didn't like it when the Catholic Youth Organization condemned Durocher for "undermining the moral training of Brooklyn's Roman Catholic youth" and threatened to remove thousands of members from the Dodger boys' club.

But what did it all add up to? Durocher slept around and may have had some questionable friends. But he was never convicted of a crime. There had been stories about Durocher's hustler associations ever since his pool-sharking days in the 1920s when Babe Ruth accused Leo of stealing his watch. Why, all of a sudden, was Durocher now being hit with the stiffest punishment since the aftermath of the 1919 Black Sox scandal?

Well, there were a couple of reasons. Firstly, Chandler, the former

governor of Kentucky, was viewed as a floundering commissioner, a hamfisted ex-politician who was afraid to place his mark on the game. There were game-fixing scandals in college basketball and minor league baseball in the mid-'40s, and Chandler was under pressure to show that the major league game was clean.

Secondly, Durocher had humiliated Chandler's friend Larry MacPhail, general manager of the Yankees. After the Raft incident, Durocher had promised Chandler that he would steer clear of all questionable associates, including a couple of gambler friends named Memphis Engelberg and Connie Immerman. So when Durocher spotted Engelberg and Immerman in MacPhail's box before an exhibition game in Havana in the spring of 1947, he was incensed. "Look over there," Durocher shouted to reporters. "He has gamblers as his guest. If I did that, I'd get kicked out of baseball." Durocher publicized the incident in his weekly newspaper column, and MacPhail went ballistic. MacPhail had engineered Chandler's appointment as commissioner two years later. Now it was payback time. Chandler muzzled Durocher with the suspension. Then he slapped a $2,000 fine on MacPhail, and called the incident closed.

The 1940s

Durocher married actress Laraine Day in 1947 and promptly began having an affair with another Hollywood star. As told in Peter Golenbock's *Bums: An Oral History of the Brooklyn Dodgers,* an astonished friend then asked the short, bald Durocher to explain his womanizing tactics, and Durocher obliged:

"Kid, when you pick one of them up at seven o'clock, you've got to make your first move fast. You make sure you put your hand on their snatch at seven oh five. Seven oh five! Now, one of two things can happen. Sure, they can knock your hand off. All right. It's seven oh five. No go? Tough, but it's still early yet. Plenty of time to call another broad. But suppose she don't knock your hand off. Well, then hello dear. You know you're in, and you ain't gonna waste the evening. Kid, you'd be surprised. Some damn famous broads don't knock your hand off."

Eddie Waitkus's Surprise

Eddie Waitkus was no matinee idol. He was a talented first baseman with a long mournful face who spent most of his career with lousy ball clubs. He hit .295 with the Chicago Cubs in 1948, when they finished in the cellar. It was only through circumstance that Waitkus achieved the celebrity the next year that has kept his name alive for almost half a century. What happened to Eddie Waitkus? If you've ever read Bernard Malamud's 1952 novel *The Natural,* you know the Waitkus story. Like Robert Redford in the 1984 film of the same name, Eddie Waitkus was a ballplayer who strolled into a hotel room in Chicago and was shot by a young female fan.

"Oh, baby, why did you do it?" Waitkus asked, clutching his gut.

The shooter was nineteen-year-old Ruth Ann Steinhagen, a typist who had built a Waitkus shrine at the foot of her bed.

She first saw Waitkus on April 27, 1947, at Wrigley Field. Some of the teenage girls sitting near Steinhagen shouted, "Hey, funny face!" at Eddie as he ran off the field. Steinhagen got hooked.

She never spoke to him, never got his autograph. But she began to spend a lot of time at Wrigley Field, studying Waitkus. In her mind, he was her man. She celebrated April 27 as their anniversary each month. She learned to speak Lithuanian, to better understand his ancestry. She collected Waitkus photographs and Waitkus news articles. She sat in her room and listened to records made in 1936, because Eddie wore the number 36 on the back of his uniform.

After the 1948 season, Waitkus was traded to the Philadelphia Phillies. Steinhagen could not handle the change. She became depressed and could think of only one way to improve her spirits: "I would shoot him because I liked him a great deal and knew I couldn't have him," she later explained. "And if I couldn't have him, neither could anybody else."

The Phillies were scheduled to play the Cubs in Chicago in June 1949. Waitkus was on a tear, batting .306 coming into the series.

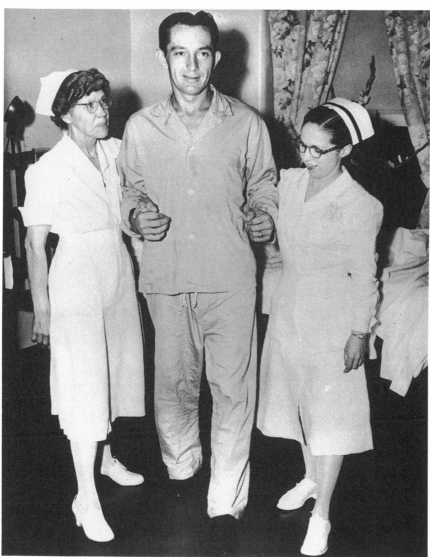

*Eddie
Waitkus's
Surprise*

*Eddie Waitkus.
Recovering from
a groupie's
gun shot:
"Baby, why did
you do it?"*

Steinhagen prepared for his return by purchasing a rifle at a pawnshop. Then she rented a room at the Edgewater Beach Hotel, where the Phillies would be staying.

    After the game on June 14, Waitkus went out with some friends. He returned to the hotel around midnight to find a stack of messages waiting for him at the front desk. They were all from a woman named Ruth Ann in Room 1297A. This is what one of the messages said: "We're not acquainted but I have something of importance to speak to you about. I think it would be to your advantage to let me explain it to you. . . . Please come soon."

Waitkus went straight upstairs.

Steinhagen opened the door. Waitkus strode past, sat down, and said, "What's up?"

"I have a surprise for you," she answered.

She opened the closet door, took out the rifle, and ordered Waitkus out of the chair and toward a window.

"Baby, what's this all about?"

"For two years you've been bothering me," Steinhagen told him, "and now you are going to die."

She pulled the trigger and the shot knocked Waitkus against the wall.

"Baby, why did you do that?" Waitkus asked. "Why did you do it?"

Steinhagen called the front desk and announced the shooting. Waitkus was bleeding profusely. The medics arrived and rushed him to the hospital for surgery. He missed the rest of the season, but was named Comeback Player of the Year in 1950 when he hit .284 and helped the Phillies win the pennant.

Steinhagen spent three years in a mental hospital. Waitkus always feared she would come back into his life. She never did. And after all these years, she's lost in the legend, like the man she shot.

The
1940s

Jake Checks Out

Jake Powell was explosive and unpredictable in his fifteen-year career with the Yankees and Senators. He was the man who rifled empty bottles at spectators and boasted about "beating niggers over the head" in his off-duty job as a cop—an admission that won him a suspension and briefly generated some real discussion about racism in professional sports. In 1948, three years after fading from the game, Powell exploded again. Arrested in Washington, D.C., on charges of writing $300 worth of bad checks at a hotel, Powell was taken to the police station for questioning. There he asked permission to speak privately to the young woman who was with him. Her name was Josephine Amber, and she later said they were to have been married that day. The police granted Powell's request, and he used his private moment to pull out a .25 caliber pistol and shout, "Hell, I'm going to end it all." Powell, forty, shot himself twice, first in the chest, then in the right temple. Ten minutes later, he was dead.

The
1950s

1950
- Billy Martin joins the Yankees.
- Walter O'Malley forces Branch Rickey to leave the Dodgers.
- Sal Maglie beans Pirates' Danny Murtaugh, fracturing his skull.
- Fan accidentally shot and killed in stands at Polo Grounds on July 4 by teenager on nearby rooftop.
- Ted Williams gives Fenway fans the finger.
- Brooklyn woman Hilda Weissman, twenty-five, says her baby was fathered by Hugh Casey.

1951
- Ford Frick is named baseball commissioner.
- Hugh Casey calls estranged wife on phone and says he'll blow his brains out if she won't have him back. She won't. He does.
- Bobby Thomson hits the shot heard around the world as the Giants win the pennant.
- Mickey Mantle trips on outfield drainpipe in Yankee-Giant World Series. Wrecks his knee.
- Shoeless Joe Jackson dies.

1952
- Branch Rickey's Pirates wear batting helmets.
- Billy Martin knees Clint "Scrap Iron" Courtney in the groin.
- Martin twice fights the mentally unstable Jimmy Piersall.

1953
- Don Zimmer is beaned in minor league game and nearly dies.
- Clint Courtney spikes Phil Rizzuto. Near-riot in New York.
- Dodger Carl Furillo attacks ex-boss Durocher in Giant dugout.
- Major league attendance drops to 14.4 million.
- Taxi driver hits Giants' Hank Thompson with sawed-off bat.

1954
- Joe DiMaggio marries Marilyn Monroe.
- Joe Adcock of the Braves hits four homers and a double in one game against the Dodgers.

- Clem Labine of the Dodgers beans Adcock the next day.
- Don Newcombe of the Dodgers hits Adcock with fastball a few weeks later. Adcock is out for season.

1955
- Minnie Minoso's skull is fractured in beaning by Yankees' Bob Grim.
- Giant pitcher Jim Hearn breaks Joe Adcock's arm with fastball.
- National League adopts batting helmets.

1956
- Rookie Frank Robinson is hit twenty times by pitchers.
- Ruben Gomez brushes back Adcock. Adcock attacks. Gomez runs.
- Hal Jeffcoat of Cincinnati beans Don Zimmer, who is nearly blinded.
- American League adopts batting helmets.
- Ted Williams spits at Fenway fans.
- Jackie Robinson retires.

1957
- Line drive hits Cleveland pitcher Herb Score in eye. The winner of thirty-six games in his first two years, Score never pitches well again.
- Billy Martin celebrates his twenty-ninth birthday at the Copacabana with Mantle, Ford, and the gang.
- Yankee–White Sox slugfest, featuring Walt Dropo, Enos Slaughter, and Billy Martin.
- Martin is traded to Kansas City two days later.
- Ruben Gomez beans Frank Robinson.

1958
- Walter O'Malley moves Dodgers from Brooklyn to Los Angeles.
- Don Drysdale knocks down Orlando Cepeda in his first major league at bat.
- Both leagues impose anti-beanball rule: pitchers are fined $50 on the first warning for throwing at a batter.
- Ted Williams throws bat seventy-five feet into stands, where it hits Red Sox general manager Joe Cronin's housekeeper.
- Ex-Giant Hank Thompson arrested for stealing a car.
- Rickey Henderson is born.

259

1959

- Boston Red Sox hire team's first black player, Pumpsie Green, twelve years after Jackie Robinson's debut in Brooklyn.
- Major league attendance rebounds to 18.3 million.

*The
1950s*

"I didn't give a shit what happened, as long as I got the job done."
—Don Drysdale

In May 1952, Joe Black joined the Brooklyn Dodger pitching staff. He stood six feet two inches tall and threw an overwhelming fastball that won him fifteen games over the next five months. But the rookie was black and subject to the gross racial slurs that still characterized the game. One afternoon, with Black on the mound, the Cincinnati bench broke out in a chorus of "Ol' Black Joe." Black responded by throwing fastballs at the heads of seven consecutive

George Brace

Joe Black
gave as good
as he got.

Cincinnati batters, who ducked and then shut up. This was the sort of
"by-any-means-necessary" retaliation that black pitchers used to
silence racial insults—and to protect black teammates from racially
motivated beanball attacks. Black batters routinely led the leagues in
being hit by pitched balls: Robinson and Campanella on the Dodgers,
Luke Easter on the Indians, Minnie Minoso on the White Sox, Monte
Irvin and Hank Thompson on the New York Giants. "We spent a lot of
time flat on our backs," said Thompson, who homered eight times
down the pennant stretch in 1951 as the Giants rebounded from
thirteen and a half games back to snatch the pennant from the
Dodgers. "One time I hit a home run and as I rounded the bases the
pitcher said, 'I'll get you next time, you black motherfucker.' "

The New York Yankees stonewalled on the racial issue. General
manager George Weiss, the man most responsible for forging the
Yankees' cold, aristocratic image, once stood up at a cocktail party and
proclaimed, "I will never allow a black man to wear a Yankee uniform.
Box holders from Westchester . . . would be offended to have to sit
with niggers." In 1953, only six of sixteen major league teams were
integrated as the season waned. Along with the Red Sox and Tigers, the
Yankees were particularly well known for unyielding support of the
color line. New York had a tremendous prospect in their farm
system—the black first baseman Vic Power, probably the smoothest
fielder at his position since Hal Chase and a .300 hitter to boot. But
Power was not a suitable talent for the Yankees, argued Weiss, who
called him hot-tempered and a showboat. Power was buried in the
minors and eventually dealt to the Athletics, who placed him in
segregated housing during spring training in Florida. Power wasn't
allowed to drink from the team water fountain in the dugout—having
grown up in Puerto Rico, where the races mixed relatively freely, he
was shocked by the meanness of American racial realities. So were
up-and-coming black stars like Frank Robinson, who went after a
heckler in Columbia, South Carolina, with a bat. When
nineteen-year-old Henry Aaron took the field for the South Atlantic
League's Jacksonville team, beer guzzlers in the stands chanted,
"Nigger! Nigger!" One of Aaron's black teammates, Horace Garner,
was pelted with rocks. Once Garner ran into a crowd to catch a fly ball
and, spotting a little white boy underfoot, scooped the child up to avoid

running him over. The child's mother shrieked, "My God! That nigger's running away with my baby!"

This was still 1953. The following year, the U.S. Supreme Court ruled that segregation in public schools was unconstitutional. As if responding to a signal, half a dozen major league teams signed black players over the next few months. But it wasn't until 1955 that the Yankees, who had been picketed for their racial policies, broke down and allowed catcher Elston Howard to wear pinstripes. As late as 1957, the year the Senate passed the first civil rights legislation since Reconstruction, Cincinnati manager Birdie Tebbetts complained that his new slugger, Frank Robinson, was being brained by pitchers because he was black. The Red Sox refused to play a black man until 1959—twelve years after Jackie Robinson's debut.

Yet even as Robinson, Campanella, and Aaron received routine death threats in the mail, there was a transformation underway.

In his book *Bums: An Oral History of the Brooklyn Dodgers,* author Peter Golenbock recounts the time in 1950 when Brooklyn pitcher Don Newcombe was baited by a racist coach on the Philadelphia Phillies. Newcombe paused to confer with teammate Jackie Robinson, then threw a fastball at the head of Del Ennis, the Phillies' most valuable batter. Ennis was big; six feet tall, about two hundred pounds, and on his way to hitting thirty-one homers and knocking in 126 runs that year. He slowly picked himself up from the dirt, went over to the dugout to have a few words with the coach, then returned to the batter's box and struck out. When Newcombe, a massive man who towered four inches over Ennis, later asked him what he had told the coach, Ennis explained, "I told that son of a bitch, 'You leave that big son of a bitch alone out there on that mound, because you don't have to go up there and hit against him. I do, and he's knocking me on my ass for what you're saying to him. Now, if that's your feeling, that's fine. But if you say anything more to him while I'm at bat, I'm gonna pull your fucking tongue out of your head and lay it in your hand. Leave that man alone.'"

The Phillies fired the coach.

Racism was becoming counterproductive. Over the next ten or fifteen years, as baseball slowly adjusted to the new social reality, it became unacceptable to insult not only blacks, but members of other ethnic groups. Leo Durocher, now managing the Giants, took the team to Japan to play some exhibition games and was nearly drummed from the stadium for calling an umpire a "slant-eyed idiot." That type of language was no longer acceptable, at home or abroad. As racist language slowly came to be frowned upon, so did racially inspired violence. It began to dawn on pitchers that it wasn't really fair to throw at the heads of black batters simply because they were black.

Baseball was acquiring a veneer.

It was being held up by its marketers as part of a grand social experiment: a model for a kinder and gentler America.

But wait.

By the mid-'50s, more than two hundred batters were being hit by pitched balls each year—up from an average of 130 before World War II.

In 1953, Brooklyn's top minor league prospect, Don Zimmer, was almost killed when a pitch fractured his skull and left him unconscious for weeks. Dodger owner Walter O'Malley warned it wouldn't be long before "some district attorney out to make a name for himself starts indicting pitchers suspected of tossing a beanball." The leagues soon decided to mandate the use of batters' helmets. But pitchers weren't deterred.

The baseball field had become a wide-open arena for settling individual scores. When New York Giant pitcher Sal "the Barber" Maglie shaved Jackie Robinson with one too many fastballs, Robinson got even by crashing like a football halfback through Giant second baseman Davey Williams on a close play at first base. The Giants' Alvin Dark returned the insult by knocking down Robinson at third base later in the game. But revenge came too late. Williams's career was ended by the collision.

The marketers could talk all they liked, but this was the new Wild West. Whites threw at whites. Whites threw at blacks. Blacks threw at whites. Blacks threw at blacks. Brothers even threw at brothers: when the Dodgers' Larry Sherry decked Norm Sherry in an intersquad game, Norm jumped up screaming, "I'm gonna tell Mom!"

And everybody threw at Willie Mays.

"I didn't give a shit what happened, as long as I got the job done," said Dodger pitcher Don Drysdale, whose headhunting career began in 1956 when Sal Maglie joined the team and became his mentor.

You may remember how the violent baseball of the 1890s was perpetrated by a legion of nasty little men.

Well, in the 1950s, the offenders were behemoths. Drysdale stood six feet five inches tall. Newcombe was six feet four. Maglie was six feet two. Robinson and Dark were former college football stars, powerfully built.

Think about the other baseball stars of the '50s: Gil Hodges, Frank Robinson, Hank Bauer, and Eddie Mathews, the great home-run-hitting third baseman and number one barroom brawler in the game. Ralph Kiner, Rocky Colavito, and Ted Kluszewski.

Bruisers all.

Maybe it was television that compelled baseball owners to put on a muscle-bound spectacle for viewers. Or maybe it was the cumulative effect of decades of baseball that emphasized clouting ever-increasing numbers of home runs. But the 1950s, more than any other decade, were a time when baseball teams were built around brute strength: "Home run hitters drive Cadillacs. Singles hitters drive Fords," reasoned Kiner. The result was a very dull brand of baseball with few refinements. Sure, there was more platooning and managers paid more attention to relief pitching. But the overall game grew less sophisticated. People sat in their seats and waited . . . and waited . . . and waited until one of their big-boned heroes parked the sucker. We think of this as the golden time of Mays, Mantle, Snyder, and Aaron. And in New York and Milwaukee, these *were* special years. But the reality is that attendance plummeted throughout most of the majors, and one reason was that there were so few surprises in the game. It all came down to this: boom!

Big men. Gross retaliation. Getting even.

It was a cruel game. Here's an example: National League pitchers used Joe Adcock of the Braves for target practice.

Adcock was a Louisiana farm boy who played basketball at Louisiana State University and arrived in the major leagues in 1950. He was a six-foot-four-inch mountain of muscle, one of the strongest men who ever played. "Toughest ballplayer I ever saw. The guy I'd want in a fight," says Earl Lawson, former sportswriter for the *Cincinnati Enquirer,* who became a connoisseur of barroom fights involving the strongest, or most headstrong, players of the era. These included shortstop Johnny Logan of the Braves, a Billy Martinish, short-fused character who was always jumping somebody, and Eddie Mathews, the team enforcer who usually stepped in and finished what Logan began. Lawson remembers ballplayers hitting cops in taverns and throwing glasses that shattered upon impact with cocktail waitresses' heads. His recollections make it sound as if the '50s were one long drunken tear for many of its most celebrated players—which they probably were. But the man who could take on any of these guys, and occasionally did, was Adcock: "He could fight," Lawson remembers. "When he swung, he didn't miss. And he didn't swing roundhouse. He swung straight from the shoulder."

Adcock could pound the baseball, too. He once hit a 483-foot shot into the deep center field seats at the Polo Grounds, the first player to reach those previously unexplored regions. On July 31, 1954, at Ebbets Field, Adcock came to the plate five times, was thrown seven pitches, and hit four home runs and a double. It was probably the most devastating offensive outburst in the history of the game, and Adcock paid for it for years to come. The next day, Dodger pitcher Clem Labine beaned him. Six weeks later, on September 11, Brooklyn's Don Newcombe threw a pitch that smashed Adcock's right hand, sidelined him for the rest of the season, and ruined the Braves' pennant hopes. The next season, on the anniversary of his four-homer outburst in Brooklyn, an erratic right-hander for the New York Giants named Jim Hearn threw an inside fastball that broke Adcock's right forearm. This

Joe Adcock shows Milwaukee manager Charlie Grimm the dent in his batting helmet—payback for hitting four homers and a double the day before.

is how it went. If Adcock was going to hit the ball out, the pitchers were going to hit him. There was "a very clear underlying message to all this," says veteran St. Louis sportswriter Bob Broeg, "that being: 'If you show us up, you're gonna pay a price with an injury, and maybe a season-ending injury.' These guys had long memories and they repaid their debts."

In 1956, the year Adcock hit thirty-eight home runs, another pitcher got even. On July 17, Ruben Gomez of the Giants brushed back Adcock, hitting him on the right hand. Again. Adcock was disturbed. On his way to first base, he exchanged words with Gomez, then charged the mound. Gomez's reaction shocked everyone in Milwaukee's County Stadium: he threw a bullet at Adcock's thigh, then ran for the hills, with half the Braves team on his heels. Gomez sprinted into the Giant dugout, hid in the clubhouse, armed himself with a bat, then grabbed an ice pick, just in case. But the fight went no further. Teammate Sal Maglie thought it was outrageous that Gomez ran away: "He showed he wasn't willing to back up the knockdown." But Gomez was no dummy. He wasn't going to open himself to one of Adcock's straight-from-the-shoulder punches: "I don't let him break my ribs," he explained. He had hit Adcock with the pitch; mission accomplished. Adcock was "a six-foot-four-inch stationary target," says Milwaukee baseball historian Bob Buege. In seventeen seasons, Adcock only twice played as many as 140 ball games. The pitchers identified his weakness and chipped away at his livelihood.

It was cruel revenge, for front offices were in the hands of numbers crunchers who brooked no sentiment and fought tooth and nail against salary advances for even established stars. The cold business mentality was best symbolized by Weiss of the Yankees and Dodger owner Walter O'Malley, who booted general manager Branch Rickey from the team in 1950 and instituted a system of fines for anyone who mentioned Rickey's name. But even Rickey, as we know, was not one to open the safe to his players. He moved from Brooklyn to Pittsburgh and turned down a request for a raise from the Pirates' Ralph Kiner, the home-run-hitting Cadillac driver: "We finished last *with* you; we could've finished last *without* you," Rickey lectured. Mind you, he was talking to the man who established the second-highest home-run-to-at-bats ratio in the history of the modern era. But that wasn't relevant. A handful of players edged past the $50,000 salary barrier, but most still clawed their way to every nickel. "The owners had the players by the short hairs," said Yankee pitcher Bob Grim. Every error by a player, every miscue at bat, was an excuse for owners to tamp down salaries at negotiation time. When an official scorer in Cincinnati took a base hit away from Red second baseman Johnny Temple, the player snapped, "You're taking bread and butter from my mouth." Pitcher Early Wynn, who won three hundred ball games and a reputation as master of the beanball, railed that "every hitter I face is a man trying to take money out of my pocket. Every hitter is an enemy."

No one stretched the us-versus-them mentality further than Billy Martin. Martin had arrived with Stengel's Yankees to stake out his position as baseball's never-ending headache. But Casey loved him. Having managed Martin in Oakland in the Pacific Coast League in the late '40s, Stengel saw in him a brash player of limited talents who loved the game so much that he would learn every imaginable angle to get ahead. Martin practiced the double-play pivot in his hotel room using a pillow for a base; he stared at walls for hours without blinking—so that he wouldn't blink and miss a fastball in the middle of a ball game. He made himself a winner. Like Durocher, Martin saw baseball and all of life as a series of battles to be won. He'd grown up poor in Berkeley, California, a real Dead End Kid who was picked on for his short stature and long nose, and spent his life straightening out personal affronts. By the time he reached the Yankees, he was always jittery, ready to explode, and he instigated a number of famous grudge fights and drunken off-the-field escapades that began his long run on the front pages of New York's tabloids.

He always seemed to be around when there was a fight. And he didn't know when to stop.

On June 13, 1957, the Yankees played the Chicago White Sox. Pitcher Art Ditmar got off to a poor start for New York, and when Chicago's Larry Doby came to the plate, Ditmar testily threw a fastball at his head, sending Doby sprawling. Doby got up, said, "If you ever do that again, I'll stick a knife in your back," then started swinging. The benches cleared. Yankee first baseman Moose Skowron tackled Doby. White Sox first baseman Walt Dropo, a gigantic man, jumped on the Yankees' Enos Slaughter, a twenty-year veteran who, as Red Smith

Battle of large lumbering men:
White Sox first baseman Walt Dropo
pounds Enos Slaughter
of the Yankees.

once wrote, had performed appendectomies with his spikes ever since his days with the Gas House Gang. Gradually the melee dissolved into a brutal, extended one-on-one slugfest between the two giants, Slaughter and Dropo. After it was over, Slaughter lumbered off the field, head bent, his jersey ripped to shreds.

With order restored, the umps prepared to resume play. But then Martin asked Ditmar, "What did Doby say to you?" Ditmar repeated the knife threat, and Martin went crazy, as if the previous twenty minutes of fighting had never occurred. He lunged at Doby, pummeling him with short stabbing punches—a technique he had acquired as a teenage gang leader—until teammates ripped him off.

The June 13 fight was one of three bench-clearing brawls the Yankees had that week. And as Martin and Doby went at it in Chicago, the Dodgers and Braves fought in Brooklyn; the very same afternoon. No surprises, just more big men proving their manhood: Drysdale plunked Johnny Logan on the back with a fastball to register his displeasure with the previous batter's home run; Logan attacked Drysdale; Eddie Mathews entered swinging; the benches cleared. A Dodger-Reds rumble in July followed a similar scenario, but grew more interesting when Brooklyn's Charlie Neal sucker-punched the Reds' Don Hoak, an ex-Marine and real '50s tough guy, who went bananas. Dodger manager Walter Alston once said: "If Hoak went out to get a bear, bare-handed, I gotta bet on Hoak." Hoak once slid so forcefully into second base that he tore his stomach lining, bled profusely, and lost sixteen pounds in a matter of days. After the fight with Charlie Neal, he fumed to reporters, "I'll get him. I'll whip his hide and his wife won't know him when I get through."

The lawlessness in the game was always a reflection of events outside the ballpark. Baseball in the 1950s was played against a backdrop of urban decay in the big Northern and Midwestern cities that had historically hosted big league teams. As neighborhoods deteriorated, so did old ballparks. As middle-class people fled the cities, they stopped going to ball games. As crime rates burgeoned, owners reconsidered their investments. The Boston Braves pulled up stakes and moved to the Milwaukee heartland. The Dodgers left poor little Ebbets Field after the 1957 season for a new, splendorous setting in Los Angeles. The fact that the Dodgers were abandoning generations of loyal Brooklyn fans whose lives were entwined with memories of their team—this meant little to Walter O'Malley, a tremendously wealthy man, who looked at his dwindling gate receipts and saw that baseball's future did not lie in Brooklyn. "I think Hemingway said it," reflected the writer Joe Flaherty, "that if you live long enough, everything you love will be sullied, and it was O'Malley who was the first one who really put the shit into the game, the one who showed everyone that loyalty means nothing."

But how loyal were the fans? Off-duty Boston cops passed out apples to children at Fenway Park with instructions to throw them at left fielder Ted Williams. Sure, Williams had legendary run-ins with spectators, flipping them the bird, spitting at them. "Those goddamn fans; they can go fuck themselves, and you can quote me in all the papers," he told reporters. But was Williams any worse than the "wolves" in the seats who cursed and insulted him, day in, day out, year after year? There was no such thing as civility at Fenway Park: Mickey Mantle received a letter saying that he would meet his death there "at the end of a .32."

It wasn't just Boston: Detroit Tiger outfielder Al Kaline took the field in Chicago and had an open knife thrown at him. That made headlines. But no one questioned why American League pitchers threw at Mantle's legs, hobbled by degenerative bone disease. No one asked whether Don Drysdale really needed to throw at Frank Robinson's head. Or at Hank Aaron's. Drysdale *owned* Aaron for a time, and Aaron briefly feared that Drysdale would drive him out of the league. He knew that Drysdale had excellent control. When one of Drysdale's pitches came close to his head, it was no accident.

"Drysdale flaunted his willingness to injure the hitter," said sportswriter Leonard Koppett, one of the game's keenest observers. "He wanted the batter thinking, 'Hey, he's willing to *kill* me!'"

Baseball was a cold, cold game. It was about winning.

Leo Durocher put it like this: "If we're spitting at a crack in the wall in this office for pennies, I want to beat you at it. Anybody can finish second."

Casey's Pearls

Casey Stengel was named manager of the New York Yankees in 1949 and promptly won the pennant—the first of ten consecutive American League flags that the Yankees captured under Stengel from 1949 to 1958. In that period, the Yanks also won eight World Series titles, usually beating the Brooklyn Dodgers.

Clearly Stengel had something on the ball.

What exactly was it?

On catcher Elston Howard, who debuted with the previously lily-white Yankees in 1955:

"When I finally get a nigger, I get the only one that can't run."

On Boston Red Sox outfielder Jimmy Piersall, who was institutionalized for psychological problems:

"He ain't crazy. He don't run to third base when he gets a hit, does he?"

Also: "He's great, but you gotta play him in a cage."

On Jackie Robinson, after he struck out three times in a World Series game against New York's Allie "Superchief" Reynolds, who was part Creek Indian:

"Before that black sonofabitch accuses us of being prejudiced, he should learn how to hit an Indian."

On Yankee pitcher Ralph Terry, after he had given up a homer to lose a game in the late innings:

"The only thing wrong with that fella is he ain't smart enough to cross the street."

*Ol' Casey's wit
could be cruel.*

On Yankee pitcher Bob Turley:

"Look at him. He don't smoke, he don't drink, he don't chase women, and he don't win."

Finally, there was this story about Stengel:

He goes to the mound to talk to a struggling pitcher. The pitcher doesn't want to come out. "I'm not tired," he tells Casey.

"Well," says Stengel, "I'm tired of you."

Leo, Leo, Leo

In 1948, Brooklyn manager Leo Durocher shocked the Bums by defecting to the New York Giants. For Leo, war was war, no matter whose troops he commanded. So he started to pick on the Dodgers. Durocher's pet target in the late '40s and early '50s was Brooklyn outfielder Carl Furillo. One time, Durocher instructed Giant ace Sal Maglie to throw some heat at Furillo's head. Furillo responded by throwing his bat at the Barber. Another time, before sending Giant pitcher Sheldon Jones to the mound, Durocher told Furillo, "You'll really be ducking tonight." One of Leo's coaches, Herman Franks, leaned into the Brooklyn clubhouse to warn Furillo, "In your ear, we'll get you tonight." Sure enough, Furillo was beaned and hospitalized.

On September 5, 1953, Furillo went four-for-four against the Giants. He wasn't surprised the next day when New York pitcher Ruben Gomez retaliated by throwing a pitch that hit him on the wrist. But then Durocher started to taunt Furillo, and the Dodger blew his cool. He charged into the Giant dugout, put a headlock on Durocher, and squeezed until his old boss's "bald head started to turn purple," sportswriter Harold Rosenthal said. In the brawl that followed, Furillo, the National League's leading hitter with a .344 average, broke a bone in his left hand. He missed the rest of the season. But when reporters asked him if he had overreacted, Furillo said no: "The newspapermen don't know the inside dope. I know Durocher throws at my head, and he knows it. Why should I be sorry for going after a guy who might get me killed?"

Mr. Sensitive: Rogers Hornsby

Rogers Hornsby arrived in Beaumont, Texas, in 1950 to manage the New York Yankees' farm club there. The team boasted the talents of Gil McDougald, the up-and-coming Yankee shortstop, and there was great excitement over the club's chances. Baseball historian Charles C. Alexander remembers the 1950 season as "a wonderful summer, and in some respects the greatest year of my life. I must have seen at least twenty-five games. I sat there and wondered how the great Hornsby wound up in Beaumont, and at the same time was delighted that he had."

Well, the great Hornsby had wound up in Beaumont by insulting one major league club owner after another for twenty-five years. He was, for the moment, between real jobs. Still, Hornsby "was a brilliant success," says Alexander, Hornsby's biographer. "After finishing last for three years, the team went to the play-offs under his leadership. To the people of Beaumont, Hornsby was above criticism. And as a token of the town's esteem, he was given a brand-new Cadillac before one of the ball games. Well, the Cadillac was brought out and Hornsby barely acknowledged it. He didn't look at it or say a word. We were all sort of struck dumb that he was so abrupt and rude about the whole business. There was just sort of an embarrassed hush in the stands, and then someone got in the Cadillac and drove it off the field, and the game started.

"He was just a stiff guy," according to Alexander. "He had no diplomacy. He was what we would today call 'insensitive.' I don't think Hornsby would've known the meaning of the word."

Dave Egan vs. Ted Williams

Ted Williams's cocksure John Wayne demeanor never went over big with the Boston press. Almost from the moment he set foot in camp as a rookie in 1939, Williams was attacked for his booming pronouncements about his hitting talents, his seeming lack of generosity toward teammates, and his overall disdain for etiquette, and the barrage didn't stop even after his retirement in 1960. Reporters didn't like his World War II draft deferment, or his failure to tip his cap to the fans after hitting a home run, or his fishing trip to Florida while his wife was in the hospital in Boston giving birth. They didn't like his divorce or his spitting at abusive spectators, an offense that earned him a $5,000 fine. They didn't like his style on the field: "The dimensions of his performance are heroic, but the effect isn't moving or genuine," wrote Joe Williams in *Sport* magazine in 1951. And when Williams returned from Korea, a war hero, they still had to slam him: "Williams is a competitor, but . . . his blood is ice cold," wrote *Boston Herald* columnist Bill Cunningham.

It's probable that no other athlete of comparable talent has ever been subjected to such unending criticism. Williams was no demigod, but he didn't deserve it. He was the victim of a twenty-year journalistic gangbang, and the worst offender was Dave Egan—"the old drunken bastard from the *Record,*" Williams called him. Egan was a Harvard Law School graduate who called himself "the Colonel"; the caricature that accompanied his columns in the *Boston Record* showed a mustachioed Confederate officer with a long beard and oversize hat. Assuming this down-home guise, Egan set about making pronouncements on big city slickers. He was a master of vituperative prose, a man who enjoyed jumping on people. When Casey Stengel, then managing the Boston Braves, was hit by a taxi in 1943, Egan hailed the cabbie as "the man who did the most for Boston in '43." Casey, meanwhile, had a limp for the rest of his life.

Boy, did Egan have a good time with Williams. He assailed him for failing to offer hearty enough handshakes to teammate Vern Stephens when Stephens homered. He decided that Williams's home runs always came when the Red Sox didn't need them. The truth is that Egan was in no position to make any pronouncements; he never went to the ballpark. Egan viewed his columns as circulation builders and free publicity for Williams; indeed, he never understood why Williams took his remarks so seriously. But, unlike Egan, Williams was a serious man.

"I am no friend of Ted Williams," the Colonel wrote time and again. He mocked Williams as "the big man," "the great man," a practitioner of "gutless baseball." He urged Boston owner Tom Yawkey to trade Williams, called him "the worst team player ever known to the major leagues," and complained that the Red Sox were blocking the development —get this—of young Marv Throneberry by keeping Williams in left field.

But Egan really pulled out all the stops on April 30, 1952, when Williams, who was about to report to the marines for active duty in Korea, was honored at Fenway Park by Boston's mayor, the governor of Massachusetts, and thousands of fans. A state senate resolution that called Williams "an inspiration not only to the youth of

Pi-tooey! Ted Williams, the greatest pure hitter in history, spits at his biggest detractors—the fans of Fenway.

Massachusetts but to the youth of the country" was read. Predictably, Egan was having none of it. This is a bit of what he wrote that day:

"It seems disgraceful to me that a person such as Williams now is to be given the keys to the city. We talk about juvenile delinquency, and fight against it, and then officially honor a man whom we should officially horsewhip, for the vicious influence that he has had on the childhood of America. . . .

"Men who call themselves community leaders insult the decent and intelligent fathers and mothers in the community, lavishing honors on a man who consistently and over a period of many years has set the poorest possible example to our children, and if this is leadership, I'll have strychnine."

Hear, hear.

Popeye: Don Zimmer

First there was Pete Reiser.

And then came Don Zimmer.

In the early '50s, Zimmer was the heir apparent to Brooklyn shortstop Pee Wee Reese. He had "an absolute gun" for an arm, said Don Drysdale. Dodger scout Al Campanis called him "a Stanky with ability . . . the outstanding man in our organization." He was tough, compact, aggressive. "Popeye," as Zimmer was known for his good looks, was going to join Hodges, Cox, and Gilliam in the Dodger championship infield.

Then he got beaned.

Then he got beaned again.

The first beaning occurred in 1953, while Zimmer was playing for the Dodgers' St. Paul farm club in the American Association. Zimmer was almost killed. Unconscious for three weeks, hospitalized for seven, he suffered horrendous skull fractures and underwent two operations to relieve pressure on the brain. The surgeons inserted plugs in his skull—to "keep my brain from jiggling," Zimmer joked, after he learned to talk again.

He came back. But around the National League, Zimmer was known as a "plate paralytic," unable to move out of the way of a threatening pitch, in the tradition of Frank Chance and Mickey Cochrane. New York Giant pitcher

Transcendental Graphics

Don Zimmer joked about the plugs that surgeons placed in his skull after one of his beanings.

Sal Maglie said he "hated to pitch against him. I didn't dare throw at him because I knew he'd freeze."

Something was always happening to Zimmer. Drysdale recalled him hobbling with pain after fouling two straight pitches off the same spot on his foot. In late 1955, while playing winter ball in Puerto Rico, Zimmer hit a 410-foot homer one game, which embarrassed the pitcher. The next time Zimmer came to bat, the pitcher threw the ball at Zimmer's right wrist, breaking it. Later in the winter, Zimmer had an appendectomy.

But he came back again in 1956. Briefly.

On June 23, he went to bat against an old friend from the winter leagues, Hal Jeffcoat of the Cincinnati Reds. Jeffcoat threw a slider that didn't break. It clobbered Zimmer in the face, broke his cheekbone, and knocked him unconscious. After Zimmer was carried off the field on a stretcher, Jeffcoat moaned, "Anybody but little Zim. It just got away from me and it seemed like he froze."

Zimmer was almost blinded. Doctors advised him not to resume his career; he might not survive another beaning.

But Zimmer came back. And when the Dodgers eventually traded him to the Cubs, Drysdale, like Maglie, hated pitching to him. "Popeye scared me half to death," wrote Drysdale in his autobiography. "He stood in there, right over the plate, daring you to come inside on him. He had a motto about that, too: 'If you're going to hit me, don't wound me. Get me good. I don't want to lie there quivering. Just end it.'"

Up to the Moon, Alice

In 1957, Philadelphia Phillies center fielder Richie Ashburn hit a foul ball that struck the face of a spectator named Alice Roth. It broke her nose and shook her up so badly that she had to be removed from the stands on a stretcher. Fate and Ashburn struck again. Against all odds, he lined another foul ball, this one striking Roth on the stretcher as she was lifted to safety.

Billy Martin 101

Billy Martin turned twenty-nine years old on May 16, 1957, and, to celebrate, he and his buddies from the Yankees took in a late show at the Copacabana nightclub. Martin, Mantle, Whitey Ford, Yogi Berra, Hank Bauer—the whole gang was there to check out Sammy Davis, Jr. Sitting at a nearby table were a couple of drunks, one of whom shouted racial insults at Davis and asked Bauer what he thought of "Little Black Sambo." Bauer took exception to this. There was a loud argument between the Yanks and the drunks—well, they were *all* a bunch of drunks—and before you knew it, one of Davis's attackers was knocked unconscious in the bathroom. Uh-oh. The Yanks decided to sneak out the back door, but someone was loitering there. Yoo-hoo! It was Leonard Lyons, gossip columnist for the *New York Post.* Lyons noted the Yankees' disheveled appearance, went inside to interview the drunks, and the story was all over page one the next morning.

Poor Billy Martin.

His jittery temperament, raucous life-style, and escalating dependence on alcohol might have gone unnoticed in the 1940s, when ballplayers still rampaged nightly and not a word of it was reported by the press. But Billy made the majors at a time when baseball players were starting to live in fish bowls, thanks to television, the newspaper gossip mill, and America's burgeoning fascination with celebrities. Sure, it was a gas for Martin to be set on a pedestal alongside television and movie stars. But it ruined his career. It convinced Yankee general manager George Weiss that Martin was trouble—a punk amid Yankee aristocracy. Martin didn't throw a single punch at the Copa, but as the media latched onto the incident, and as a grand jury convened to investigate it, Weiss blamed Martin. Who was always around when Mantle and Ford went boozing? Who accompanied them on their nutty hunting expeditions? Who was there when Mantle crawled onto a window ledge twenty-two stories above the street to watch a teammate fornicate in the next room? Martin was there, of course. And while

*Opposite:
Billy Martin
was never
a class act. Here
he plants a knee
in the groin of
St. Louis Brown
catcher
Clint Courtney.*

some of those incidents remained hidden for years, there was enough of an odor to alert Weiss and the public that a rascal was on the loose. Martin was born ten years too late. The media watched him, and his reputation preceded him, even when he was innocent. None of his baseball predecessors, not even Durocher, got called on the rug like Martin.

He was so much like Durocher.

Years later, after Martin clawed his way back to prominence as a manager, he said, "I would play Hitler, Mussolini, and Tojo on my team if I thought it would help me win." He laid five $20 bills on Yankee pitcher Bob Kammeyer as thanks for knocking down Cliff Johnson, an ex-Yankee whom Martin hated. Like Durocher, Martin came to kill. His arrival with the Yankees in the early '50s—wisecracking with veteran teammates, calling rival Jackie Robinson "a big clown" in the World Series—recalled Durocher's rookie year in New York more than two decades earlier. Like Durocher, Martin was short, funny-looking, not a natural athlete. Like Durocher, he spent years learning every esoteric nuance of the game—and all the dirty tricks to put his team over the top. Casey Stengel came to rely on Martin as a second manager, the only man who could impress fundamentals on the undisciplined Mantle. It was Martin who saved the 1952 World Series in the seventh game with a diving, fingertip catch of a windblown pop-up by Robinson with the bases loaded. He led New York to the 1953 pennant with his clutch hitting, even though his average was only .257. Martin was an unspectacular player who accomplished spectacular things: "My one-for-four would kill ya," he said.

But he was out of control, always fighting. And, again like Durocher, he became a cancerous presence in the game. The headlines never stopped. He wouldn't go away.

Martin grew up in the flatlands of Berkeley, California, a working-class neighborhood that was home to immigrants and San Francisco Bay dockworkers. His father was a truck driver who abandoned the family when Martin was an infant.

His mother told Billy, "Take shit from no one."

That became his credo.

He was a noted street fighter before junior high school, later a neighborhood gang leader and an "enforcer" on the Berkeley High School basketball and baseball teams. He was the guy who planted a tag extra-hard on the mouth of a troublesome opponent or cold-cocked a rival wise guy after the game. Martin beat up spectators, and he was a wicked puncher. He was frequently taunted for having a big nose: "Pinocchio," people called him, or "flag nose." He got even. Every acquaintance was a potential adversary, every one of their actions a potential affront. Martin was "an injustice collector," writes his biographer, David Falkner. "People did things to Billy Martin; he was nearly always blameless. He never started a fight in his life, he said—he just never backed down from one."

A childhood friend named Rube DeAlba described Martin's fighting mode: "His temper became uncontrollable. It was something that just seemed to come over him, like demons or whatever, and then when it was over, he would often get this look on his face, like, 'What have I done?' As if it had been someone else who had done it. He was also someone who bore a grudge. He wouldn't let you know right away. . . . It would just fester until one day it would explode."

In 1947, when Martin played for Phoenix in the Arizona-Texas League, a rival catcher named Clint Courtney spiked Martin's teammate Eddie LeNieve, an old friend from Berkeley. Five years after the collision, when Martin was on the Yankees and "Scrap Iron" Courtney on the St. Louis Browns, Billy got even. Courtney slid into second base and Martin slammed the ball into his mouth. When Courtney rose to fight, Martin dropped him. Courtney got up, and Martin dropped him again. The next year, 1953, Courtney pressed two deep spike wounds into the leg of Yankee shortstop Phil Rizzuto. But little Rizzuto was inviolate on the Yankees; hurting him was like hitting a cop. Martin leveled Courtney, and a seventeen-minute fight broke out between the clubs.

There were other fights, including two with Boston Red Sox outfielder Jimmy Piersall, who was under psychiatric treatment and on the verge of hospitalization. "I'm ashamed of that," Martin said afterward. "I didn't know Piersall was on the verge of cracking up. My only excuse is that I was only a jump away from the guys in the white coats myself."

Martin's marriage was breaking up. He was moody, unable to

sleep, and reliant on pills throughout the '53 season. He channeled all his nervous energy into baseball; this was his best year. In 1954, he applied for a hardship deferment from the draft board in Berkeley, claiming that his mother and stepfather depended on his baseball salary and that he was broke himself. But Martin arrived for his hearing in a new baby-blue Cadillac; the board turned down his request and Martin spent the next two years in the Army.

Returning to the Yankees in late 1955, Martin resumed partying with Mantle and Ford. They would have dinner and drinks and pretty soon they "skipped the dinner part," Mantle said. Billy, Mickey, and Whitey gallivanted about town like rock stars. But there were press rumors that Martin welshed on child support payments, and fans responded by sending him hate mail and death threats. He wasn't performing well on the field. Bobby Richardson was moving in on the second base job. The stage was set for the Yanks to dump Martin when he showed up at the Copacabana for his birthday party. The next morning, seeing the headlines, Martin packed his bags: "I'm gone," he told Mantle. A month later, George Weiss swept Martin from his pedestal and traded him to the Kansas City Athletics. The Yankees' brash, "big-nosed kid," as Stengel had called him, languished there for a couple years, was dealt to Cleveland, got beaned, and woke up in the hospital one day with seven broken bones in his head, wondering how he was ever going to get back on top.

innie Minoso was known as the "Cuban Flash." But if he
moved so fast, why couldn't he get out of the way of a pitched
ball? For ten of eleven years from 1951 to 1961, Minoso led the
American League in being hit by pitches. Some said Minoso was
constantly dinged because he crowded the plate. But others, including
Minoso, said it was because he was black. "There's nothing wrong with
me that a bucket of whitewash wouldn't take care of," Minoso said.

The only time Minoso didn't lead the league in getting hit was
1955—the year that a pitch by the Yankees' Bob Grim fractured
Minoso's skull. But Minoso came back in 1956 and set a league record
by getting hit twenty-three times. Here are his season-by-season totals:

1951: 16
1952: 14
1953: 17
1954: 16
1955: 10
1956: 23
1957: 21
1958: 15
1959: 17
1960: 13
1961: 16

Ding!
Ding!
Ding!

National Baseball Library

Minnie Minoso in a characteristic pose.

The Barber: Sal Maglie

S al Maglie was known as "the Barber" because of his ability to
shave a batter's stubble with his fastball. During his ten-year
career, which ended in 1958, Maglie sent hundreds of hitters sprawling
in the dirt. How did he get away with it? In 1959, he divulged his
secrets in an article for *Cavalier* magazine entitled "I Always Threw
Beanballs." Maglie told how manager Leo Durocher complained,
"You're in the strike zone too much"—another way of telling the
pitcher to stick it in the batter's ear. Maglie gave blow-by-blow
accounts of how he threw at Musial (Stan was unperturbed), Jackie
Robinson (it made him a more aggressive hitter), and Roy Campanella
(the knockdown scared him badly). He demystified the knockdown
pitch: In Maglie's hands it was simply "a tool of the trade like a
carpenter's hammer or a barber's scissors . . . the best pitch in baseball.
. . . The batters expected me to knock them down. I didn't want to
disappoint them.

"I couldn't stop throwing the knockdown," Maglie pleaded. "That
would be the same as if Marilyn Monroe stopped wearing sweaters."

Here are some excerpts:

On his rivalry with Brooklyn:
"When I was pitching for the New York Giants in the early 1950s,
my friends used to warn me never to walk across the Brooklyn Bridge.
. . . Dodger fans hated me then the way they hate Walter O'Malley
now. They believed that when I pitched against Brooklyn, I threw at
the heads of the Dodgers. This was their belief and I can't really blame
them for it. *They were 100 percent correct.*"

On anatomy:
"Why didn't I throw at, say, batters' chests, instead of their heads?
I threw at the head because I knew that a batter could see a pitch up
around his face better than he could see a pitch to any other spot. It's

no trick to hit a batter in the ribs. Any pitcher with decent control can do it. It's a bigger target than the head and, besides, it's a lot tougher for a batter to move his body than his head. So I aimed at the head. The pitch served my purpose. It kept the hitter loose. It made him move. But at the same time there wasn't much chance of my beaning the batter. The pitch was effective without really being dangerous."

And yet:

"Beaning [Danny] Murtaugh and [George] Strickland was no fun. I felt sick when I saw them go down."

On Don Zimmer:

"This was the guy you couldn't possibly throw at. He froze."

On Campy:

"The Dodger I threw at most often was Roy Campanella. Roy was a great ballplayer and a good guy but I found out that he wasn't the same hitter after you brushed him back. . . . Sometimes with Campanella, I could see that he was so sure I was going to knock him down that he'd practically be backing away before I pitched."

On baseball at the turn of the decade:

"I think the whole game of baseball has been sissified. The men who run the sport are trying to make it a delicate game, and it's not. I'm a pitching coach now and, when I'm working with young fellows in the Cardinal farm system, I'm not going to tell them to be polite to the batters. I'm teaching them to be tough."

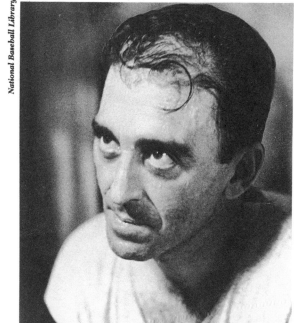

National Baseball Library

The Barber shaved 'em close.

The
1960s

292

*The
1960s*

1960
- Billy Martin fights six-feet-eight-inch pitcher Gene Conley.
- Billy Martin breaks pitcher Jim Brewer's cheekbone.
- Jimmy Piersall throws temper tantrum in Chicago. Fan abuse escalates.

1961
- American League institutes the 162-game season.
- Teenagers attack Jimmy Piersall in center field at Yankee Stadium. Piersall decks one, kicks the other in the can.
- Roger Maris hits sixty-one home runs.
- Ty Cobb dies.
- Frank Robinson arrested for carrying gun in restaurant.

1962
- Maury Wills steals 104 bases.
- Minnie Minoso crashes into concrete wall in St. Louis.
- Hot dog Joe Pepitone is a rookie.
- Future hot dog Darryl Strawberry is born.

1963
- July: Bob Gibson breaks Jim Ray Hart's shoulder in Hart's second big-league at bat. In August, Hart returns. Curt Simmons beans him.
- Ex-Giant Hank Thompson sentenced to prison for holdup.
- Pete Rose is a rookie.
- Rogers Hornsby dies.

1964
- Phillies blow ten-game lead and pennant.
- Dock Ellis swings leaded bat at racist heckler in Batavia, New York.
- San Francisco manager Al Dark disparages intelligence of black and Latin players.
- CBS buys the Yankees.

1965
- August 22: Juan Marichal brains John Roseboro with bat. Marichal is suspended nine days and fined $1,750.
- Yankee dynasty collapses.

1966
- Marvin Miller elected executive director of Major League Players Association.
- Koufax and Drysdale hold out for three-year, $1 million pact.
- Merritt Ranew brained with bat during Pacific Coast League game. Santiago Rosario, brandisher of bat, suspended for a year.
- Cleveland shortstop Larry Brown and outfielder Leon Wagner collide chasing pop fly. Brown suffers multiple skull fractures.
- Ron Santo beaned by Jack Fisher. Cheekbone fractured.
- Eddie Stanky becomes manager of Chicago White Sox.
- Leo Durocher becomes manager of Chicago Cubs.
- Phillie-Met doubleheader: Dick Allen of Phillies hits home run; pitcher Dick Selma of Mets hits Allen; pitcher Bob Buhl of Phillies hits Selma; pitcher Jack Fisher of Mets hits Buhl.

1967
- Tony Conigliaro beaned by Jack Hamilton.

1968
- Number of batters hit by pitches spirals to twenty-year high.
- K.C. Athletics owner Charles Finley moves team to Oakland.
- World Series riot in Detroit after Tigers beat Cardinals.

1969
- Bowie Kuhn takes over as baseball commissioner.
- Players threaten spring training strike.
- Billy Martin becomes manager of Minnesota Twins. Beats up Minnesota pitcher Dave Boswell.
- Mets clinch pennant; thirty-one fans injured in celebrations at Shea.
- Curt Flood objects to his trade by St. Louis to Philadelphia. Files lawsuit challenging the reserve clause.

293

I think I spiked more guys than Ty Cobb.
I did it in a way that appeared accidental.
It wasn't.
  —*Maury Wills*

The Lords of Baseball attempted a renewed cleansing of the game. These powerful businessmen saw themselves as the new tribunes of the national pastime, and they proceeded with their work on two levels. First, they carried out bold business decisions to increase markets and paint a middle-class sheen on the game. Men like the Dodgers' Walter O'Malley built massive new stadiums, surrounded by parking lots the size of small cities, to reattract the many suburban fans who had abandoned baseball in the 1950s. They expanded the leagues to twenty-four teams, and the game became entrenched, coast-to-coast, even in Canada. Here was democracy in action: a franchise for every man or corporate sponsor with sufficient capital! CBS even bought the Yankees. An indoor stadium was built in Houston; baseball in a shopping mall. Artificial turf was laid, auguring the elimination of metal spikes; while it had long been permissible for players to rip one another's flesh, they would not be allowed to tear apart the costly new artificial surfaces. Besides, the game was being beamed into millions of living rooms—there were 78 million television sets in the U.S. by 1968—and no one, certainly not O'Malley, wanted viewers to sit there and watch bloody base-path collisions in color. This was the second part of the owners' grand plan: arranging the marriage of baseball to television. The '60s were about Sundays in the den with Dad, watching the ball game on the boob tube: baby boomer days with Clemente and Koufax, Drysdale and Gibson, Mantle and Mays. It was a game of titans, played in the sunshine on lazy afternoons, beamed into distant suburban homes where fathers snoozed in front of the screen and attentive children pounded fists into gloves.

The closest thing to on-field homicide in baseball history: Juan Marichal of the Giants brains Dodger catcher John Roseboro with a bat. That's Sandy Koufax looking on.

Take a deep breath and dispel the illusion.

These were the '60s, after all, and baseball lost whatever innocence it had left. The violence was mind-blowing: Juan Marichal's bat attack on the Dodgers' John Roseboro stunned not just the 43,000 spectators who witnessed it, but the entire country, and it only incited further violence in the game, rather than penance or reflection. There was a new crop of ballplaying gamblers and criminals in the 1960s who couldn't resist the company of bookies, racketeers, and other marginal characters; the parallel to ballplayers a half century earlier is uncanny. But most of all, the 1960s were a time when the game, like the country, lost its pluck and exuberance.

Remember the youthful Mantle's shining baseball card smile? It dimmed as Mantle ran too many gauntlets of autograph hounds who grabbed at his glove, spat at him, body-blocked him as he tried to cross the street to his parked car outside Yankee Stadium. Soon Mantle was telling kids to beat it, shutting bus windows on their outstretched fingers. The smile was fading. His body grew hobbled. In the '61 World Series, his uniform was soaked with blood from an oozing abscess on his buttocks—there it was for all to see, in color, alas. In '62, he dropped "like a shot rabbit" on the way to first base, as one reporter

Don Drysdale drops Vada Pinson of Cincinnati in the dirt.

put it, when he wrenched a thigh muscle. He broke his foot in '63, when it became caught in a wire fence in Baltimore. Mantle underwent one knee operation after another, lost all his cartilage, and played in a "bone-on-bone situation," as Yankee manager Johnny Keane described it in '65. Once the fleetest man in baseball, Mantle now had to hoist himself up stairways with his strong arms. He grunted with every swing, and could barely run to first base. "I used to love to run. It was fun," he told Arnold Hano of *Sport* magazine. "Now it hurts to run." Mickey Mantle was America's tragic hero, persistent, playing in pain; a war veteran. He was light-years removed from the boozing, happy-go-lucky strongman who had to be fished naked out of St. Petersburg bay in 1960, with Whitey Ford and a few of their friends, when the boat on which they had been partying caught fire and sank.

297

The game could not be reduced to a strict business proposition, as O'Malley and his cronies found out. It was still a game played by flawed individuals, men like Billy Martin, who shattered pitcher Jim Brewer's jaw in a fight in 1960. When Brewer sued him for $1 million, he joked, "How does he want it? Cash or green stamps?" Like Pete Rose, a rookie with the Reds in 1963, already hanging out at River Downs, the thoroughbred track in Cincinnati. He met his first wife there and became a gambling addict, like John McGraw years earlier, befriending criminals and failing to pay his debts. Like Denny McLain, who apparently ran afoul of Detroit mobsters in 1967 and had his feet stomped by the thugs so that he couldn't pitch effectively for the Tigers down the pennant stretch. These stories sound like they are out of baseball's dark ages, but they happened only a few years ago, at a time when corruption and casual violence had supposedly been drummed out of the game. They augured more problems for baseball in the decades ahead: Martin, Rose, and McLain would all badly sully the game's public image. And there was absolutely nothing Walter O'Malley could do about it.

But baseball was more than a menagerie for animals like Martin and budding criminals like Rose and McLain. It was a looking glass for the culture, reflecting the social revolution that swept the country in the '60s, and O'Malley could do nothing about that, either. There was violence in the streets of Chicago in '68; on the field that year, there were more beanballs thrown than ever before, and attendance plummeted. Fans sensed it; baseball didn't seem like a game anymore. There were racial divisions in the streets; there were black and white cliques in locker rooms; and players groused, like Mantle, that the game was no longer fun. There was the coming of the union, money wars, and agents, angry owner responses to union demands, the penalization of players who spoke their minds too freely: "Baseball is a form of slavery," said Phillie third baseman Dick Allen. "Once you step out of bounds, they'll do everything to destroy your soul."

Allen was the most changed man in baseball. He arrived in Philadelphia in 1963, an enthusiastic, twenty-one-year-old black kid ready to play some ball. He won the Rookie of the Year award the next season, almost carried his team to the pennant, and then started to buck the system. Why? Maybe it had to do with the segregated hotels and restaurants he was sent to in Florida during spring training. Maybe it had to do with the Philadelphia press who started to portray him as a bad guy; the city's first black superstar, he was said to be brash and unaccountable. The fans threw garbage at him in the field, even as he batted .300 each year, so Allen took to wearing a helmet in the field. He was one of the ten best hitters of his time, but played by his own rules off the field. He missed team flights, refused to ride the team bus, drove his own car to out-of-town games, and at times arrived late, if at all. In 1969, he would cruise into the clubhouse at Philadelphia's Connie Mack Stadium twenty minutes before game time, dressed in Edwardian hippie garb, like Jimi Hendrix, then jump into his uniform and take the field in the middle of the national anthem to thunderous boos. He enraged the hardhats who ran the game and became the premier antiestablishment figure of the decade. Philadelphia finally dumped him, and he left town an angry man, an emblem of tensions in the game.

Allen's experiences were typical. Well into the decade, black players still couldn't safely bring their families to Florida for spring training. The Birmingham bombings in 1963 reminded black athletes of the tenuousness of their positions. "We knew we were being watched," said Hank Aaron. There were few areas of American life outside baseball where blacks performed so visibly alongside whites. Black athletes were at times personally reminded of this by Martin Luther King and other civil rights leaders. Violent reactions to the

*Dick Allen likened
major league
baseball to
slavery.*

struggle for equality motivated men like Aaron to perform to their
utmost. In the National League, which integrated more quickly and
willingly than the American League, blacks won the Most Valuable
Player award seven times during the decade. They would have excelled
anyway, but the incitement to perform at the highest level was almost
palpable to these men.

National events impinged on the game in the summer of 1965.
From August 11 to August 16, riots in the Watts section of Los Angeles
resulted in the deaths of thirty-five people, the arrests of four
thousand, and $40 million in property damage. Days later, the most
violent on-field incident in baseball's history occurred: San Francisco

Giant pitcher Juan Marichal's August 22 bat assault on John Roseboro, catcher for the Los Angeles Dodgers. If you doubt that there was a connection between Watts and Marichal's assault, consider the fact that these were emotionally supercharged times. The whole country was talking about Watts and had watched the looting and burning on television. National League president Warren Giles's nine-day suspension of Marichal was timed to make sure that he would not pitch later in the month when the Giants played in Los Angeles; there was widespread fear of new violence at the Dodgers' stadium that could potentially reincite riots in Los Angeles itself.

The attack on Roseboro occurred in a 2–1 ball game that matched the two dominant pitchers in baseball: Marichal and Sandy Koufax. Played on a Sunday afternoon at Candlestick Park in San Francisco, the game was the fourth in an emotional series between the clubs. Moreover, it took place amid an almost unbearably tight five-team pennant race. From the moment the Dodger-Giant series began, there were provocations, knockdowns, and other retaliatory moves by both teams. And Sunday's game began on a sharp note when the Dodgers' Maury Wills bunted his way to first base and went on to score the first run. Wills was one of the most confrontational players of the era; fashioning himself after Ty Cobb, he mastered the nuances of sliding and casually spiked fielders with the most subtle of foot movements. "Hey, big fella, you all right?" Wills would ask, pretending the whole thing was an accident. Other times he was less subtle, bowling through fielders or twisting his spikes into their feet. When Wills came up in the second inning on August 22, Marichal, an intimidator with an unmatched history of throwing at the Dodgers and *beating* them, reared back into his high-kick delivery and delivered a head-high fastball that "spun" Wills into the dirt. This set the stage for the infamous event.

When Marichal came to bat the next inning, Koufax threw an inside curveball in the dirt. Roseboro scooped it up and whizzed the ball back to the mound in such a way that it nicked Marichal's nose. That did it. Marichal stared at Roseboro in disbelief, then launched three overhead swings of the bat onto the catcher's head. Umpire Shag Crawford tackled him, but Marichal got back on his feet. "You want some more?" he taunted Roseboro. "Come on! Come on!" Willie Mays ran out of the Giant dugout and cupped Roseboro's bleeding head in his hands; his intercession probably stopped the incident from escalating further. Roseboro, lucky not to have been killed, was only briefly hospitalized. And while Giles's punishment of Marichal—the suspension and a $1,750 fine—seems absurdly mild in retrospect, it helps to remember that there was no precedent for dealing with such an incident. Baseball had a motherlode of violent events buried in its past, but nothing like this had ever happened before.

The attack was more than the result of escalating tit-for-tat tempers in a pennant race. It was the culmination of a blood feud between the Dodgers and Giants that began in the 1920s when McGraw's championship Giants regularly beat up on their lowly Brooklyn rivals. The feud escalated during Durocher's beanball regimes in the '40s and '50s, and more than survived the move from New York to the West Coast, where a new generation of Dodgers and Giants upheld the tradition. All of this came to bear on August 22, 1965: baseball is a game that honors its history. The legacy of bad feelings between the clubs, the immediate frustrations of the 1965 pennant race, the rioting in Watts that had the entire country on edge—all these events came into play as Marichal raised his bat over Roseboro's head. One of the premier pitchers in the national pastime appeared ready to murder an opponent in full view of a stadiumful of spectators. Freeze-frame photos of the bloody spectacle were published all over the country. People were shocked, puzzled, unsettled by the affair. The Vietnam War was escalating like mad. There was violence in the streets. Now what was happening to baseball?

Spectator abuse was nothing new, of course, but there was a callousness to the latest rash of incidents that was disturbing. Do you recall the knife being thrown at Al Kaline in Chicago? That happened in 1959. In 1960, Mantle was punched in the jaw by a teenager in a crowd of autograph seekers in New York. Detroit fans threw jagged wooden slats torn from grandstand chairs at Yankee right fielder Roger Maris that year, driving him from the field. The Detroit Common Council passed an ordinance calling for ninety-day jail sentences and $500 fines for spectators who threw objects at sporting events. But that didn't stop one Tiger fan from hurling a hammer at Cleveland outfielder Jimmy Piersall, still fighting mental illness after a decade: "Here's something you can use to knock some brains into your head," read the inscription on the handle.

One psychoanalyst tried to explain spectator belligerence like this: "A person goes to a ball game for a very elemental reason. He goes to enjoy the conflict. Baseball is essentially like a war . . . a case of 'Good' against 'Bad.' "

Half a century had passed since Ty Cobb likened baseball to war, and now everyone bought into the idea: the fans, the players, the therapists.

The warrior mythology was borne out on the field, all right. Forty years after Babe Ruth's power revolution, speed again became an important factor. Jackie Robinson's run-rabbit-run style of play finally came into bloom: nervous, dancing, diving, sliding baseball, a game of chicken in which people got hurt. The new breed of black athletes ran full tilt and hit with power, pushing major league baseball toward the sort of balanced, strategically varied offense that had characterized play in the Negro Leagues. Black ballplayers reinvigorated the game, brought it new style and excitement and prowess, while ensuring that baseball would remain a hard-nailed and at times injurious pastime—not what O'Malley had hoped for. Dodger shortstop Wills ushered in the new age of speed, stealing a record-breaking 104 bases in 1962. That's how the public remembers him—the kinetic little runner who drove opposing pitchers to distraction on the base paths, played the ukulele in his hotel room, and dated Doris Day on the sly. But in his time, among his peers, Wills was known as someone who took pleasure in humiliating opponents, stealing bases even when his team was too far ahead for it to matter. He wanted "to make them hate me more; just to rub it in," he explained, with Cobbian logic. Wills was a grudge settler, sharpening his spikes to get back at Milwaukee first baseman Joe Torre for some rough play. When he reached first base, Wills took his lead, lunged back to the bag to beat the pitcher's pick-off throw, and plunged his spikes into Torre's leg: "I pull them out like the cork out of the bottle and blood starts running all over the place."

Later they made this guy a manager.

Frank Robinson, too. He eventually became an establishment man, front-office poo-bah, and manager. But in the early '60s,

Robinson was hell-bent; threatened with a butcher knife by a fast-food restaurant cook in Cincinnati, Robinson pulled out a .25 Beretta and got himself arrested. On the field, Robinson went after Milwaukee third baseman Eddie Mathews, baseball's most accomplished brawler, in the first game of a doubleheader in 1960. "Robinson came in high with his slide," remembers Cincinnati beat reporter Earl Lawson, "and Eddie said something, and Robinson swung and missed. And Eddie *didn't* miss. He hit 'im one punch and laid Frank down; closed Robinson's right eye. Second game of the doubleheader, Frank came back and hit a double and a home run, and made a streaking, diving catch over the railing to rob Mathews of a homer."

That's what made Robinson special: he never let up, never backed off. Phillie manager Gene Mauch instituted a $50 fine for any pitcher who knocked Robinson down with a pitch, because it only fired him up and made him a more dangerous batter. It was this quality that enhanced Robinson's already extraordinary skills and made him a Hall of Famer. Arguably the most aggressive base runner of the decade, he barreled into Mets second baseman Ron Hunt on a double play in 1963. Hunt leaped to avoid Robinson's slide, then "came down on my left arm," Robinson recalled, "and his spikes punctured my biceps." Thirty stitches and ten days later, Robinson was back in the lineup. There was also the time he plowed into White Sox shortstop Al Weis, as he put it, "like the Marines storming Inchon." Weis's left knee whacked Robinson in the head, knocking him out. He woke up in the hospital, with no recollection of the collision, suffering

George Brace

***When Frank Robinson got brushed back,
it only made him a better hitter.***

from double vision that took two years to clear up. But Robinson kept playing after the collision and batted .311 that year, hitting thirty home runs. Weis ripped ligaments and damaged blood vessels inside his knee, and was out of action for months. "The player should realize the risks involved in his position," reasoned Robinson, who said he never deliberately tried to hurt an opponent. If anyone thought otherwise, or hated him for his aggressiveness, that was "their privilege," he said. "I hate, too. I hate all the fellows around the league who are wearing the other uniform."

Well, Juan Marichal presumably felt some hatred toward John Roseboro in the summer of 1965, too. In the nine months following Marichal's assault, there were two more bat attacks, the worst occurring in the Pacific Coast League in May 1966. Seattle Angels pitcher Jim Coates—an ex-Yankee who looked like an undertaker—threw a high inside fastball that struck batter Ricardo Joseph of the Vancouver Mounties on the shoulder. This was not unexpected; Coates was said to dislike Latins and blacks and threw at them habitually. A fight broke out. Seattle catcher Merritt Ranew joined in. So did Vancouver's Santiago Rosario, who rushed out of the on-deck circle and slammed Ranew over the head with a bat, opening a deep three-inch gash. The left side of Ranew's face was temporarily paralyzed. He was rushed to the hospital and underwent brain surgery to remove a blood clot, then remained there for six weeks, before returning to his chosen profession.

But Ranew's ordeal was just a minor league sideshow. In the American League, Eddie Stanky was back: the biggest pest in baseball now managed the White Sox. What a summer it was in Chicago! Leo Durocher took over the Cubs across town, kicking umpires in the shins, berating his players, and screaming his head off. And Stinky Stanky announced that his pitchers would throw at any team whose pitchers threw at the Sox. "I'm a retaliation manager!" Stinky said, happy as a clam. Twenty years had passed since Stanky roared into Brooklyn, and baseball was still thick with beanballers. Brothers Gaylord and Jim Perry once took turns knocking each other down in spring training. Just for fun. Drysdale was still around. So was Jim Bunning. Bob Gibson of the Cardinals was doing his Terminator impersonation, turning every at bat into a confrontation of fear. He even knocked down his best friend, Bill White, when the Cards traded the first baseman to Philadelphia in '66.

The following season witnessed the transformation of Gentleman Jim Lonborg, Stanford biology major and Boston Red Sox pitcher. The Sox' new backup catcher, Russ Gibson, remembered Lonborg from the minor leagues: "He was the shyest guy you've ever seen in your life. Then I came here to Boston and the first night I caught him we were playing Kansas City. I said, 'Lonnie, you want to go over the hitters?' . . . He said, 'Campaneris is leading off. I'm going to hit him in the head with the first pitch.' He didn't miss by much, I tell you! I think the ball went between his head and his helmet. I just couldn't believe it—the change! He turned into just a complete guerrilla."

Lonborg had come under the influence of Red Sox pitching coach Sal "the Barber" Maglie. Presto! Gentleman Jim's record improved from ten wins and ten losses in 1966 to twenty-two wins and nine losses

The Cardinals' Bob Gibson was the ultimate intimidator.

in 1967, when he helped lead Boston to its first pennant in close to twenty years. But there was a price to pay for all this euphoria over knockdown pitching. One of Boston's most talented and charismatic players was twenty-two-year-old Tony Conigliaro. In 1964, still a teenager, he had won the Rookie of the Year award by batting .290 and hitting twenty-four home runs. In 1965, he led the league with thirty-two home runs. In 1967, Conigliaro became the youngest player ever to reach homer No. 100. There was much talk about Conigliaro's Hall of Fame potential, but also concern about his proneness to injury. In the spring of 1967, Conigliaro's shoulder bone was fractured by a pitch. For the fifth time in his short career, he was sidelined with a bone break as a result of being hit. He healed and played strongly in the regular season. But on August 18, Conigliaro came to the plate against California Angel pitcher Jack Hamilton and was beaned. The ball's impact sounded "like a melon hitting a pavement off the back of a truck," wrote *Los Angeles Times* columnist Jim Murray. Conigliaro slumped to the ground, his cheekbone broken, his jaw dislocated, his retina damaged. He made a number of fitful comebacks, but Tony C.'s career was effectively over.

And the pitchers didn't stop throwing at batters.

In 1968, they threw at *more* batters. This was the so-called Year of the Pitcher. For five years, pitchers had been taking ever greater control of the game, driving down batting averages, run production, home run totals, and attendance—fans were turned off by the lack of offense. It started happening in 1963. Concerned over escalating batting averages and the burgeoning home run totals of Maris, Mantle, and Mays, major league baseball decided the pitchers

Tony Conigliaro's beaning in 1967 effectively ended his climb toward the Hall of Fame.

needed some help. A decision was made to expand the strike zone—giving pitchers a wider target—and offenses immediately fell off. New stadiums were built with higher mounds that suited the new breed of power pitchers like Gibson, Koufax, Bob Veale of the Pirates, Dick Radatz of the Red Sox. By 1968, the balance had shifted totally toward the pitchers. In the American League, Denny McLain posted thirty-one wins, six losses, and a 1.96 ERA. In the National, Gibson won twenty-two games, lost nine, and posted a frightening 1.12 ERA. The pitchers had become near-invincible, and hyperaggressive knockdown pitching was part of the reason.

Bill James has computed that in 1968 there were forty-eight batters hit by pitches in every hundred games played—a near-doubling of the totals from twenty years earlier. On his very first at bat as a National Leaguer in spring training of '68, Tommy Agee of the Mets was beaned by Bob Gibson. The much-touted Agee went on to hit all of .217 that season, and didn't regain his confidence at the plate until the middle of the next season. But he was only the first beanball victim of 1968. After Agee came Don Mincher, Paul Schaal, Bill Voss, Don Wert, Pete Ward. Sitting ducks all.

It was the Year of the Pitcher and the fractured skull.

It was the year that Martin Luther King and Robert Kennedy were murdered. And it was the year that spectators at Shea Stadium in New York City watched a cop fight a fan in the upper deck. The cop almost knocked the fan over the railing, then grabbed him to prevent his fall. "Let him go! Let him go!" the crowd chanted. Around the league, there were similar stories.

"They tell us we are becoming a violent society," wrote Detroit sports columnist Joe Falls, "and you wonder if maybe they're right. I don't mean what's happening nationally or internationally. I mean what's happening in our ballparks."

Before the start of the 1969 season, the St. Louis Cardinals sent former MVP winner Orlando Cepeda to Atlanta. It wasn't long before Cepeda came to bat against his old friend and teammate Bob Gibson. "The first time I went to the plate, he knocked me back," Cepeda recalled, shrugging his shoulders. "It was mandatory, know what I mean? In fact, Bob came to my house for dinner after the game and my son said, 'How come you threw at my dad?' And Bob said, 'It's a game. Baseball.' "

Old Macho Man: Ty Cobb
(Won't this guy ever go away?)

In the last year of his life, Ty Cobb still slept with his faithful Luger. He still railed against his "enemies": McGraw, Landis, Ban Johnson, all dead for decades. He cut the phone lines to his Tahoe hunting lodge because he thought he was being tapped. He drank a quart of whiskey a day, accused bartenders of watering the Scotch, and hurled drinks against the wall. He gambled relentlessly in Reno, accused the help of touching the dice, swung his seventy-three-year-old fists at them, and got thrown onto the street. He was sick; dependent on Librium, codeine, and insulin. No matter. He drove Sierra mountain passes at night in the middle of snowstorms and cracked up his car. Stopping at a motel, he shot his Luger at drunks in the parking lot who disturbed his sleep. Returning to his mansion south of San Francisco, he sat alone in the gloom with no light, heat, or hot water because he was in the midst of suing the utility company. He was Ty Cobb, an old man in a Stetson hat with no friends.

In the spring of 1961, he went to Scottsdale, Arizona, for what would be his last spring training. He didn't like the way a Mexican cab driver handled the taxi. Cobb threw the fare on the ground, and when the man bent over to pick it up, kicked him in the stomach. "What's your sideline?" Cobb shouted. "Selling opium?" When a lawyer threatened to sue him over the matter, Cobb snarled, "Get in line. There's five hundred ahead of you." Al Stump, who ghosted Cobb's autobiography, witnessed all of it, wrote about it for *True* magazine, and decided that Cobb was "the most violent, successful, thoroughly maladjusted personality ever to pass across American sports." Cobb's long, sick journey ended on July 17, 1961, when he died at age seventy-four. His funeral was notable for the almost total nonattendance of friends from the world of baseball.

The Target: Jimmy Piersall

Jimmy Piersall continued to battle mental illness in the early '60s, a decade after his institutionalization. "Hey, bugs!" fans shouted at the Cleveland outfielder. "Hey, crazy, are they coming after you with the net today?" "When are they puttin' you back in your straitjacket?" In a series of interviews, Piersall listed the various objects thrown at him by fans around the American League: golf balls, metal tape measures, pennies, a hairbrush with a rock tied to it, paper cups filled with ice cubes. Oranges in Chicago. More rocks in Baltimore. Bolts in Detroit: "All the time bolts," he mused in May 1961. "I used to wonder about that, and I figured they must be unemployed autoworkers throwing them." The fans, he said, "have the cruelest way of talking about my illness."

National Baseball Library

Taunted by fans for his history of mental illness, Cleveland's Jimmy Piersall lets a heckler have it at Yankee Stadium in 1961.

Casey's Pearls

On Met outfielder Ron Swoboda:

"Amazing strength, amazing power. He can grind the dust out of the bat. He will be great, super, wonderful. Now if he can only learn to catch a fly ball."

On Choo Choo Coleman, Chris Cannizzaro, and Jesse Gonder, three early catchers on the Mets:

"I got one that can throw but can't catch, and one that can catch but can't throw, and one who can hit but can't do either."

On Cannizzaro:

"He's a remarkable catch, that Canzoneri. He's the only defensive catcher in baseball who can't catch."

To Met pitcher Tracy Stallard, at the Polo Grounds in 1963:

"At the end of this season they're gonna tear this place down. The way you're pitchin', that right field section will be gone already."

Casey Stengel—always the kidder.

Scary Steve Dalkowski

Meet the most frightening pitcher who ever walked onto a mound. Faster than Ryan, faster than Koufax, faster than Gossage or Dibble: little Steve Dalkowski, a man with thick glasses and steel-belt biceps, threw a 110-mph fastball, but couldn't find home plate. Teammates dared him to throw balls through wooden fences. He did it in Stockton and Elmira, then threw one through a welded mesh screen sixty feet behind home plate in Wilson, North Carolina. A batter in Knoxville had to return to the clubhouse to change his pants after Dalkowski found his range and threw a fastball past the man's head. "I threw so hard that night that I scared the whole town," Dalkowski remembered. He tore part of a batter's ear off with a fastball in Kingsport, Pennsylvania. In a tryout with the Baltimore Orioles, he hurled a fastball past Ted Williams that dazed the greatest pure hitter in history. "Fastest ever," Williams said, shaken as he left the batting cage. "I never want to face him again."

The fastest pitcher alive was also the wildest, so Dalkowski couldn't make the majors. But his legend grew. There was no explanation for his thunderbolt arm: "I just got faster and faster every year, and I could do nothing to stop it," Dalkowski said. His pitches might go anywhere: up, down, through the screen. One time, he shattered the umpire's mask. In 1959, he pitched a no-hitter, striking out twenty-one batters. His next time out, Dalkowski walked the first eight hitters. There was no rhyme or reason to his success, or lack of it. "I'd strike out nineteen batters and lose," he told journalist Pat Jordan, who pitched minor league ball in the late '50s and early '60s when Dalkowski made his reputation. "He only had one struggle—to get the ball over the plate," said Jordan, who wrote about Dalkowski for *Inside Sports* in the early '80s when he found the long-vanished Dalkowski working as a migrant farmworker in Bakersfield, California, by day, hanging out at the local ballpark in an alcoholic haze by night. "It was never a question about batters rippin' his stuff. If you're throwing the

*Duck!
Steve Dalkowski
reputedly threw a
110 mph fastball,
but couldn't
find home plate.*

ball 100 miles an hour—or 110—you don't even think about the batter.
You're only battling yourself, trying to get the ball near the plate."

Dalkowski couldn't do it. In his ten-year career with eleven teams
in nine leagues, Jordan wrote, "Dalkowski managed records like 1–8
with an 8.13 ERA at Kingsport, 0–4 with a 12.96 ERA at Pensacola,
7–15 with a 5.14 ERA at Kennewick. Dalkowski never pitched an
inning in the major leagues, and pitched only twenty-four innings as
high as Triple A, where his record was 2–3 with a 7.12 ERA." But
Harry "the Cat" Brecheen, an old Cardinal pitcher and keen judge of

talent, said Dalkowski had "the best arm in the history of baseball." Despite what may have been the worst pitching record in baseball history, Dalkowski's employers stuck by him, and kept hoping for a change.

Dalkowski was raised in New Britain, Connecticut. His father was an alcoholic who "never said nothing. He just worked and gambled and drank." By his junior year in high school, when Dalkowski's fastball was starting to attract attention, he was drinking, too. The Orioles gave him a $4,000 advance and sent him to Kingsport, where he threw the pitch that took off part of the kid's ear, gave the batter a concussion, and sent him to the hospital. Suddenly aware of the potentially lethal effects of his pitching, Dalkowski became depressed. There are those who say it was his fear of killing someone that undermined his confidence and contributed to his wildness as time passed.

The young Joe Pepitone faced Dalkowski in '59 and was alarmed. "He struck me out five times in one game," Pepitone told Jordan. "I was scared to death. Here I was with a chance to make some progress in the minor leagues and I had to face this guy who could kill you."

In Pensacola that year, Dalkowski drank and lived it up at night with fellow left-handers Bo Belinsky and Steve Barber. In '60 and '61, he set league records for the most walks ever given up by a pitcher. In 1962, Dalkowski pitched for Earl Weaver in Elmira and started to find the plate, even as he drank more heavily. Finally, in the spring of '63, Dalkowski seemed poised to break through to the majors: "I don't know why," he said, "but it was easy to strike out major leaguers." He threw three straight strikes past Roger Maris in an exhibition game against the Yankees. Later in the afternoon, Yankee pitcher Jim Bouton laid down a bunt. Dalkowski fielded it, threw to first, and felt something pop in his arm. *Finis.* His fastball leveled off at 90 mph and Dalkowski drifted from team to team before San Jose released him in 1966. Dalkowski, twenty-seven, headed south, started picking peaches, and disappeared from baseball history.

Hardhead Jim Ray Hart

In July 1963, in his second big league at bat, San Francisco Giant third baseman Jim Ray Hart's shoulder was broken by a pitch thrown by the Cardinals' Bob Gibson. Hart sat out five weeks, then returned to the lineup. Four days later, the Giants once again played the Cardinals. Curt Simmons was on the mound. Hart got into the batter's box. Simmons skulled him. Hart was out for the year.

The following spring, manager Al Dark drilled Hart on how to get out of the way of a pitch. He set up a pitching screen fifteen feet in front of home plate and fired one ball after another under Hart's chin. The exercise worked. Not once in 1964 was Hart injured by a pitch. In August, however, Hart slid into second base to break up a double play against the Dodgers, and shortstop Maury Wills pegged a relay throw directly into his forehead. "You ever see a duck-hunting film where somebody shoots the bird and it folds up and falls?" Wills asked in *On the Run,* his autobiography. "That's the way Jim Ray Hart went into second. He was lying there with his eyes rolled up into his head and his mouth open. I thought I'd killed him."

Hart was carried off the field on a stretcher and hospitalized. Discharged the next morning, he returned to the lineup. "You could hit Jimmy with a sledgehammer and it wouldn't hurt him," said Bobby Bonds, his former teammate. "It's like hitting concrete. You put a few cracks in it, but you put some plaster over it and you go right ahead."

Jim Ray Hart played twelve seasons in the major leagues.

Yogi Berra on autograph hounds:

"What bothers me most are the little sharp pencils they jab into you. Into your back and into your neck and right up your nostrils."

Joe Pepitone's repartee with a heckler at Yankee Stadium:

Heckler: "Hey, Pepitone, you bum! Is that your nose or are you eating a banana?"

Pepitone: "If you think it's a banana, why don't you come down and peel it?"

Roger Maris on baseball, 1961:

"It's a business. If I could make more money down in the zinc mines, I'd be mining zinc."

Mickey Mantle on his impending retirement, 1968:

"I can't play anymore. I can't hit the ball when I need to. I can't steal second when I need to. I can't go from first to third when I need to. I can't score from second when I need to. I have to quit."

Here Comes Billy!

Billy Martin's playing days ended ingloriously in 1961. But he was hired as a scout by the Minnesota Twins and began his long, slow trip back to the front pages. In 1965, he became a coach. In 1966, he made news by beating up Twins traveling secretary Howard Fox. "I'd like to get you outside, you sonofabitch," Martin told Fox, taking umbrage at some perceived slight on an airplane trip. After Harmon Killebrew pried Martin off Fox, Billy fell to the ground, where he kept throwing punches "into the concrete," team press officer Tom Mee told Martin's biographer, David Falkner. "He had no idea who he was swinging at. He was just blind with rage."

In 1968, Martin was named manager of the Twins' struggling Triple A farm team in Denver and advanced to the parent club in '69. Instantly controversial, he ordered Minnesota pitchers to throw at the head of Oakland slugger Reggie Jackson, who was on his way to a forty-seven-homer season—Martin hated Jackson long before they occupied the same Yankee clubhouse. Martin returned to the front pages by beating up his own pitcher, Dave Boswell, outside a Detroit bar: "I started to hit him in the stomach. I worked up and hit him in the mouth, nose, and eyes. He bounced off the wall and I hit him again and he was out cold before he hit the ground. . . . I didn't start the fight. I've never started one in my life."

The innocent Martin led the Twins to the divisional playoffs. But they lost the pennant to Baltimore, and Minnesota owner Calvin Griffith fired his troublesome manager pronto.

In 1969, the average major leaguer earned $19,000. The combined salaries of all the New York Mets totaled $650,000—which is about what a mediocre utility infielder earns today.

But the revolution was coming to baseball. It surfaced in 1966 when Sandy Koufax and Don Drysdale held out for a joint, three-year $1 million contract. They settled for a one-year, joint $235,000 pact, but the Dodger pitchers had started something. The Major League Players Association hired labor negotiator Marvin Miller as its first full-time executive director later that spring, and the war to improve pensions and salaries was on. Miller chipped away at the owners' traditional power to make unilateral financial decisions. He forced them to bargain collectively with the players' union, convinced the players to threaten a strike in the spring of '69, and won concessions from the owners that set the stage for the greenbacking of the game in the 1970s.

But for the moment, the owners still held the ultimate power: they still had the reserve clause. It bound every player to the team that signed him until the team decided it was ready to trade or sell the player. The courts had always upheld the reserve clause, making baseball a monopoly, with the blessings of the federal government. Curt Flood decided to change it.

Flood was a career .293 hitter, a perennial Golden Glove outfielder, who had just finished his twelfth season with the St. Louis Cardinals in 1969. In October, he received a two-sentence memo announcing his trade to the Philadelphia Phillies. Flood said, "No, thanks." On Christmas Eve, he mailed a letter to baseball commissioner Bowie Kuhn announcing that he rejected the trade and planned to challenge the game's legal framework in court. This is what Flood told Kuhn:

"After twelve years in the major leagues, I do not feel that I am a piece of property to be bought and sold irrespective of my wishes. I believe that any system which produces that result violates my basic rights as a citizen and is inconsistent with the laws of the United States. . . . I am a man, I live in a democratic society, and I believe that I am entitled to participate in our free enterprise system."

Flood sacrificed his career by turning down the trade. The owners no longer wanted his services. But his words changed baseball. Free agency was on its way.

The
1970s

320

*The
1970s*

1970
- Denny McLain suspended twice by Commissioner Bowie Kuhn: for role in '67 bookmaking scandal, and for dumping water on reporters.
- Kuhn investigates Leo Durocher gambling allegations. Innocent.
- Kuhn begins decade-long investigation of gambling by Pete Rose.
- Bill Lee attacked and beaten by Ellie Rodriguez and friends outside ballpark in Caguas, Puerto Rico.
- Yucatan police subdue baseball crowd with tear gas.
- Baltimore's Paul Blair is beaned.
- Pete Rose crashes into catcher Ray Fosse to win All-Star game.

1971
- Carl Mays dies.
- Alex Johnson of Angels fined twenty-nine times for not hustling. Johnson says teammate Chico Ruiz pulled gun on him in locker room.
- Vida Blue goes 24–8, posts 1.82 ERA for Oakland A's.
- Thousands riot and loot in Pittsburgh as Pirates win Series.

1972
- Jackie Robinson dies.
- U.S. Supreme Court rejects Curt Flood's challenge to reserve clause. But baseball's antitrust exemption is called "aberration."
- Vida Blue feuds with Oakland owner Charles Finley over salary.
- Players strike for thirteen days.
- Oakland's Bert Campaneris throws bat at Tiger pitcher Lerrin LaGrow in American League playoffs.
- Roberto Clemente dies in plane crash.

1973
- American League introduces designated hitter.
- George Steinbrenner and partners buy Yankees.
- Woman, nineteen, dies of gunshot in Cesar Cedeno's Santo Domingo motel room.
- Hank Aaron breaks Babe Ruth's all-time home run record amid racist abuse.
- Pete Rose collides with and creams Met shortstop Bud Harrelson during National League playoffs. Met fans drive Rose from field with garbage.
- Oakland A's beat Mets in seven games in World Series. Reggie Jackson plays amid death threats.

1974
- Houston outfielder Bob Watson crashes into center field wall in Cincinnati. Fans pour beer on him as he bleeds on warning track.
- Ten Cent Beer Night in Cleveland: 25,000 fans consume 60,000 ten-ounce beers and stage riot that threatens Texas Rangers.
- Yankee Bill Sudakis threatens Lou Piniella with hatchet.
- Pittsburgh fans hurl whiskey bottles at Cubs in NL playoffs.
- Ron Hunt retires: hit by 243 pitches in twelve-year career.
- Catfish Hunter becomes baseball's first unofficial free agent.

1975
- Casey Stengel dies.
- Orlando Cepeda arrested in Puerto Rico for importing marijuana.
- Houston pitcher Don Wilson dies of carbon monoxide poisoning.
- Frank Robinson of Indians becomes baseball's first black manager.
- Billy Martin becomes Yankee manager in August.
- Pitchers Andy Messersmith and Dave McNally win lawsuit challenging reserve clause. Free agent era begins.

1976
- Owners stage spring training lockout.
- Charlie Finley sells Vida Blue, Joe Rudi, and Rollie Fingers to Yankees and Red Sox for $3.5 million. Bowie Kuhn blocks the deals.

1976
- Reggie Jackson hit in face by Dock Ellis fastball.
- Lou Piniella crashes into Red Sox catcher Carlton Fisk. Graig Nettles slams pitcher Bill Lee's pitching shoulder into ground.
- Joe Ferguson of Dodgers breaks arm in brawl with Padres.
- Chris Chambliss of Yankees nearly trampled by fans after hitting pennant-winning home run in playoffs against Kansas City.
- Steinbrenner signs Reggie Jackson to five-year, $3 million deal.
- Nolan Ryan becomes first $1-million-a-year player.

1977
- Lenny Randle of Rangers punches out manager Frank Lucchesi.
- Reggie Jackson: "I'm the straw that stirs the drink."
- Billy Martin pulls Jackson out of nationally televised ball game for failing to hustle after fly ball.
- Yankee fans shower Dodgers with garbage during World Series. Los Angeles manager Tommy LaSorda calls then "animals."

1978
- Kuhn consults with owners on crowd control, a growing concern.
- Thurman Munson accused of choking University of Minnesota student with one hand after game against Twins.
- July 24: Billy Martin is fired by Steinbrenner.
- July 29: Steinbrenner announces Martin will return in 1980.
- California Angel Lyman Bostock murdered accidentally in another couple's domestic dispute.

1979
- Bill Lee says he smokes pot, then changes story: he only sprinkles it on his organic buckwheat pancakes.
- Major league umpires strike until mid-May.
- Mike Jorgensen of Mets almost killed in beaning.
- Disco Demolition night at Comiskey: thousands riot on field.
- Reds trade pitcher Pedro Borbon, who has been arrested in discotheques for fighting and biting patrons.
- Thurman Munson killed in private plane crash.
- Riots in Pittsburgh after Pirates beat Orioles in World Series.
- Billy Martin beats up marshmallow salesman Joseph Cooper.

Pete Rose has contributed too much to baseball to be allowed to die in left field at Shea Stadium.
    —*Cincinnati manager Sparky Anderson*

On July 27, 1976, Dock Ellis of the New York Yankees threw a fastball that hit Reggie Jackson, then playing for the Baltimore Orioles, in the face. Jackson slumped, his glasses shattered, and Ellis trotted in to home plate to check out the damage. "Is he dead?" Ellis asked the ump. It was the most frightening thing that ever happened to Jackson in twenty-two years of baseball. Years later, there was still numbness in his cheek, and Jackson never totally overcame the fear of being hit. Why did Ellis do it? "I owed him one," Dock explained matter-of-factly. Five years earlier, in the 1971 All-Star game, Jackson had launched a home run into the light tower above the right field upper deck at Tiger Stadium in Detroit. Running around the bases, Jackson pumped his fists in the air, putting on a show for the crowd, as Reggie was wont to do, and caused Dock to lose face on national television. Ellis, as temperamental a player as Jackson was egotistical, stored up the affront, waited five years to get Reggie back, and beaned

George Brace

Dock Ellis threw a fastball that hit Reggie Jackson in the head. "I owed him one," he explained.

him in a meaningless ball game. The Yanks were delighted. Crisp $20 bills were left anonymously in Ellis's locker and "certain guys bought me drinks the rest of the year," he later wrote.

Everybody hated Reggie. "There's not enough mustard in the world to cover that hot dog," mused pitcher Darold Knowles, who played with Jackson on the World Champion Oakland A's in the early '70s. Jackson was the most media-savvy player of his generation, a charismatic publicity hound who was despised by teammates and opponents alike. He was the original prime-time player in a decade that saw baseball transformed into prime-time entertainment, its players blown up into larger-than-life celebrities with fat paychecks and no privacy, living in a media fishbowl. The media seized on Jackson; he was going to be bigger than DiMaggio, bigger than Ruth. Every Monday night on national television, the cameras bore down relentlessly on Jackson and everyone else in the dugouts. See Reggie spit! Curse! Fight! Spin those cameras! Can we have one more look at Pete Rose obliterating Ray Fosse at home plate in the All-Star game? Does anyone have footage of Lenny Randle belting his manager, Frank Lucchesi? Those fans aren't really pouring *beer* on Bob Watson of

UPI/Bettmann

*George and Reggie,
the game's most
infamous couple.*

the Astros, are they? Watson's bleeding badly; the poor guy just crashed into the center field wall. Can we get a close-up?

Every foible was ripe for media exploitation. Bill Lee of the Red Sox called Billy Martin a Nazi? Print it. Mickey Rivers's wife was playing bumper car with her husband's Cadillac in the Yankee parking lot? Beautiful! Baseball was a soap opera. When New York Yankees owner George Steinbrenner flew Reggie to Manhattan in November 1976 to wine and dine him at "21," then offer him a $3 million five-year contract and a free Rolls-Royce, there was really no question that trouble lay ahead. "I'm the straw that stirs the drink," Reggie announced. "I didn't come to New York to become a star. I brought my own star." Was this big-money, college-bred, yuppie ballplayer with the bloated ego really supposed to get along with the liver-impaired Billy Martin, who'd been ordering his pitchers to throw at Jackson for years? And how long would the gutsy little Martin stay on Steinbrenner's good side, anyway, without suffering a nervous breakdown and kissing George's meddling, millionaire ass?

325

No, Reggie had it all wrong. Steinbrenner was the straw who stirred the drink.

With the busting of the reserve clause in 1975 and the coming of free agency and million-dollar ballplayers, there was a popular misconception that the players now ran the show. The tables had been turned, the fans assumed; ballplayers were like pigs feeding at the trough, deserving of popular abuse for their greed, sloth, and newfound power. And there was some truth to this; the nouveau riche boys of summers were, at times, repulsive. Money, money, money was all they ever talked about. But the players were *not* in command. Although inflated to legendary proportions by the media, the porcine athletes were actually treated as dependent children by the owners. In fact, the owners were the story of the '70s. *They* were the biggest egomaniacs in the business, and the new belligerence between managers and employees became an unremitting theme of sports coverage.

Consider Steinbrenner, the Cleveland shipping magnate, telling Billy Martin, the most knowledgeable baseball man around, how to manage the New York Yankees. It was a bald absurdity, yet there was Steinbrenner, giving the players pep talks in the clubhouse, hounding them, sending them tape-recorded harangues about their lack of a winning attitude, publicly criticizing individual players for miscues on the field. He was "George III," in the words of sportswriter Red Smith, a tyrant who mistreated the help and ran through "front-office people and p.r. men the way the rest of us go through pistachio nuts," Jackson said. Every day during the game, the red telephone in the Yankee dugout jingled. Once. Twice. Three times. Martin shuddered. It was Steinbrenner again, screaming, "I told you to bat Jackson clean-up! . . . I told you *not* to change the starting lineup. . . . I told you . . ." He wore Martin down, wrecked his health, drove him to drink. He promised team captain Thurman Munson that he would always be the highest-paid Yankee, then reneged. He built Jackson up, then jerked his string when Reggie assumed that George was his ally: "You better get your head on straight, boy. When I need your help running the New York Yankees, I'll let you know."

Steinbrenner's Yankees were the baseball equivalent of a high-powered yuppie law firm. He ran the club on creative tension, making promises, breaking them, playing one man off the other, fostering dissension. He sucked all the fun out of the game with his mind games, but left the players with one choice if they wanted to keep feeding at the trough: to channel their anger into a championship style of play on the field. Which the Yankees did for a time, winning three pennants and two World Series in the late '70s, before the whole thing imploded.

But Steinbrenner was not the only owner who played hardball in the clubhouse. Before George, there was Charles O. Finley, owner of the Oakland A's. As a boy in Alabama, Finley bought discolored eggs for a nickel, turned around, and resold them for pennies profit. He made his millions selling liability insurance to doctors, then bought his ball club, and spent years fighting with players over nickels and keeping tabs on the phone bill in the trainer's room. In one sense, he was a throwback; he resembled Chris Von der Ahe of the old St. Louis Browns, who turned part of his ballpark into an amusement park to lure fans in the 1880s. Faced with lagging attendance in Oakland ninety years later, Finley resorted to his own publicity gambits: he sent his relief pitchers to the mound on the backs of mules, paid his players $300 apiece to grow Gay Nineties handlebar mustaches, and dressed them in silly kelly-green-and-gold uniforms. But Finley wasn't all fun and games. Like Steinbrenner, he understood modern management psychology, knew how to turn the screws, and exerted top-down pressure on the club that simultaneously enraged players and incited them to win. "Charlie O. made us tough," Jackson wrote, even though the whole team knew "he was paying us slave wages."

Finley once took away free passes from Oakland city council members when they failed to pass a measure renaming the Oakland Coliseum as Finley Stadium. Folksy and charming one moment, he held people in his clutches the next . . . and the next. Jackson once lamented that he would "die in the green and gold." Finley phoned manager John McNamara daily through the 1970 season, dictated the batting order to him, then fired him when the team finished second. He hired Dick Williams as manager in 1971 and badgered him constantly, even as Williams led the team to three successive first-place finishes. Finley was a phone freak; he had telephones built into the trees on his estate. When Williams spent a rare day off at Disneyland with his family, he returned to his hotel at night and was confronted with an inch-thick stack of phone messages from Finley at the front desk. This control was numbing. When catcher Dave Duncan bitched about it to reporters, Finley struck back by firing Duncan's roommate

Charlie Finley, cheapskate owner of the A's, poses with the team mascot. Two stubborn asses.

and coach, Charlie Lau. When pitcher Vida Blue feuded with Finley over salary, the owner retaliated by firing Blue's roommate, the veteran Tommy Davis, who had batted .324 the year before. His mistake was introducing the young pitcher to a lawyer-agent in Los Angeles.

In 1971, Blue was a shy, charming twenty-one-year-old and the owner of a fastball that led him to one of the great seasons of any modern pitcher: twenty-four wins, eight losses, and a 1.82 ERA. At one point he won ten games in a row, going the distance each time, never allowing more than six hits, and shutting out his opponents five times. Blue was a media phenomenon and the biggest attendance draw in the American League. Big Daddy Finley decided he would exploit his hired hand, who was earning all of $14,750, to the fullest. He told Blue he would reward him with a baby-blue Cadillac with personalized plates. Blue said he "wasn't a Cadillac kind of guy," but Finley went ahead with the plan, flew Blue's family to Oakland from Louisiana, and presented the Caddy to Blue at the ballpark. Sportswriters quipped that the only thing Finley forgot to bring was the watermelon. Embarrassed, Blue gave the car to his mother. Then Finley tried to pay Blue $2,000 to change his name to "True Blue." Blue objected: "Why doesn't he change his name to True Finley? I like my name. It was my father's name. It's Spanish. It means 'life.' "

In the spring of 1972, Blue figured he was worth a lot more than $14,750. He had just been named the youngest winner ever of the Cy Young Award, so he asked for $115,000. Finley laughed, Blue sulked, Tommy Davis got fired. The public standoff lasted for weeks—much longer than the major league players' strike that spring—until Blue settled for about half of what he had asked. "Charlie Finley has soured my stomach for baseball," he declared. Blue couldn't get it out of his system, had a lousy year, and wouldn't celebrate with the A's when they won the World Series, fighting instead with teammate Blue Moon Odom moments after the final game ended. Blue never quite recaptured his early success or the thrill he had once felt while throwing a baseball. There were others like him, players slapped around by management as the game moved into the big-money era. The owners were ruining baseball for these men. Playing ball was the only thing they knew how to do, and they were finally becoming well compensated for it, but it was no longer any fun. It was a job.

All these episodes were plastered across the sports pages: stories of psychological violence in the clubhouse. There were also myriad stories about rampant physical violence in the stands. The owners were confounded by increasing security problems: they had reached out to the middle-class market, built comfortable new stadiums, and added amenities to make the trip to the game safe and hassle-free. But the rowdiness and outright violence that ushered in the decade were undeniable; violence in the stands hadn't been so endemic since the first part of the century. Sociologists pointed to the general breakdown of authority in society, the glorification of violence on television, the envy fans felt toward the newly rich ballplayers. But there was another explanation, usually overlooked: the owners, by treating the players with disdain, were setting an example for the fans. If management continued to handle the players like so much high-paid property, why shouldn't fans do the same?

They did.

The Pittsburgh Pirates doubled security in 1970. In a move redolent of 1890s paranoia, the Chicago Cubs built a forty-two-inch steel-mesh screen in front of the center field bleachers to contain the wild Wrigley Field "Bleacher Bums." At Yankee Stadium, relief pitcher Steve Hamilton complained about fans who dropped billiard balls from high above into the New York bullpen. And left fielder Roy White told reporters about fans who perched on the outfield wall before the conclusion of a game. They threw bottles at him, and laughingly warned him that they would give him a running start, before sprinting after him to try to knock him down and steal his glove. "It doesn't make any difference how many police are on hand," moaned Yankee general manager Lee MacPhail. "It is impossible to stop a mob."

In 1971, Chicago White Sox fans threw rocks at Baltimore Oriole Don Buford. As Buford knelt in the on-deck circle, a jagged-edged slat from a chair in the upper deck sailed over his head and impaled itself in the dirt in front of him. The barrage continued, along with taunts from the stands, and finally Buford went after a fan along the third base line, hitting him in the nose and bloodying his lip. Fans around the country were just following the old baseball adage that you can say anything to a ball player with impunity, but the players weren't buying it. More and more, there were reports of players storming into the stands after hecklers. And more and more, there were reports of players donning batting helmets for protection in the field against beer showers and debris thrown by spectators, even in their own parks.

Baseball fans were also staging celebrations known as "victory riots." In 1971, after the Pirates beat the Orioles in the World Series, tens of thousands of fans rioted in downtown Pittsburgh, smashing store windows, overturning and burning taxis, dancing in the nude, and having sex in the streets.

When the Cincinnati Reds won their division title in 1973, a mob rushed the field and went wilding through the stands, forcing the evacuation of Reds executives. When the Reds traveled to

Pete Rose flattens Bud Harrelson at second base in the 1973 National League Playoffs between the Reds and Mets.

Shea Stadium in New York to play the Mets in the national League playoffs, there was more trouble. It started after the 200-pound Pete Rose flattened the 146-pound Met shortstop Bud Harrelson at second base, inciting a fight between the teams, during which the fabled Red pitcher Pedro Borbon, a man infamous for biting people on and off the field, marched around carrying a thatch of Met hair like a trophy. There were three hundred cops in the park, but they couldn't stop the spectators from hurling garbage at the Reds. And the fusillade only intensified when Rose returned to his position in left field. The garbage attack was not unlike that by Detroit fans against Joe Medwick in the 1934 World Series. The Mets ran out toward Rose and pleaded with the fans to desist, but they would not. Finally, Cincinnati manager Sparky Anderson pulled Rose out of the game: "Pete Rose has contributed too much to baseball to be allowed to die in left field at Shea Stadium," he said.

And it only got worse. "Fans or felons?" one headline inquired. In Cincinnati, Bob Watson of the Astros really *was* showered with beer as he lay bleeding on the warning track after running into the center field wall. Following a game in Pittsburgh in which fans hurled whiskey bottles at the Cubs, Chicago outfielder Jose Cardenal remarked that he felt lucky to have escaped with his life. Cardinal pitcher Al Hrabosky, known as "the mad Hungarian," quipped that his U.S. Army weapons training came in handy every time he pitched at Shea. Harrelson agreed: "Our lives are in danger out on the field."

But all this mayhem found its focus on a single night: June 4, 1974. Ten Cent Beer Night in Cleveland. On this night, 25,000 Indian fans consumed 60,000 ten-ounce beers, and many of them stormed the field to attack Billy Martin's Texas Rangers. "They were drunk all over the place," said umpire Nestor Chylak. "We would have needed twenty-five thousand cops to handle it." Texas outfielder Jeff Burroughs looked up to see "about five hundred of them coming at us. It was Custer's last stand. We thought we were goners." Some of the marauding fans brandished knives, but Burroughs and his teammates were saved thanks to a joint counterattack by the Indians and Rangers. The teams charged from their dugouts, leveling bats at the attackers. A steel chair sailed onto the field and hit Indian pitcher Tom Hilgendorf

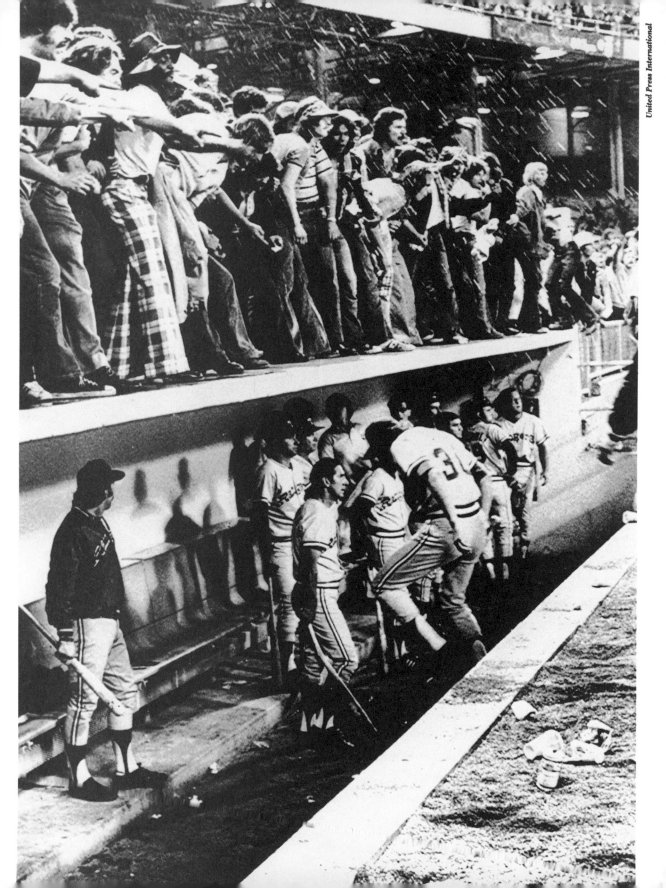

in the head. "I've been in this game twenty-five years," Martin said, "and that was the closest I ever saw to someone getting killed in baseball."

Remarkably, the owners at this very time were conceiving new TV marketing strategies to depict baseball as the quintessential American game—simple, pure, rooted in old-fashioned values. As the fans rampaged in Cleveland, the Lords of Baseball were wrapping the game in an aura of nostalgia. All the images we've grown used to of players loping in slow motion across green grass while pastoral classical music plays in the background date from the mid-'70s when television became a sophisticated marketing tool for the game. Baseball, we were told, was like milk: healthy, clean, and uncontroversial. Obviously, that was a lie. No one was selling milk at the ballpark.

It should have been enough to sell baseball on the basis of the extraordinary level of play during the '70s. A rejiggering of the strike zone and the lowering of pitching mounds had tipped the power balance toward batters, and offenses took off. The installation of artificial turf at many stadiums made the game noticeably faster as balls whizzed like marbles across the carpet—to be snared by wizards like St. Louis Cardinals shortstop Ozzie Smith. There was a pleasing variety of offensive styles: power offenses, speed offenses. It varied from club to club. The introduction of the designated hitter in the American League added more heavy artillery to lineups and drew fans to the ballpark. Attendance soared through the decade in both leagues: a total of 330 million people passed through the turnstiles. Fans watched relief pitchers emerge as superstars: Rollie Fingers, Goose Gossage, Bruce Sutter. And they saw some of the greatest athletes in the game's history take the field for the first time: Smith, Dave Winfield, George Brett, Mike Schmidt. For many students of the game, the 1970s represented a pinnacle for strategy and quality of play.

But was the game pure?

The California Angels locker room was an armed camp ready to explode in 1971, the *Los Angeles Times* said. Former hitting champion Alex Johnson, fined twenty-nine times early in the season for loafing, accused teammate Chico Ruiz of pointing a gun at his head and saying, "I'm as black as you and I hate you . . . I could kill you." One of the team's Latin players supposedly asked a broadcaster to explain the

Opposite:
Whoopee!
It's ten cent
beer night in
Cleveland. The
Texas Rangers
get drenched.

penalty for shooting someone in self-defense. Knives and rifles were stashed in lockers by a multiethnic cross section of the psychotic Angels, who finished the season more than twenty-five games out of first place. Manager Lefty Phillips, no rocket scientist, remarked, "I'm afraid there's going to be violence in the clubhouse."

In the spring of 1974, Pirate pitcher Dock Ellis sensed that his team had lost the aggressiveness that drove it to three straight division flags from 1970 to 1972. His teammates no longer felt invincible and, far worse, seemed scared of Cincinnati's "Big Red Machine." To break Pittsburgh out of its emotional slump, Ellis announced in spring training that he would mow down the entire Cincinnati lineup the first time he faced the Reds in the regular season. "I'm going to *hit* those motherfuckers," he told his teammates.

On May 1, Ellis faced the Reds. The first batter was Pete Rose; Ellis hit him in the ribs. The second batter was Joe Morgan; Ellis hit him in the kidney. The third batter was Dan Driessen; Ellis hit him in the back. The bases were now loaded, with no one out. Tony Perez came to the plate, dodged a succession of Ellis pitches, and walked, forcing in a run. Then came Johnny Bench: "I tried to deck him twice," Ellis said. "I threw at his jaw, and he moved. I threw at the back of his head, and he moved." At this point, Pittsburgh manager Danny Murtaugh, who had been the victim of a Sal Maglie beanball in his playing days, walked to the mound, noted that Ellis was having trouble finding home plate, and removed him from the ball game.

The Pirates, incidentally, won their division that year. The Reds did not.

Pennant winners thrived on overt aggression. "Athletes talk about aggressiveness the way businessmen talk about profit margins," the writer Donald Hall once observed. The New York Yankees, playing under Billy Martin in 1976, offered a compelling example of the aggression obsession. On May 20, in a game against Boston, New York's Lou Piniella rounded third base, put his head down to charge home—and realized that he was going to be out by a mile. Piniella simply accelerated, and attempted to run straight through Red Sox catcher Carlton Fisk. In the ensuing fight between the clubs, Yankee center fielder Mickey Rivers punched Boston pitcher Bill Lee in the back of the head. "Spaceman" Lee was Boston's resident hippie-intellectual—Billy Martin called him "the lady" and "the fag"—and had won seventeen games the year before when the Red Sox won the pennant. Yankee Graig Nettles now lifted Lee up, turned him over, and slammed his pitching shoulder into the ground. Lee, who later said he was "jumped by Billy Martin's Brown Shirts," suffered a near-career-ending shoulder separation. His arm felt dead and he started screaming at Nettles: "How could you do this to me? I played ball with your brother Jimmy in Alaska, you no-good prick! How could you be such an asshole?"

The Yankees won the American League's eastern division in 1976; they left the Red Sox in the dirt. Then the Yankees won the American League pennant and there was more craziness. In the final game of the playoffs against Kansas City in New York, the umpires had to stop play nine times as Yankee fans pelted the Royals with bottles and garbage. When Yankee first baseman Chris Chambliss hit a home run to win the game and the pennant, the fans swarmed onto the field and nearly trampled him before he reached home plate. The fans had become the mirror reflection of their team—obnoxious and aggressive. Of course, players and spectators all took their lead from Martin and Steinbrenner, the masters of bad form.

As the Yankees advanced to the World Series against the Reds, baseball commissioner Bowie Kuhn collected $700,000 from the networks as payment for moving a World Series game to a Sunday night—that way the networks could televise an afternoon football game without a conflict. But playing a World Series game on a freezing October night in New York City was one more defilement of the summer game and its rituals—what some people had once naively called the Temple of Baseball. In the months ahead, a long line of players entered the temple and cashed in their free-agent chips. Outfielder Lyman Bostock, who earned $47,000 with the Minnesota Twins in 1976, jumped to a $450,000 contract with the California Angels. Cincinnati pitcher Don Gullett, fresh from the Reds' World Series sweep of the Yankees, jumped into Steinbrenner's arms and signed a six-year $2 million contract to play for New York. No one knew that his arm would go bad after a year and that Gullett would become one of the first high-paid, free-agent burnouts whom sports fans cursed over morning coffee.

Gullett was joined in New York in 1977 by Reggie Jackson. Sometimes Reggie batted cleanup, sometimes he batted sixth or seventh, and sometimes he sat on the bench. It all depended on the state of his feud with Martin, and the state of Martin's feud with Steinbrenner. Billy called Reggie "George's boy." Martin and Jackson fought on national television one night in June during a game in Boston. After the country watched the squabble, Jackson retired to his hotel room, where he wept to reporters: "I'm a Christian and they're fucking with me because I'm a nigger, and they don't like niggers on this team." Emotionally unbalanced, the Yankees fought on to win the pennant anyway. And one of the enduring memories of modern sports fans is that of Jackson hitting three consecutive home runs on three pitches to win the final game of the World Series against the Dodgers at Yankee Stadium. Missing from this memory is context. Yankee fans terrorized the Dodgers during the Series, throwing beer cans, fifths of whiskey, brandy bottles, smoke bombs, and hard rubber balls at the enemy. The stadium was a shooting gallery, the Dodgers were the ducks, and Los Angeles manager Tommy LaSorda grimaced, "You talk about America and all the great things it's provided us, and then you see animals who throw bottles and things at another human being. How can people do that?"

The next season, Kuhn again tried to formulate effective regulations for crowd control. He failed. Tommy John of the Yankees suggested that the teams might try using attack dogs.

The league presidents tried to control violence *on* the field. They announced that runners would no longer be allowed to veer out of the base baths to take out infielders. There were a lot of base runners who still enjoyed hunting for second basemen. "Rip 'em up," says former pitcher Andy Messersmith, who was one of them. "I *loved* goin' into second base. That was *fun*. I remember one game, I was up about nine-nothing, going into second base, and knocked Davey Johnson into left field. Hank Aaron looked at me and said, 'The fucking guy's nuts.' It really was war out there." He describes the operating pitching philosophy of the era: "If a batter went four for four with three dongs, you could count on going down, pal."

But the game's arbiters wanted to expunge such unconcealed aggressiveness. "There is no place for violence in baseball," declared Fred Fleig, supervisor of National League umpires, echoing the sentiments of baseball officials going back a century. He complained that the frequency of beanballs had tripled in 1977 over previous years.

Sorry, Fred. As the decade drew to a close, Boston manager Don Zimmer—the old beanball victim who sported steel screws in his skull—kept telling his pitchers to knock down opponents. Dwight Evans, one of Zimmer's outfielders, was knocked unconscious by a pitch. Mike Jorgensen of the Mets was nearly killed by a pitch; he went into convulsions and suffered a blood clot on the brain.

Baseball was a circus. Thousands of Chicago White Sox fans rioted at a "Disco Demolition" night at Comiskey Park, stoking a bonfire in the middle of the field to burn their vinyl. Pedro Borbon of the Reds was arrested for biting people in Cincinnati discotheques. Goose Gossage and Cliff Johnson of the Yankees beat each other up in the team shower, and the Yanks shipped Johnson to Cleveland. In September, Billy Martin was said to have slipped $100 to one of his pitchers, Bob Kammeyer, to hit Johnson with a pitch. Martin hated Johnson. Like he hated Jackson. Like he hated Bill Lee. He was on the downslide again, on the verge of one more nervous breakdown induced by Steinbrenner. Thurman Munson was dead—fleeing the Bronx Zoo on an off day a few weeks earlier, Munson had flown his private plane home to Akron to see his family and crashed. The Yankees had reached critical mass. They finished fourth, thirteen and a half games behind the Orioles, and everyone went home for rehabilitation outside Steinbrenner's cellblock. Reggie Jackson went to his vacation home in Carmel, California. Imagine Reggie relaxing in tony Carmel-by-the-Sea, playing with his antique cars in the intense sunshine, kicking back, flipping on the radio, and hearing this report from the real world: Billy Martin had just been arrested for beating up a marshmallow salesman named Joseph Cooper in a bar in Minnesota. Jackson broke up laughing. In New York a few days later, George Steinbrenner announced that Martin was out of a job. Steinbrenner was afraid Martin's drinking would end tragically, with either Martin dead or Martin killing somebody. Cooper, it seems, had narrowly escaped serious injury. "When Billy hit this guy," Steinbrenner told reporters, "he fell down inches away from one of those huge metal andirons. If the guy hits his head on that, he's dead. Wouldn't that be something, the manager of the Yankees on trial for murder?"

Return of the Gamblers

Poor Bowie Kuhn. In 1970, the baseball commissioner was faced with *three* gambling investigations involving three high-profile figures in the game.

Denny McLain—Kuhn suspended McLain until July 1 after concluding that the Detroit pitcher had been the "victim of a confidence scheme" in 1967. These were kind words. McLain had, in fact, been in over his head with a bookmaking ring whose members apparently stomped his feet in the middle of the '67 pennant race when McLain didn't repay a debt. He was suspiciously ineffective down the stretch.

After Kuhn announced the suspension in 1970, McLain admitted he had been "double dumb," a favorite expression of his. After returning to the Tigers in midseason, though, he was not contrite. McLain got into trouble for carrying a gun on a team flight and dumping ice water over a couple of reporters' heads. He had won thirty-one games in 1968 and twenty-four more in 1969. But he was highly unpopular with teammates and management and now bounced from team to team, before fading out of sight in 1972. The rest of the decade was a disaster for McLain. He played the organ in nightclubs, cooked up business schemes, went bankrupt twice, and

*Denny McLain.
Baseball's last thirty-game winner
hung out with the wrong crowd.*

started playing golf for $50 a hole in 1979 after his family's house burned down.

Leo Durocher—One more time. Kuhn investigated rumors, first heard by the FBI, that Leo was playing footsie with Chicago hoodlums and gambling heavily. As was the case in 1947, when gambling rumors led to Durocher's suspension from baseball for the season, the proof was elusive. The commissioner concluded that the Cubs manager was innocent, and accepted Durocher's statement that his only gambling took place in Las Vegas casinos. Durocher liked to visit Las Vegas to see his friends Frank Sinatra and Dean Martin, and had won $25,000 during one recent stay.

Pete Rose—Rose's gambling debts were often forgiven during the 1960s by the old Cincinnati bookies who had known him as a boy. But in 1970, Kuhn, on the personal recommendation of J. Edgar Hoover, hired an FBI man named Henry Fitzgibbon to assist with baseball gambling investigations. Fitzgibbon soon began to hear that Rose associated regularly with known gamblers, a violation of baseball rules. He received tips that Rose gambled large sums of money through bookies and was a regular at the racetrack. In *Hustle: The Myth, Life, and Lies of Pete Rose,* author Michael Y. Sokolove details Rose's growing addiction, Fitzgibbon's efforts to discuss it with him, and Rose's assurances that he never bet on baseball and didn't gamble illegally. The investigation continued for ten years, with questionable effectiveness, for incriminating evidence was never gathered even as Rose's life careened out of control.

Aaron's Tribulation

A s Hank Aaron closed in on Babe Ruth's all-time home run record in 1973, he was besieged with racist hate mail. "Dear Nigger." "Dear Jungle Bunny." "Dear Nigger Scum." "Hey nigger boy." A quarter century had passed since Jackie Robinson's entry into the national game, but tens of thousands of Americans abhorred the idea that a black man might break baseball's most cherished record, set by its most cherished hero, the great (white) Ruth.

Aaron went public with the problem in May. "I never said I was as good as Babe Ruth," he told reporters, "but what am I supposed to do, stop hitting? . . . Put it this way: the more they push me, the more I want the record."

He received 930,000 pieces of mail during the year he pursued Ruth. In the early stages, before Aaron brought the racism into the open, much of the correspondence was sickening. "You may beat Ruth's record but there will always be only one Babe. You will be just another black fuck down from the trees." "How about some sickle cell anemia, Hank?" "Beware of the white man's wrath." "I hope you join Dr. Martin Luther King in that Heaven he spoke of." Some of the letters informed Aaron he would be killed on specific dates in specific ballparks with a .22 or a .45, fired from the upper deck. "BANG BANG YOUR DEAD."

A kidnapping plot against Aaron's daughter Gaile was uncovered; FBI agents were stationed at Fisk University to protect her. The city of Atlanta assigned a policeman named Calvin Wardlaw to act as Aaron's own bodyguard; he carried binoculars and a gun at all times. And while Atlanta Braves teammates and manager Eddie Mathews formed a support network for Aaron, Atlanta fans screamed "nigger" at him so often that he felt as if it were 1953 and he were still playing for Jacksonville in the Sally League. Later, the crowds came around for Aaron, and along with them the mail. But baseball commissioner Bowie Kuhn was conspicuously absent from the ballpark when Aaron hit his seven hundredth homer in late '73 and when he finally broke the record early in '74.

"It should have been the most enjoyable time in my life, and instead it was hell," Aaron wrote years later in *I Had a Hammer,* his autobiography. "I'm proud of the home run record, but I don't talk about it because it brings back too many unpleasant memories."

*The
1970s*

"I'm a Yankee"

Imagine Billy Martin's sense of triumph in 1975, the year he was named manager of the New York Yankees. As a high school student in California, Martin had boasted to friends that he would someday play for the Yanks. He became Casey Stengel's protégé in the Pacific Coast League in the '40s, joined the Yankees under Stengel in the '50s, and found a family there, the first real family he had ever known. Tough little Billy Martin, the dead-end kid with the big nose, had finally crossed over to the right side of the tracks. Suddenly he was pals with Mantle and Ford, and his knee-in-the-crotch style of play helped

United Press International

*Billy Martin in
the umpire's face,
as usual.*

lead the team to a couple of pennants. But Yankee general manager George Weiss dumped Martin in 1957, traded him to Kansas City, because he thought Martin was a troublemaker, a burr on the smoothly functioning Yankee pennant machine. Overnight, Martin was wrenched from his family, stripped of his Yankee pedigree, and returned to his previous identity as an undistinguished street-fighting punk. He was once more a man with no home, no class, living on the wrong side of the tracks.

And here he was in '75, back at the top in pinstripes! Martin had spent close to twenty years fighting his way back to the Apple, and now he was about to reclaim the Yankee championship tradition by refashioning the Bronx Bombers in his image. The team once likened to U.S. Steel would now be compared to the Bronx Zoo; Billy's gorillas were going to beat up the American League.

He was praised for his tactical brilliance on the field, his psychological gambits in the clubhouse. Martin was like McGraw. There was always tension in his locker room. There were cliques. There were fist fights in the showers. The idea was to keep the team on edge so that it would careen onto the field and outnerve the opposition. Dock Ellis, an almost surreally violent '70s character who by his own admission once pitched a no-hitter on LSD, played for Martin in 1976 and enjoyed that season like no other. Martin was a wild-eyed competitor. "We didn't take no shit," Ellis said, sounding a lot like Martin's take-shit-from-no-one mother. What's more, Martin was "the *smartest* manager I ever played for," Ellis said in *The Country of Baseball,* his biography. "One guy, if Billy didn't smell whiskey on his breath, he didn't play. When he had a hangover—really *loud,* red-eyed, still staggering—Billy would say, 'You're in there, big guy.' He'd get three or four hits."

More than just hard-nosed, Martin was a psychologist. Largely because of him, the Yanks won three straight pennants from 1976 to 1978.

But there was one person tougher and shrewder than Billy Martin, and that was Yankee owner George Steinbrenner. The owner browbeat his famous manager, even as the team rose to championship heights. He second-guessed Martin, dictated lineups to Martin, overruled Martin whenever he disciplined Reggie Jackson. Steinbrenner constantly called Martin to his office for nasty little talks about what a shitty job he was doing and how he'd better get with the program. By the summer of 1978, Martin was gaunt, hiding behind dark sunglasses, fearful of losing his job if he didn't behave like Steinbrenner's lapdog. He fell to uncontrollable sobbing about Steinbrenner one night in his hotel room in front of Yankee beat writer Maury Allen, shouting, "Why should I have to take all this shit? I'm a Yankee. I've been a Yankee all my life. What's he been? Rich. He's not a Yankee. I'm a Yankee. I don't have to take this. . . . I don't have to listen to this crap, take his phone calls, ruin my life and my health. What for? I'm a Yankee."

Martin "burst into deep, excruciating sobs," Allen wrote in his book *Damn Yankee*, "his arms flailing, his head in his chest, his hands squeezing his legs, his hair disheveled, his face sallow, and his skin pulled tight. 'I'm a Yankee, I'm a Yankee.' "

Here are some further highlights and lowlights from his decade:

October 2, 1970: named manager of Detroit Tigers.

August 8, 1971: restrained by police from fighting Boston's Reggie Smith, who is approximately twice Martin's size. Billy fumes, "Reggie has one problem—his mouth. I used to run over tougher guys getting to a fight."

1972 season: threatens to levy $2,000 fines on Tiger pitchers who won't throw at opponents.

August 31, 1973: suspended for three days for ordering pitchers to throw spitballs.

September 2, 1973: fired as Tiger manager after leading club to AL division title.

September 8, 1973: named manager of Texas Rangers.

July 16, 1974: suspended and fined for ordering knockdown of Milwaukee batters. Martin says the pitches were in retaliation for Milwaukee pitches thrown at Ranger shortstop Toby Harrah. "I had to protect him," Martin explains, "to keep peace in the family."

October 24, 1974: named AL manager of the year after leading Rangers to second place.

July 21, 1975: fired as Ranger manager.

August 2, 1975: named manager of New York Yankees.

October 28, 1976: named AL manager of the year after leading Yankees to first pennant in twelve years.

Spring training 1977: curses Steinbrenner in Yankee locker room: "You fat bastard, I don't give a shit what you say!"

May 14, 1977: fined $2,500 for insulting Steinbrenner publicly.

June 19, 1977: dodges firing by Steinbrenner, who tells him, "The next time you drive me to the wall, I'll throw you over it."

October 18, 1977: leads Yankees to first World Championship in fifteen years as they beat Dodgers in six games.

July 17, 1978: demolishes his office after game against Kansas City in which Reggie Jackson ignores Martin's instructions to swing away and instead strikes out, trying to bunt.

July 23, 1978: says of Jackson and Steinbrenner, "They deserve each other. One's a born liar, the other's convicted."

July 24, 1978: resigns as Yankee manager.

July 29, 1978: participates in Old-Timers' Day at Yankee Stadium, where cheering crowd is told he will manage again in 1980.

June 18, 1979: returns ahead of schedule to manage the Yankees. Jackson says, "I can't play for that man. He hates me."

September 18, 1979: accused of paying Yankee pitcher Bob Kammeyer $100 to hit ex-Yankee Cliff Johnson, now playing for Cleveland, with a pitch. League investigation clears Martin.

October 22, 1979: beats up marshmallow salesman Joseph Cooper.

October 29, 1979: fired as Yankee manager.

Pepi in the Fast Lane

He was Joe Pepitone from Brooklyn, a street guy. Got shot in the stomach with a .38 when he was in high school and spent his life showing off the scars. Arrived at spring training with the Yankees in '62, a rookie, driving a fancy new car, towing a motorboat with a dog yapping on its bow. He had a quick, sweet left-handed swing that might have taken him to Cooperstown—Pepi popped twenty-eight homers for the Yanks in '64, driving in 100 runs. But he always wanted to impress the fast crowd more than his managers or the fans. Whenever he went AWOL from the Yanks, his bosses wondered if he might show up at the bottom of the East River with his spiked shoes in cement. Still, he was funny, likable, a card: "Pepi could start an argument in an empty room," joked Joe Garagiola.

It was in the mid-'60s that Pepi bumped into Leo Durocher in the lobby of the Eden Roc Hotel in Las Vegas. Leo introduced Pepi to Frank Sinatra. "Hey, paisan!" Frank greeted him. Friends from the get-go. As the years moved on, Pepi partied at Frank's house. He hung out at nightclubs with important men in fine suits. "These were kings of the racket trade, superstars, and they all wanted to be my friend," he explained in his autobiography, *Joe, You Coulda Made Us Proud.*

Trouble kept finding him.

He always promised to grow up, to reform, but never did, and the Yankees finally traded him to Houston in 1969.

George Brace

Pepi was in heaven under Leo Durocher.

With the Astros, Pepi demanded a private room on the road. When the team assigned him a roommate, he threatened to retire. He was traded to the Chicago Cubs after 75 games.

This was heaven. Pepi's manager was Durocher. Leo understood Pepitone. He understood the yen for fine clothes, night life, women. (Pepitone's second wife, Diane, discovered slips of paper on which the names of 150 women with whom her husband had slept were painstakingly recorded. These included some of her closest friends.)

It was under Durocher that Pepitone arguably had his best year, batting .307 in 1971, the only time in twelve seasons that he broke .300.

But Durocher left the club in '72. Pepitone moved on to Atlanta in '73. In '74, he moved to Japan and joined the Tokyo Yakult Atoms who offered him a two-year contract at $70,000 a year. It didn't work out.

"No one spoke English," he complained.

And there was his apartment: "I swear the door was 4 feet 5 inches high."

He didn't last the season.

Dick Young: Conscience of Baseball?

Dick Young was a visionary who pushed baseball writing well
beyond the mere cataloging of runs, hits, and errors. Almost
from the time he joined the *New York Daily News* in the 1940s, he
took his craft into the locker room to question the athletes about their
performances and to consider the personalities behind the game. He
became a guru to the new breed of sportswriters of the '60s who saw
baseball as a subculture to be explored and analyzed. But maybe
because his impact was so great, he started to take himself pretty damn
seriously. Young, arrogant to begin with, had always feuded with
individual players, like Jackie Robinson, whom he despised. But by the
'70s, his tough guy routine and I-know-the-score attitude were wearing
thin with some colleagues. He was "a jut-jawed little man," wrote
journalist Pat Jordan, "who always seems to be arguing with cab drivers
and who considers himself the moral conscience of sport."

In the late 1950s, Young came up with a name for the new
generation of bottom-line businessmen who took over the game: the
Lords of Baseball. For years, he attacked them for remaking baseball as
a corporate enterprise, unsentimental and without loyalty to fans or
cities. But in the mid-'70s, Young made an about-face. He became a
shill for M. Donald Grant, the New York Mets owner who was
wrecking the team's popularity with his pomposity and poor handling
of players. In the spring of 1976, Grant publicly humiliated Tom Seaver
during contract negotiations. Simultaneously, Young began publishing
a series of personal attacks on Seaver that justified Grant's actions,
shaped public opinion, and eventually drove Seaver out of New York.

Seaver was asking for an $800,000 three-year contract, a lot of
money at the time. Only three months had passed since a federal labor
panel decision established free agency and turned player salaries on
their ears. Young had been in baseball for thirty years, and it's
understandable that he might have been disturbed by the drastic
changes in his world; that's only human. But the viciousness with which

he went after Seaver was extraordinary. Seaver was the best pitcher in baseball, a three-time Cy Young Award winner, a cornerstone of the franchise, respected by his peers and the public. Yet Young never quoted Seaver in his columns, never summarized Seaver's position. He just railroaded the guy, week after week. Young, whose son-in-law worked in the Met front office, sang praises to Grant's generosity. He harped on Seaver's old back injuries as a potential liability to the club, even though the pitcher had won twenty-two games the previous season. He quoted club officials as saying they wouldn't mind trading Seaver if that's what it came down to—and, with Young cowriting the script with Grant, it inevitably did.

But first Young laid the groundwork: "Tom Terrific is a holdout, a serious, gen-u-wine holdout." Seaver was "too damn greedy." Seaver was "coddled . . . spoiled, spoiled, spoiled." He was sodden with "self-pity that trickles down each cheek while he's picking up huge paychecks."

A year later, Young was still at it: "Let's all have a good cry for Tom Seaver. The poor guy is moping around camp with a long face, telling any newspaperman who's chump enough to ask, how unhappy he is, how put upon he is, how miserable the Mets' front office has made his life."

Young couldn't understand "the strange sourness of Tom Terrific . . . constantly sniping at the bosses who have been rather good to him. I would say he is more ingrate than victim."

"Poor Tom Terrific."

It was around this time that Young dragged Seaver's wife, Nancy, into the fray. He claimed that Nancy was jealous over Nolan Ryan's contract with the California Angels and that *this* was the

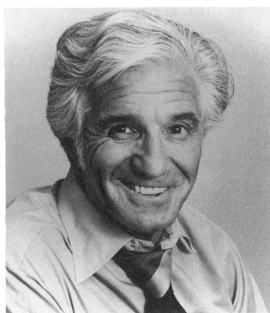

National Baseball Library

Mean-spirited in his later years, columnist Dick Young drove the Mets' Tom Seaver out of New York.

reason her husband argued over money with the Mets' front office. Now this statement *really* ticked off Seaver, which only pleased Young, who checked around the league and wrote that there was no market for baseball's best pitcher: "I have sad news for Tom Seaver. No one wants him."

Shortly afterward, the Mets traded Seaver to Cincinnati.

"Enough already of Tom Seaver's crocodile tears," Young wrote in his next column. "My personal role in this has been grossly exaggerated."

Seaver finished the 1977 season in Cincinnati with a 21–6 record, went on to win about 115 more games, and sailed into the Hall of Fame with 311 career victories.

Years after he helped evict Seaver from New York, Young tried to rewrite the history of the affair. He crafted a column stating that Seaver had agreed to the trade because he was afraid of waiting to test the free-agent market: "He didn't have the business acumen or the guts to find out how high teams would bid for him," Young said, hoping no one would remember the truth.

But this was now the 1980s, and Young's reputation was shot. The man who spent years lecturing free-agent players about loyalty—excoriating them as they jumped from team to team to capture the big money—abandoned the financially troubled *Daily News* to sign a fat contract with the *New York Post*. Not long after, Young started to pick on another celebrated Met pitcher, Dwight Gooden, who had drug and drinking problems in the late 1980s. Young wrote that Gooden was a "druggie" and a "graduate of Smithers U. [a famous rehab center in Manhattan]." No longer the sportswriters' guru, Young was just old and mean. He died in September 1987 at the age of sixty-nine.

Macho Man:
Q&A with Bobby Bonds

hen Bobby Bonds debuted with the San Francisco Giants in 1968, the press called him "the next Willie Mays." Even if he didn't live up to the hype, Bonds was one of the most roundly talented and aggressive players of his era. Four times during his fourteen-year career, he hit more than thirty home runs while stealing over forty bases.

We spoke to Bonds, the father of Barry Bonds, about aggressive baseball in the 1970s. He says there's something missing from today's game: "The knockdown pitch—it's part of baseball. That's just like taking apples out of an apple pie. You've just got crust."

Q: Did pitchers throw at you much?

A: Are you kidding? Knocked us down like crazy. You kidding? Brushed us back like crazy. Ooooh, if they had the rules then that they have now about brushbacks—Jesus Christ, I'd love to hit today. If you hit a home run when I played, you'd get drilled the next time you came up. You got sent on your butt. Sometimes it was kind of difficult to stand up in that batter's box knowing that a guy was throwing in the nineties and you were gonna get it.

Q: Tell me about Gibson.

A: I hit two home runs off him one day and I got up the third time. I was scared to death. Not so much like fear, or nothing like that, but I knew what was gonna happen. I knew that I wasn't gonna get hit in the head, because Bob wasn't really a headhunter. But I knew I was gonna get hit. I didn't know where and I didn't know how much it was gonna hurt. But I knew it was gonna be over ninety-five and I knew I was gonna get it.

I wasn't intimidated by Bob. It was an anticipation of getting the shit knocked out of you. It's no different than a guy standing up there, and you know he's gonna hit you in the jaw. It's not that you're afraid; you just know it's gonna hurt.

Q: How big a part of the game is intimidation by the pitcher?

A: It's a big part, because it's a mental game. I can remember playing with Nolan Ryan one day. And I remember we were playing against Oakland, and Nolan threw a pitch up and in against Bert Campaneris. And Campy went down, and he was shaking his bat at Nolan, like, "If you're gonna get me, this is what I'm gonna do." And the next pitch, Nolan spun him. And I'm talking about *spun* him, buddy. He threw it right at his noggin. He must've thrown it a hundred miles per hour. And Campy went down and the ball went between his helmet and his hat. Yeah, I mean, he *threw* it.

And that day, Nolan struck out Campy the rest of the times he was at the plate. So I think that pitch intimidated Campy, because he didn't know if he was gonna do it again.

Q: Besides Gibson, who were the most intimidating pitchers?

A: I never faced an intimidating pitcher, because I can't be intimidated.

Q: Who were the—

A: Seaver would send you down. Jerry Koosman wasn't afraid to knock you down. Bill Singer. Steve Carlton. I mean, there's a lot of them. We used to call it "chin music." The closer the pitcher threw to me, the closer I got to home plate. If I was standing on the line and they knocked me down, I would almost put my feet on home plate. I didn't care. I'd stand as close as I could. I'd just keep moving up, because I had no fear.

Q: How were you at breaking up the double play?

A: I spiked people and I got spiked. I only went after one person, really: Larry Cox, a catcher for Philadelphia. I slid into home plate one day—1973, I think it was, or '74. Larry had offered me a part of the plate, and I went after it. And he put down his shin guards in front of me and got me pretty good. My knees were bleeding and everything.

He hurt me. Not to the point where I had to leave the game. But I was in some pain. So I went after him to get him back, and I broke his leg. I wanted to hurt him. I mean, not to the point of breaking his leg, because that's a person's career. But I wanted to let him know, "Don't do this. If you wanna play this way, this is the way I can play. You wanna have rough baseball? Well, let's have rough baseball."

Q: Was it a violent game?

A: I don't think I would use that word: "violent." That's a pretty strong word. It's been a very competitive game. A tough game.

Like I've said, going up standing sixty feet six inches from Bob Gibson or Don Drysdale and not knowing if they're gonna throw the ball at your chin or on the outside part of the plate was tough.

I've seen pitchers throw at people's heads. I've had eighteen managers,

Macho Man:
Q&A with
Bobby Bonds

and I've heard managers say, "I want his head taken off." I don't think they meant that literally. That means "spin 'em" or "separate 'em"—separate his helmet from his head.

Q: Isn't that a fine line?

A: No, it's not a fine line, because you have enough time to get out of the way. Billy Martin, I was with him, and I know that he told pitchers to hit players. Never in the head, though. Because that's life-threatening. You know, "Hit 'em. Hit 'em in the knee. Hit 'em in the leg." I think a manager should be able to say, "Get him off the plate." I don't think there's anything wrong with that.

We played harder than they do today. We played the game the way it was supposed to be played.

354

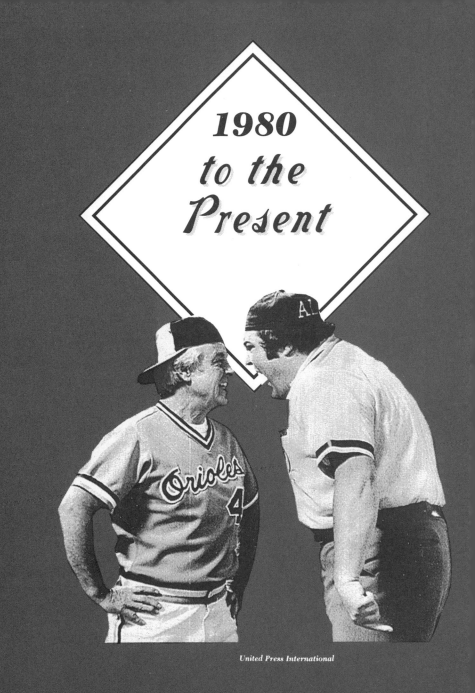

1980
to the
Present

United Press International

1980
- Charlie Finley hires Billy Martin to manage Oakland A's.
- Joe Charboneau is AL Rookie of the Year: opens beer bottles with his eye socket.
- Willie Stargell Day in Pittsburgh: fans attack Dave Parker.
- Philadelphia mayor Frank Rizzo stations police attack dogs at Veterans Stadium to control crowd at final game of World Series.
- Charlie Finley sells Oakland A's.

1981
- Dave Winfield signs ten-year $23 million deal with Yankees.
- Reggie Smith decks heckler who blows kisses at him during Dodgers' spring training workout in Vero Beach, Florida.
- Players walk out: fifty-day midseason strike.
- Ron Cey hit in face by Goose Gossage's 94-mph pitch in World Series.
- Yankees lose World Series to Dodgers. Steinbrenner apologizes to the people of New York for his team's performance.

1982
- Steinbrenner fires manager Bob Lemon and hires Gene Michael. Fires Michael and hires Clyde King.
- Alan Wiggins of Padres arrested for cocaine possession.
- Steve Howe of Dodgers goes into rehab for cocaine addiction.
- Lonnie Smith of Cardinals attacks the Phillie Phanatic.
- Average player salary nears $250,000.

1983
- Steinbrenner hires Billy Martin to manage Yankees.
- Dave Winfield kills sea gull in Toronto outfield while playing catch.
- Willie Aikens, Jerry Martin, and Willie Wilson of Kansas City Royals are suspended for drug use. Go to jail.
- Lonnie Smith of Cardinals enters drug rehabilitation.

1984
- Yogi Berra replaces Martin as Yankee manager.
- Pasqual Perez jailed in Santo Domingo for cocaine possession.
- Vida Blue suspended for drug use.
- Tigers win World Series. Fans riot in Detroit: forty-one arrests, eighty-two injuries, one man shot dead, two cars set afire.
- Peter Ueberroth hired as baseball commissioner.

1985
- Steinbrenner fires Berra. Rehires Martin.
- Denny McLain found guilty of cocaine trafficking and possession, loan sharking, extortion, and bookmaking.
- Joe Pepitone arrested for possession of cocaine, Quaaludes, heroin, and a loaded handgun. Jailed for two months.
- Pete Rose gets his 4,192nd hit, breaking Ty Cobb's record. He sells the record-setting bat for $129,000 to pay off gambling debts.
- Billy Martin fights Yankee pitcher Ed Whitson at Baltimore hotel.
- Pittsburgh drug trials reveal massive cocaine use in baseball.

1986
- Commissioner Peter Ueberroth announces one-year suspensions of Dave Parker, Keith Hernandez, Lonnie Smith, and others for drug use.
- Lou Piniella replaces Martin as Yankee manager.
- Red Sox lose World Series to Mets after Bill Buckner commits the most famous error in the history of baseball.
- Dwight Gooden fights with Tampa police.

1987
- Commissioner Ueberroth dedicates the season to Jackie Robinson on fortieth anniversary of Robinson's debut with the Dodgers.
- Dodger general manager Al Campanis goes on national TV, says blacks lack "some of the necessities" for baseball management.
- First of three collusion rulings against major league owners: conspiracy to limit free-agent salaries will cost owners millions.

357

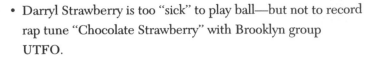

- Darryl Strawberry is too "sick" to play ball—but not to record rap tune "Chocolate Strawberry" with Brooklyn group UTFO.
- Dwight Gooden enters Smithers Alcoholism and Treatment Center.

1988

- Billy Martin hired to manage Yankees.
- Martin nearly killed during brawl at Texas strip joint.
- Pedro Guerrero throws bat at pitcher Dave Cone.
- Pete Rose incites Cincinnati fans against umpire Dave Pallone. Bombarded with garbage for fifteen minutes, the umpire leaves the game.
- Margo Adams files $6 million palimony suit against Wade Boggs.
- June: Martin is fired by Yanks.

1989

- A. Bartlett Giamatti becomes baseball commissioner. Investigates Pete Rose's gambling.
- Jose Canseco arrested for driving 125 mph in suburban Miami—and for keeping loaded semiautomatic gun in his Jaguar near Oakland.
- August: Pete Rose accepts lifetime suspension from baseball with right to apply for reinstatement after one year.
- Earthquake rocks World Series between Giants and A's.
- Billy Martin killed in Christmas Day car crash.
- Mark Langston, with 86–76 lifetime record, becomes highest-paid player ever by signing $16 million deal to pitch for Angels.

1990

- Darryl Strawberry booked for assaulting wife, Lisa, with deadly weapon. Checks into Smithers Alcoholism and Treatment Center.
- Tony Conigliaro dies.
- Owners lock players out of spring training camps.
- Pete Rose pleads guilty to two felony counts of failing to file income tax.
- Eight days later: baseball commissioner A. Bartlett Giamatti drops dead.
- George Steinbrenner is ordered to give up majority

ownership and day-to-day management of Yankees. He paid
mobster $40,000 for dirt on Dave Winfield.

1991
- Average player salary rises to $851,383.
- Major leagues set new attendance record: 56.8 million.
- Lenny Dykstra testifies at trial of Mississippi bookie to whom
  he owes $78,000 in poker money.
- Roger Clemens charged with assaulting off-duty cop in
  Houston.
- Rob Dibble throws 95-mph fastball behind head of Eric
  Yelding.
- Drunken Dykstra smashes Mercedes in late-night crash.
- Albert Belle throws ball at taunting fan in Cleveland.
- Mets sign Bobby Bonilla to five-year $29 million deal.
- Cubs sign Ryne Sandberg to four-year $28.4 million pact.
- Kevin Mitchell arrested and accused of forcible rape; woman
  doesn't press criminal charges. Giants trade Mitchell to
  Seattle.

1992
- Canseco arrested for ramming his Porsche into wife's BMW.
- Angels pitcher Matt Keough undergoes brain surgery after
  line drive hits him flush in face in dugout during spring
  training.
- Gooden, Strawberry, and Vince Coleman of Mets accused of
  raping woman in Florida. Lie-detector test indicates sex was
  consensual.
- Yankee pitcher Steve Howe pleads guilty to misdemeanor
  after buying cocaine from DEA agent in Montana.
- Yankee pitcher Pasqual Perez suspended for cocaine use.

1993
- Average player salary rises to $1,116,353.
- National League expands: Colorado Rockies and Florida
  Marlins.
- Barry Bonds joins the Giants: six-year $43.75 million deal.
- Cincinnati Reds owner Marge Schott suspended from
  baseball for racist comments about players and employees.
- Jesse Jackson calls for boycott of game.
- George Steinbrenner is given a reprieve: returns to Yankees.
- Vince Coleman throws explosive device at autograph seekers
  in L.A.

> **If they don't pay me what I deserve, I'm going to become a pain in the ass. Maybe I'll have some unexpected medical problems that will keep me out. If they're going to keep treating me like a dog, I'll be a dog.**
> —*Rob Dibble, after rejecting a $475,000 contract offer from the Reds*

The last decade and a half have been tiring for baseball. Exhausting for the players, who now earn more than $1.1 million apiece on average, and have to put up with all the abuse that fact brings from fans and the media. Tiring for the fans, who have to open the papers each morning and read about the millionaires' salary complaints, along with the rape charges and drug arrests that

Associated Press.

*Dar-ryl!
Strawberry
is unhappy
with the call.*

proliferate against them, the out-of-wedlock children they father, the Rolex-laden mobsters they hang out with, the trees they crash into with their high-priced cars. In a single week in January 1990, Darryl Strawberry of the Mets was in the headlines for fathering an out-of-wedlock child in St. Louis, hitting his wife, Lisa, and allegedly threatening her with a .25 caliber semiautomatic pistol in Encino, California, and being admitted to the Smithers Alcoholism and Treatment Center in New York. Is this the same game you dreamed about as a child when you fell asleep with a transistor radio pressed between your head and the pillow?

It's hard on the fans.

But let's be fair: the fans are suspect, too. You go to a ballpark nowadays and you often find one of two things. You find uninterested spectators who wouldn't dream of looking up from their sushi—$6.00 at Anaheim Stadium—to scream at the umpire. In Oakland, in the midst of the most hair-raising playoff contests, the crowd is silent, as if at a tennis match. Spectators rub on the sun block, preen, and stream from their seats to line up at concession stands to buy $20 T-shirts. But why complain about the Californians? If you prefer action, you can always go to Wrigley Field in Chicago where a couple of inebriated men fell 35 feet from the upper deck while wrestling at a Cubs game a few years ago. Or you can take the subway to Yankee Stadium where California Angel first baseman Wally Joyner was grazed by a foot-long butcher knife thrown from the upper deck in 1986. And then you can swing by Shea Stadium, where fans perched high above the visitors' bullpen once urinated onto the head of Houston Astro pitcher Dave Smith.

Macho New Yorkers laugh about such incidents. But they're not limited to New York, and they're not funny. Casual violence, unbridled boorishness, and excessive materialism are the hallmarks of contemporary life. And they're all on exhibition at the ballpark: once again, the National Pastime mirrors society. Old-timers say today's wealthy ballplayers have gone soft; that they "respect" one another too much to risk hurting an opponent. "There's so much money to be made, so much glory for every guy," Dibble, one of the "Nasty Boys" of the Cincinnati Reds, said a couple of years back. "There's enough room for everybody." But those are mere words. If modern "country club" baseball is such a pale imitation of the hard-bitten game of yore, then why does Dibble throw 95-mph fastballs behind batters' heads? Why do so many batters take umbrage at inside pitches and charge the mound, risking injury to themselves, the pitchers, and the various players who join in the fights that invariably break out?

Big-money baseball has had the paradoxical effect of creating a generation of preening, thin-skinned, and often *violent* millionaires. They are short-fused and overly sensitive to any affront to their celebrity status or money-making capabilities: this is what charging the mound is all about. It's a form of reverse, or preemptive, intimidation. For a century, the pitchers ruled by intimidating the batters with the brushback pitch. Now the batters are turning the tables, saying, "Don't even *try* it." It used to be if you threw at a guy's head, you threatened his safety and career. Today, you do the same, but you're also endangering his $8 million contract, his accountant, his two agents, and his investment counselors. They've all warned him: "Don't get hurt." And by charging the mound, the player is passing the warning along to the pitcher: "Don't *fuck* with me. Don't hurt me. Don't make me look bad in front of all these people and, especially, in front of all these television cameras." It's a hair-trigger response, patterned after the unprovoked, tough-guy violence you see on television and in the street. Do you remember George Bell charging the mound in 1985 to plant a karate kick in the stomach of Red Sox pitcher Bruce Kison, known in his younger days as "the Assassin"? Do you remember Kevin Mitchell's attack on San Diego Padre pitcher Bruce Hurst in 1991? Hurst threw a pitch that hit Mitchell in the *foot*—enough to enrage Mitchell, who charged and threw a roadblock tackle at an amazed Hurst, knocking him to the ground. "Mitch was gonna kill him," said San Diego first baseman Fred McGriff, who pulled Mitchell away and stopped the incident.

As the millennium approaches, Mitchell may be the quintessential baseball antihero. He's said to be a congenial man in the locker room, but his exploits on and off the field are not exactly wholesome. He was accused by one girlfriend of beating her and pulling a gun on her; no charges were filed, but an out-of-court settlement of a civil suit stipulated that he enter a domestic violence counseling program. Another accused him of raping her, and this time he was arrested,

UPI/Bettmann

*The sweet
follow-through of
Kevin Mitchell.
Off the field,
he's no angel.*

though criminal charges were again not pressed when the woman
declined to cooperate with prosecutors. He reportedly test-fired an Uzi
in the desert during spring training while playing with the Padres.
When he was with the Giants, he was once dropped off at Candlestick
Park by an old friend named Kyle Patrick Winters. Later that night,
Winters was arrested by police in connection with the slaying three
years earlier of a twenty-four-year-old San Diego police officer.
Mitchell was not implicated, of course, but people were shocked by his
associations. If anyone still thinks that baseball exists in a vacuum,
unsullied by life outside the ballpark, Mitchell is as good an example as

you will find that it does not. He bounces from team to team, a man with no professional roots and, like the country itself and most of his colleagues, no sense of history. During the 1989 season, when Mitchell won the National League MVP award and hit forty-seven home runs, reporters asked if he thought he might break Roger Maris's all-time record for homers in a single season. Roger who? Mitchell had never heard of him.

Where have you gone, Joe DiMaggio?

Willie Mays, we miss your power and grace.

Not that they didn't have their own skeletons. But at least they stayed in the closet.

One could argue that in this age of media overkill, the ballplayers don't stand a chance. Who, after all, is a good enough person to escape the media inquisition? Like the President, baseball players are held up to impossible standards, and must inevitably fall to earth. We live in an age of fallen heroes. Columbus is trashed. JFK is trashed. So when Steve Garvey—the first baseman who would be U.S. senator—turns out to have fathered three children with three different women in the late '80s, should we be shocked? And when Pete Rose—good ol' Charlie Hustle, who loved the game to death, played harder and better than almost anyone, and worshiped the stars who came before him—winds up surrounding himself with "a creepy entourage of body builders, baseball memorabilia hustlers, and drug dealers" (as his biographer Michael Y. Sokolove puts it), what are we to think? Is it the media's fault that Rose, the player/manager of the Cincinnati Reds, gave his criminal friends the run of his office in Riverfront Stadium? That he almost certainly placed bets on his own team? That his gambling addiction and criminal associations landed him in jail and resulted in his banishment from baseball? Was it the media's fault? Or was it Rose's?

Even as the owners and media preach doom-and-gloom, lamenting the game's failure to groom young fans and its loss of a billion-dollar network television contract, the American public retains a residual love for the game. A record 56.8 million people visited major league ballparks in 1991. Baseball has returned to the tooth-and-nail running game that established its popularity decades ago. The leadoff men are magnificent: Rickey Henderson may be the best ever. The home run hitters are still legion: Jose Canseco, Cecil Fielder, Barry

Bonds, Fred McGriff. The pitchers continue to expand their
repertoires; the split-fingered fastball, when properly thrown by the
likes of Mike Scott or Jack Morris, is said to be almost unhittable. Yes,
the recent baseball landscape has been pretty exciting, if you can brush
the dirt aside. And, yes, there are ballplayers who are as yet untainted
by scandal: Bo Jackson, Orel Hershiser, Tony Gwynn, Ken Griffey, Jr.,
John Smoltz, Kirby Puckett, Cal Ripken, Jr., Ozzie Smith, Don
Mattingly, McGwire.

Still, the good guys seem to be in the minority these days—while
the bad guys make good fodder for a nasty game of Baseball Jeopardy.

Are you ready to play?

The first answer is: Tim Raines.

"Who kept toots of cocaine in his hip pocket and always slid
headfirst to avoid damaging his stash?"

Correct!

The next answer is: Rickey Henderson.

"Who threatened to have a lousy year if management didn't
renegotiate his $12 million contract?"

Correct!

Now: Wade Boggs.

"Who was sued for $6 million by Margo Adams, his on-the-road
girlfriend, sex toy, and good-luck charm
for years?"

Outstanding!

Go ahead: David Cone.

"Who was accused of masturbating
in front of a young woman who visited
the Mets bullpen?"

That's it.

Faster: Bobby Bonilla.

"What 230-pound superstar grabbed
a much smaller club executive by the
necktie and threatened to strangle him in
an argument over parking spaces for
wives of players?"

Associated Press

Rickey Henderson, unhappy as usual.

You're on a roll.

Now: Canseco.

"Who bashed his wife's BMW with his Porsche and bought a new $250,000 Lamborghini?"

Good detail.

Try this: Lenny Dykstra.

"Which drunken player broke his collar bone, bruised his heart, and punctured a lung late one night after leaving a bachelor party in suburban Philadelphia and wrapping his new, bright red Mercedes 500 SL around a couple of trees?"

One more: Dave Parker, Keith Hernandez, Pasqual Perez, Dwight Gooden.

"Who are prominent examples of cocaine abusers?"

Sad, but true.

Gooden was the one whose downfall hurt the most. We loved you, Dwight. You were young, innocent, unhittable. And when you got into the fight with the cops in Tampa, we believed that it was purely a racial thing; violently unjust on their part. And when you committed yourself to the rehab program at Smithers, we pulled for you. And we still pull for you. We check the box scores every time you pitch, hoping for evidence that you are recapturing your lost greatness. You probably never will, but you keep plugging, you pitch respectably, sometimes extremely well, and that's a lot to ask from a ballplayer in this Era of the Fallen Hero.

Cocaine became baseball's scourge during the '80s, dragging down literally dozens of players. Darrell Porter was one of the first to acknowledge his problem

Cool Canseco.

and seek help, in 1980. Steve Howe's addiction surfaced in '82; he went through rehab six times and doesn't seem to have licked his problem yet. The cocaine roll call included three members of the Kansas City Royals in '83—Willie Mays Aikens, Jerry Martin, and Willie Wilson, all suspended from the game and jailed. In '84, Vida Blue was suspended and jailed—another heartbreaker. In '85, a couple of old-timers had their names called. One was Denny McLain, jailed for coke possession and trafficking, loan sharking, and extortion. Joe Pepitone, who had boasted about his big-shot racketeering friends since his days with the Yankees in the early '60s, was arrested in Brooklyn with a bunch of small-time hoods. Pepi paid the piper: arrested for possession of cocaine, Quaaludes, heroin, and a loaded handgun, he spent two months in jail.

Dwight Gooden answers reporters' questions after being placed on probation in Tampa. He pleaded no contest to charges of battery on a police officer and resisting arrest.

Fans were perplexed by these developments, but they hadn't seen anything yet. In September 1985, the Pittsburgh drug trials dragged baseball through the mud. An array of stars testified about cocaine sales in clubhouse bathrooms, and the exploits of a Philadelphia caterer named Curtis Strong who hand-delivered bags of coke, wrapped in the pages of girlie magazines, to your favorite ballplayers. Lonnie Smith of the St. Louis Cardinals, the first to testify, named Keith Hernandez, Joaquin Andujar, and Gary Matthews as cocaine users. Smith, the only man ever to attack the Phillie Phanatic, revealed that the 1980 World Champion Philadelphia Phillies were amphetamine freaks: Schmidt, Rose, Bowa, and Luzinski were among those he named. As the trial wore on, Dave Parker, Jeff Leonard, Dale Berra, and a host of others took the stand to discuss the C-word. Baseball commissioner Peter Ueberroth responded quickly with a heavy round of fines and suspensions, announced plans for mandatory drug testing, and declared baseball's drug problem licked in 1986. But St. Peter was only kidding himself, as the roll call grew longer: LaMarr Hoyt, Otis Nixon, Gooden, Leon Durham . . .

. . . and Pasqual Perez, one of the more intimidating, coked-out figures in the game. Perez was always feared because of his reputation as a headhunter. But his image grew more menacing as his drug habit became known throughout the National League: it was assumed that when Perez threw at an opponent, he was not quite in control of himself. His career dipped, rose, and fell along with the patterns of his drug abuse. In 1983, while pitching for the Atlanta Braves, he won fifteen games and lost eight. The next winter, he was arrested for cocaine possession in the Dominican Republic and spent three months in jail there. Returning to the Braves after the start of the '84 season, he went on to post fourteen wins against eight losses. In one infamous contest against the San Diego Padres, Perez threw his very first pitch into the back of Padre infielder Alan Wiggins. This unleashed a flurry of beanballs as the game wore on—several directed at Perez himself—and provoked a fight between the teams that drew a cadre of fans onto the field, resulted in the ejections of sixteen players and the levying of $10,000 in fines against them, and was described as one of the ugliest scenes in the game's modern history. "It took baseball down fifty years, the worst thing I've ever seen in my life," said umpire John McSherry.

In retrospect, the fight was most interesting for its symbolism. Wiggins was a player whose drug addiction was well reported in the press; his numerous rehabilitations and declarations of sobriety were invariably followed by heartbreaking relapses. As for Perez, his fortunes fell in 1985 when he won a single game and lost thirteen. In 1986, he dropped out of baseball. At the end of '87, he resurfaced with the Montreal Expos, posted seven wins without a loss, and was briefly touted as the best pitcher in the game. But his career started to fizzle again in 1988, and was finally extinguished in 1991—the same year that Wiggins died of AIDS in a Los Angeles hospital at age thirty-two.

Baseball's tragic story line is always underlined by the game's obsession with money. There was a fifty-day players' strike in 1981, followed by spiraling salaries as the result of arbitration settlements, and the owners' subsequent conspiracies to limit free-agent salaries. When this collusion was discovered, federal arbitrators ordered the owners to pay $100 million in penalties to aggrieved players, who today earn enough money to individually rebuild entire city neighborhoods. The fans increasingly recognized that the national game was no longer played by people like *us;* it was played by plutocrats who were to be judged on a play-by-play, or even a swing-by-swing, basis and then cheered or harassed accordingly. If Albert Belle of the Indians, a man with a history of alcoholism, didn't pull his weight, the fans would loudly invite him to keg parties at their homes. The game was depersonalized, the players treated like commodities. At Yankee Stadium, security guards hauled away as many as fifty fans a night. In Boston, a new "subculture of dangerous people" filled the right field bleachers which had once been "a friendly place where people stretched out and schmoozed," lamented Stanley Cheren, an associate professor of psychiatry at the Boston University School of Medicine. The fans were drunk or stoned—and mean, artfully choosing the most hurtful epithets to shout at opposing players. The spirit of bench jockeying, lost in the dugout, was resurrected in the stands: "You gotta get under their skin. You have to break their mental barrier," explained Yankee fan Rich Mondragon. He succeeded in breaking the concentration of California Angel batter Luis Polonia by screeching "jailbait," a reference to Polonia's conviction for having sex with a fifteen-year-old girl. Polonia was an easy target. But when this rough treatment was generalized, and combined with the demands and abuse of owners, the game became a hellish pressure cooker for even the coolest, most highly paid athletes. "No matter what you read about the 'boys of summer,' professional baseball is rarely fun," wrote Dave Winfield, who signed a ten-year contract with the New York Yankees in 1980 and was immediately dubbed "the $23 Million Man."

The class warfare between fans and players took on an even more disturbing dimension when matters of race entered the picture. In the late 1970s, Dave Parker of the Pittsburgh Pirates was such

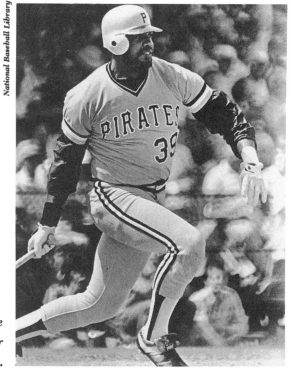

National Baseball Library

Pittsburgh fans couldn't handle Dave Parker, a wealthy black superstar with an attitude.

an unrelentingly effective hitter that he was described by sportswriters as one of the hundred greatest players to have ever walked onto a ball field. Unfortunately, as the decade closed, two things happened: Parker's salary soared astronomically, and Pittsburgh's blue-collar steel-based economy collapsed. "Here comes Dave Parker," says Pirate baseball historian Paul Adomites, painting the scene, "a six-foot-five-inch black man with a large attitude and a diamond in his ear, making a million dollars, and the people were being laid off at the mills, and it was a little too much for them to handle." On Opening Day 1980, someone threw a bag of nuts and bolts just past Parker's head in right field. On a Sunday in July, 43,194 Pirate fans poured into Three Rivers Stadium for Willie Stargell Day and a doubleheader against the Dodgers. There were more missiles thrown at Parker, and when, in the eighth inning, a nine-volt transistor radio battery hummed past his cap, Parker left the game. "It could have put his eye out," said Pirate manager Chuck Tanner. The greatest Pirate outfielder since Clemente was under physical attack by his hometown fans, and he didn't forgive them. He attacked them in the press, and as his batting average plummeted over the next couple of years, and as word spread that Parker had a drug problem, the fans of working-class Pittsburgh grew more belligerent. Parker became "the all-time Pittsburgh bad guy," says Adomites. "He always tried on the field, but he was overweight and had a cocaine habit and the fans felt let down. He could've been such a great ballplayer. This town was going down the tubes economically and Parker was blowing all this money on cocaine and hitting .240 and he was snotty about it as hell. And this town hated him forever because of it."

Some field of dreams.

Matters of race continued to emerge. In 1987, Ueberroth announced that the season would be dedicated to the memory and achievements of the late Jackie Robinson, who had debuted with the Dodgers forty years earlier. On Opening Day, Dodger general manager Al Campanis, a teammate of Robinson in the minor leagues, appeared on ABC-TV's *Nightline*. Ted Koppel lobbed him a question about the paucity of black managers in baseball and Campanis responded with his infamous bombshell remark that blacks "may not have some of the necessities to be, let's say, a field manager or general manager." A stunned Koppel tried to let Campanis extricate himself, but Campanis—a man *truly* lacking in certain necessities—jabbered on about the peculiarities of black people, including their inability to swim well, he said, because they lacked buoyancy. The Dodgers fired Campanis. But his ignorance was a fitting reminder of the grand baseball tradition: 1987, in fact, marked the hundredth anniversary of the setting of the game's first official color line, a fact that went unnoticed by the media.

Ex-Cardinal first baseman Bill White was named National League president in the post-Campanis era, and black and Latino former players like Cito Gaston, Felipe Alou, and Don Baylor became managers. But it all seemed to come too late. There was a belief among black ballplayers that they were routinely held to double standards. A black player with drug problems was seen as confirming stereotypes about his race; a white player with a similar problem was viewed as an isolated case. A black player who was injured was assumed to be jaking it; an injured white player was not. Houston pitcher J. R. Richard began the 1980 season with ten quick wins and a 1.89 ERA, but when he complained of pain in his arm, teammates and the media were incredulous. "Who Shot J.R.'s Arm?" quipped one headline. Richard pressed on, not wanting to be called a malingerer, and collapsed from a stroke while warming up in July. The career of one of the greatest modern pitchers—a six-foot-eight-inch intimidator—was suddenly finished. The symbolism of such an incident wasn't lost on young black athletes, who were now streaming away from baseball in ever greater numbers, opting to play professional basketball and football instead. Baseball front offices were largely bereft of blacks. Black faces were almost entirely absent from the stands: one newspaper report said the crowd at Boston's Fenway Park resembled one at "a rugby match in Pretoria." When Cincinnati Reds owner Marge Schott was suspended from baseball in 1993 for making racist comments about black employees and players, these trends seemed to be drawing to a logical conclusion. Schott had reportedly described star outfielder Eric Davis as a "million-dollar nigger," but said such remarks were not meant hatefully. She kept Nazi paraphernalia in her home, but didn't understand why anyone should be offended by that. In fact, Schott said, she was the victim of a witchhunt. She insisted that the very

*Cincinnati Reds
owner Marge
Schott brought
racism out of the
front office closet.*

notion of racism, on her part or anyone else's, was a fiction invented by the media.

Baseball had tried to portray itself for years as a beacon of racial enlightenment. But now the truth was out: the systemic racism of American society remained woven into the fabric of the game.

Today we are constantly told that baseball has become less violent and more humane. But try telling that to Houston shortstop Dickie Thon, coming into his own as a star in 1984 when he was hit in the left temple by a Mike Torrez fastball that April. "It was like a dead sound," Thon recalled in the midst of his years-long comeback. "Like a thud."

Try telling it to Ron Cey, Terry Steinbach, or Andre Dawson, who, in an earlier era, before the advent of batting helmets, might have been killed by the beanballs that left them slumped in the dirt beside home plate.

Mandatory helmets have made batters cockier. There is no longer an institutional memory of Ray Chapman, killed by a pitch in 1920, so today's hitters don't see death lurking behind every pitch. They dig in and act like the inside of the plate is a sacred territory that belongs to them—not to the pitchers who assumed ownership for decades. In recent years, hitting coaches like Charlie Lau and Walt Wreniak have taught batters to crowd the plate and slap pitches, including outside breaking balls, to all fields. Many of the best power hitters, including Darryl Strawberry and Eric Davis, go for full arm extension when they hit, and so they edge close to the plate to protect the outside corner. As these practices grow more common, the confrontation on the inside corner escalates. Retired players, like broadcaster Ron Fairly, fear there's a disaster waiting to happen as batters dig in and hang over the plate. To forestall this, umpires are ejecting pitchers who throw inside—taking away the most basic technique of pitching strategy. But many pitchers will not be restrained from blowing the hitters off the plate, and the batters keep retaliating by charging the mound. Former Baltimore Oriole pitching coach Ed Farmer, now a radio broadcaster for the Chicago White Sox, has suggested that every pitcher should be taught kung fu for protection, so he can break the jaw of every batter who charges. Farmer insisted he was serious.

373

The country club where baseball is played today is like a fashionable neighborhood going to seed. Everybody's fighting and the fans are distressed—heartbroken if they live in Chicago, Cleveland, or Boston. Imagine the pain of being a fan in those towns. The Cubs haven't won a World Series since 1908, the Indians since 1948. The Red Sox last won in 1918. The year after that, the team sold Babe Ruth to the Yankees. Four times since, the Red Sox have been in the World Series. Four times, they have folded in the seventh game, sometimes in improbable fashion. Boston sportswriter Dan Shaughnessy calls this effect "the curse of the Bambino." It was never more evident than in October 1986, when the Red Sox, with two strikes, two outs, and a two-run lead against the New York Mets in the tenth inning of game six of the World Series, could not secure the last strike to win the championship. The Mets toughed out three hits to score a run. Boston reliever Bob Stanley, a perennial loser who shouldn't have been on the mound, threw two quick strikes to Mookie Wilson. Then he threw a wild pitch, and the score was tied. Mookie fouled off a few pitches, then chopped a grounder to first base. It looked like the rally was over—until the ball dribbled between the legs of Bill Buckner, Boston's hobbled first baseman, and the Mets scored the winning run. The next day, the Mets won game seven and the Series.

The city of Boston let out one long, collective howl, but there were those who had very nearly anticipated the outcome. One was Yale University president A. Bartlett Giamatti, a lifelong New Englander and Red Sox fan, who had stated the following about the Sox and their fans during the fall pennant race: "There's an almost Calvinistic sense of guilt at success, that we must reenact the Garden of Eden again and again. There's a sense that things will turn out poorly no matter how hard we work. Somehow the Sox fulfill the notion that we live in a fallen world. It's as though we assume they're here to provide us with more pain."

Three years later, Giamatti became the commissioner of baseball. He added a touch of class to the game, but was hopelessly out of touch with its soulless reality. Giamatti continued to believe that baseball was an "enduring" and "quintessentially American" institution that embodied all the best things about democracy and our nation. Giamatti didn't see knockdown pitches on the field; he saw cooperation. He saw poetry in motion. He was a good soul, and the depraved behavior of Cincinnati manager Pete Rose drove him to distraction. Giamatti's team of investigators nailed Pete for cavorting with hoodlums and dropping thousands nightly on illegal sports bets, many of them presumably on his own club. "No, no, no!" shouted Rose, the weasel, who feuded with Giamatti through the media. He said the commissioner was biased and a liar, but ultimately accepted a lifetime suspension from the game. This was a triumph for Giamatti, but he couldn't save baseball. In October 1989, one of the century's most destructive earthquakes rocked the World Series between the San Francisco Giants and Oakland A's. In December, Chicago White Sox infielder Carlos Martinez was jailed for allegedly beating a stadium security guard with a bat in Venezuela—and a drunken Billy Martin was killed in a car crash in upstate New York. The following April, Rose pleaded guilty in federal court to two felony counts of failing to report $348,720 in taxable income from card shows and memorabilia sales.

374

1980
to the
Present

Eight days later, Bart Giamatti dropped dead. What sort of justice were the gods exacting here? At the very least, they were even-handed: George Steinbrenner was kicked out of baseball in July for paying $40,000 to a mobster named Howard Spira to dig up dirt on Dave Winfield, the player Steinbrenner hated the most in the 1980s.

Every time you turn on the television set, the baseball news is about everything *but* baseball. The Mets sign Bobby Bonilla to a five-year $29 million deal. The Cubs sign Ryne Sandberg to a four-year $28.4 million deal. The Giants sign Bobby Bonds to a six-year $43.75 million deal. The numbers no longer seem real. At what point do the fans become so weary or jealous or disbelieving that they tune out for good? The golden, nostalgic haze that marketers have tried to wrap around the game has turned bright green. Thirty years ago, children collected baseball cards and memorized every statistic on their backs: Vic Power's home run totals. Dave Nicholson's strikeout totals. Lou Brock's stolen base totals. Today, children memorize the market values of the cards, which fluctuate monthly, like stocks and bonds, depending on how well the players have performed lately or how much publicity they've received. Fandom has been commercialized. The children are mercenaries. And why not? So are the owners and players.

Several years ago, a friend returned to the newspaper office where we worked after attending an American League playoff game at the Oakland Coliseum between the A's and the Boston Red Sox. He was from Boston, the loyalest of Red Sox fans, and thought there was no greater person in the world than Dewey Evans. He had also become an A's fan since moving to Northern California, so the playoff series was a delicious source of pleasure and conflicting allegiances for him. But my friend Dave returned to work feeling depressed over something he had seen outside the ballpark. He had watched Reggie Jackson, broadcasting the game for ABC-TV, shove his way through a crowd of children and teenagers who asked for his autograph. He couldn't believe the way Jackson had spoken to the children: "Fuck you . . . fuck you," Reggie had said, pushing one kid after another out of his way. "Fuck you. Can't sign without a pen. . . . Fuck you. . . . Can't sign a ball with a pen. . . . Fuck you." Several hours later, it was all Dave could talk about. He wasn't a sanctimonious person. He knew how to drink. He had spent years as an investigative reporter, and understood that people in public positions aren't always what they seem to be. But he couldn't believe the magnitude of Jackson's rudeness. He had heard stories about this side of baseball, but had never come face to face with it before.

With role models like Jackson, Dykstra, Mitchell, and the rest, it's no wonder that Little Leaguers, amateur ballplayers, their coaches, and the people who watch them are operating on short fuses. In the last year, a teenage umpire in East St. Louis was shot by a coach who didn't agree with a call. A coach in Whiteville, North Carolina, pulled a knife on the opposing team's coach and slashed his throat in front of a bunch of nine-year-olds. A seventeen-year-old high school student attending a game in the Oakland suburbs was accidentally clubbed to death with a bat when the opposing team's catcher started swinging at hecklers in the crowd. One of the police officers who investigated the case had a ready explanation for the violence: "They see sports heroes beat up on each other at will," said Lieutenant Ted Nelson of the Alameda County Sheriff's Department. "If a kid's a good athlete, never mind that he's a punk. The Jose Cansecos of the world, no one ever disciplined them because they could hit a baseball."

The game for poets?

I'd settle for a few "classy people," as my grandfather might have put it.

Where are they?

Bo Jackson injures his knee and the owners of the Kansas City Royals release him, seemingly, within minutes. Hey, thanks for four years out of your life, Bo. Thanks for bringing this team more publicity than it's ever had in its history. Now . . . fuck off.

Jack Morris signs with the Minnesota Twins in 1991. He grew up in St. Paul, and returning home to play is the thrill of his life, he says. Morris leads the team to the World Series championship. He is ecstatic. Then what? Two months later, he abandons the Twins and signs a $10.85 million two-year contract with Minnesota's archrivals, the Toronto Blue Jays. A year earlier, Morris beat the Jays twice in the American League playoffs.

Where's the loyalty?

Where's the good news?

Darryl Strawberry says he's born again. But it hasn't done the Los Angeles Dodgers any good. The last time I looked, Darryl was still sitting on the bench with a sore back. He's been sitting there for more than a year.

Baseball is waiting for its messiah.

The Militant Midget: Earl Weaver

Earl Weaver badgered and feuded with more umpires than any manager of his time. He wasn't Durocher. But his remonstrations—kicking dirt, jabbing fingers, screeching jowl to jowl with the umps—made him famous, won him innumerable enemies in blue, and resulted in his ejection from dozens of games during the seventeen years that he managed the Orioles. His antics were calculated to have a psychological effect—to fire up the Orioles, who won six division titles, three American League pennants, and one World Championship during Weaver's tenure from 1969 to 1986.

Associated Press

Earl Weaver's so mad, his cap pops off his head.

The five-foot-seven-inch Weaver's most famous feud was with umpire Ron Luciano, who once told a banquet audience, "I hate Earl Weaver with a passion. . . . He's about three foot one, I tell him to get his nose off my kneecap, and I call him Mickey Rooney." In 1980, during an Oriole-Tiger game, Weaver went at it with another old rival, umpire Bill Haller. When Haller called a balk on Baltimore pitcher Mike Flanagan, Oriole first baseman Eddie Murray objected, as did Weaver, who joined the fray spewing obscenities. What Weaver didn't know was that Haller had been wired for sound by a Washington, D.C., station, WDVM-TV. The following transcription of their conversation was published in *Sports Illustrated* in October 1980:

EDDIE MURRAY: "That is not a balk."

HALLER: "Behind the rubber."

MURRAY: "He did not go behind the rubber."

HALLER: "For me he did."

WEAVER (ARRIVING ON THE SCENE): "Aaah, bleep."

HALLER: "Bleep yourself."

WEAVER: "You're here and this crew is here just to bleep us."

HALLER (WITH A JERK OF THE THUMB, INDICATING WEAVER'S EJECTION): "Boom!"

WEAVER: "You couldn't wait to get me out."

HALLER (POINTING A FINGER AT WEAVER): "Oh, Earl, you run yourself."

WEAVER (SWATTING AWAY HALLER'S HAND): "Get your finger off me."

HALLER: "You hit me?"

WEAVER: "Yeah, because you put your finger on me. . . . You do it again and I'll knock you right on your nose."

HALLER: "I didn't touch you. You're lying."

WEAVER: "You ain't no good."

HALLER: "Nah, you aren't either."

WEAVER: "What're you doing here now?"

HALLER: "Well, why don't you call the league office and ask them?"

WEAVER: "Don't you think I won't."

Boom! It was the seventy-eighth ejection of Weaver's blustery career.

Bird Killer: Dave Winfield

It's August 4, 1983, a night game in Toronto between the Yankees and Blue Jays. New York center fielder Dave Winfield is warming up before the Jays come to bat in the bottom of the third inning. He's playing catch with left fielder Don Baylor, tossing the ball back and forth, nice and easy, part of the ritual of the game. But there's a large, elderly sea gull sitting inside the left field foul line—Exhibition Stadium is only a stone's throw from Lake Ontario—and now it's time for play to resume. So Winfield throws the ball to the ball boy along the foul line. He bounces it in front of the bird to scare it away. Only the bird doesn't move. "The ball takes a short hop off the artificial turf and *wop!*—it flattens the bird," Winfield says. "Right away I know he's a goner. I feel awful. He was a big, old seagull and now he's a big white pile."

Dave Winfield is in big trouble. In New York, the fans would be in fits, convulsed with laughter. "Awright, Dave! Kill another one!" But here there is silence. The ball boy runs out, lifts the corpse, and ceremoniously carries it off the field. The crowd starts to boo Winfield, the volume increases, the fans rise to their feet, and now they're throwing garbage at the killer. The hostilities continue for the next six innings.

In the dugout after the game, which Winfield wins with a home run, manager Billy Martin walks over to his star and announces, "The police are waiting for you in the clubhouse." It's true. Winfield is arrested for cruelty to animals. He's booked at the station house, where the dead bird has been brought as evidence; the stiff is lying on a table, its legs sticking upward. The photographers have the police station staked out, and the flash bulbs are popping as Winfield exits. Charges are dropped once he convinces the cops that the bird's death was an accident. But he's booed at the park the next day, and when the Yankees move on to Detroit, there's a stadium full of fans who flap their arms whenever Winfield comes to the plate. The sea gull affair has taken on a life of its own. Yankee third baseman Graig Nettles says Winfield "should have been given a medal for killing the damn thing." But the best line comes from Martin: "First time he hit the cutoff man all year."

381

Bird Killer: Dave Winfield

Nasty Boy: Rob Dibble

Rob Dibble was the low man on the totem pole in the Nashville bullpen in 1987, the year before he was promoted to the Cincinnati Reds. Toward the end of the season, Nashville was getting creamed at home one night in a long, rain-delayed game when the manager called on Dibble. "I guess he figured, 'Why not humiliate Dibble once more before the year is over?' " he reminisced a few years later. "I told one of the pitchers in the bullpen, 'Get all the balls out, because we're going to run out of balls real quick.' I threw the first four balls into our dugout and cleared it out. Then I threw the fifth pitch off the press box, which is about a three-hundred-foot throw. It hit the top left-hand corner of the box, and everybody looked out and had to wonder about my mentality at that point."

People have been wondering ever since.

As baseball's most infamous loose cannon, Dibble understands the unsettling effect he has on batters. "Anybody in his right mind is going to be a little leery to go in against somebody who appears to be crazy and throws hard. . . . I wouldn't want to hit off me, because I wouldn't know what to expect."

He came into his own with Cincinnati in 1988, throwing a consistent 95-to-100-mph fastball, and striking out fifty-nine batters in the same number of innings. His intimidation and mastery of National League hitters took hold the next season when he won ten games coming out of the bullpen, striking out 141 batters in ninety-nine innings. This was the year that Dibble began to rack up fines and suspensions for his conduct on the mound. In April 1989, after giving up four straight hits to the Dodgers, he decided to end the uprising by throwing a fastball behind L.A. second baseman Willie Randolph. In May, after giving up a run-scoring hit to the Cardinals' Terry Pendleton, Dibble picked up Pendleton's bat and flung it high into the batting screen behind home plate. In July, he threw a pitch that hit the Mets' Tim Teufel between the shoulder blades. Teufel charged the

*Opposite:
The Nasty One
has just
delivered
a 100 mph
fastball.*

mound. "I looked up," Teufel recalled, "and there he was, spittin' and grinnin'."

In 1990, Dibble was part of the Reds' "Nasty Boys" relief corps, which also included Norm Charlton, perhaps the only modern pitcher who admits to intentionally throwing at hitters, and Randy Myers, who reputedly carried a knife in his hip pocket while pitching for the Mets in the late '80s. Dibble was called a "walking time bomb set to explode at any time" by umpire Gary Darling, but he steered clear of violent controversy this season. He, Charlton, and Myers were virtual guarantors of a Cincinnati victory if they entered a ball game with a lead. They put on "an almost maniacally inspired run of macho intimidation," one columnist said, "that carried Cincinnati right through the World Series," in which the Reds flattened the Oakland A's in four straight.

But 1991 was a different story: Dibble was out to lunch. On April 11, after giving up a run-scoring single to Houston pitcher Curt Schilling, he threw a pitch behind the Astros' Eric Yelding, who sprinted toward Dibble and threw his batting helmet at the pitcher. After the game, Dibble defended himself: "I've pitched like that my entire career. . . . I didn't hit him. He hit me. . . . If I hit a guy in the head and he dies, is that a good Christian thing to do?"

Dibble did the good Christian thing one week later, no doubt, when he hurled a ball four hundred feet into the stands, where it struck first grade teacher Meg Porter on the elbow. This incident was widely reported as the press made a sport of questioning Dibble's sanity. He feuded openly with National League president Bill White and was suspended in July. His first game back, Dibble fielded a bunt by Expo batter Doug Dascenzo and—unless videotape lies—took dead aim at Dascenzo as he raced to first base. Then Dibble threw a perfect strike at the runner's legs. Suspended once more, denounced by players around the league, and under pressure from all the bad publicity, Dibble agreed to see a therapist. "It has become apparent to me," he told reporters, "that I need professional counsel dealing with some of my emotions."

Bo Belinsky, the playboy pitcher who toiled for the Phillies in the mid-'60s, once said that Philadelphia fans would boo the Easter parade. They didn't hesitate to attack their own Joe Cowley, a Phillie pitcher who self-destructed before their eyes in 1987 and never recovered his confidence under the pressure of their loud, hooting vituperation. The bullpen gate would open, out would come Cowley, and the stands would gleefully explode with "COW-LEE! COW-LEE!" as he began his death march toward the mound. The Phillies were a lousy team anyway, and the fans became Cowley's happy executioners, enjoining him to walk the opposition around the bases.

For two years, 1984–85, Cowley had been a respectable starting pitcher for the New York Yankees, winning twenty-one games and losing eight. In 1986, he pitched a no-hitter and won eleven games for the Chicago White Sox, more than anyone else on the staff. But Cowley was just barely holding it together. In one three-inning stretch for New York, he walked four, and was pounced upon for seven earned runs; Billy Martin lost confidence in him that day. Even Cowley's no-hitter for Chicago was a cliff-hanger: he walked seven. A fragile specimen from the start, Cowley was traded to Philadelphia in 1987. Poor Cowley. Nothing works in Philadelphia. The streets are filled with windblown garbage. Crater-sized potholes go unfixed for years. People ride the city buses, hoping for traffic accidents—and profitable lawsuits against the transportation authority. It's a city that revels in laying itself to waste. It was no place for Cowley. In his first start, he couldn't find home plate and lasted less than an inning. The war cry began: "COW-LEE! COW-LEE!" The same thing happened in starts two, three, and four. The fans loved it: they were thirsty for this comic new pitcher. Cowley was demoted to the bullpen, and when he was brought in to relieve starter Kevin Gross in a May game against Cincinnati, he was, by his own admission, "petrified. As soon as that gate swung open in right field and the fans saw who it was, you wouldn't believe the boos I heard. So I ran to the mound to kind of hurry up the boos a little bit, to get it over with."

He walked two, gave up a couple of hits, and was demoted to the International League's Maine Guides. These were his stats with the Phillies: a 15.43 ERA, and a record of twenty-one hits and seventeen walks allowed in eleven and two-thirds innings.

In Maine, it got worse.

"I set the record for most consecutive walks," he recalled, in an interview with the *New York Times*. "I walked eleven in two and a third innings. Nobody walks eleven in two and a third innings unless they have a severe problem. I'm not out there trying to embarrass myself. Two and a third innings . . . walked eleven. Figure that one out. I couldn't. I'm trying to adjust every pitch. But hell, when you're around your seventh or eighth walk, you start to cringe a little out of embarrassment."

These were his stats in Maine: seventy-six walks allowed in sixty-three innings during which he gave up sixty-three hits. He won three, lost nine, and posted a 7.86 ERA. Cowley couldn't get the jeers of the Philly fans out of his head. "When I threw in the bullpen, I was fa-a-a-ntastic, couldn't beat it. Then I'd go into a game, I'd walk somebody, and I'd say to myself, 'Here we go again.'"

The Phillies sent him to a therapist. No help. Hypnosis? No help. Cowley visited Art Fowler, his old Yankee pitching coach, in Tennessee. That didn't help, either.

Cowley never came back. Yo, Philadelphia: thanks for the memories.

Joyless George

George Steinbrenner only grew more vicious in the 1980s, if that's possible, firing more managers than ever, trading Reggie Jackson, but abusing Dave Winfield, who, when asked how he prepared for each new season, said, "I get my lawyers ready, my accountant ready, and my agent ready because that's what I need to play Yankee baseball." Joyless George reamed out parking lot attendants and players' wives and shuttled Yankees up and down between the Bronx and Columbus so frequently that they had no time to prove themselves, and the team had no chance to find a groove. At long last, George managed to ruin the Yankee championship chemistry, alienating even the company men in the dugout. That didn't stop him

*George and Billy,
the best of friends.*

from visiting the Yankee locker room to insult his players while admonishing them to "have fun," to dub Winfield "Mr. May," to say the team's hitting "sucks," to announce "I'm the leader, I'm the admiral" of the club, and to apologize to the people of New York City for substandard performances by his Yankee millionaire indentured servants. "George wants to 'own' his players, wants them up on their flippers barking for fish like trained seals," said Winfield.

Finally, George went off the deep end, like Nixon. Forget the morality of it all. He hired someone to do his dirty work—to dig up information on Winfield's alleged gambling activities. Winfield was no angel, but this was a smear campaign. And the man George hired was a gambler with mob connections. George couldn't cover it up. In 1990 our prayers were answered when Steinbrenner was kicked out of baseball.

But remember: like Dracula, George always returns.

Some highlights:

1980

Steinbrenner fires manager Dick Howser, who won 103 games and the division championship, but not the pennant. Not good enough, Dick.

1981

Steinbrenner hires Gene "Stick" Michael as Yankee manager and fields an expensive team with Dave Winfield, the so-called $23 Million Man, as its new centerpiece. Reggie Jackson is slumping, and Steinbrenner rags on him in the press, then humiliates Reggie by sending him to the doctor for eye tests.

With twenty-eight games left in the season, Steinbrenner fires Michael and brings back Bob Lemon, fired two years earlier, as manager. Lemon leads the team to the pennant. During the World Series against the Dodgers, Steinbrenner breaks his hand in a hotel elevator in a fight with a couple of Los Angeles fans, then lies about it to reporters. The Yankees lose the Series, with Winfield's .045 batting average standing out conspicuously, and Steinbrenner offers a public apology to the City of New York. George guarantees it won't happen again.

1982

George boasts this year's team is the best he has ever put together. It includes expensive imports like Dave Collins and Ken Griffey, speedsters who will turn the Yankees into a swift, running team. But the season starts slowly, and after fourteen games, Steinbrenner fires Lemon and rehires Michael as manager. In the middle of the season, he fires Michael and hires Clyde King. The Yankees keep losing, George desperately turns the roster over a couple times, and almost no one steals a base.

Reggie Jackson is now playing for the California Angels. When he visits Yankee Stadium and lofts a tremendous home run, a stadium full of Yankee fans turns on Steinbrenner in his box seat and chants, "STEINBRENNER SUCKS! STEINBRENNER SUCKS!"

389

Joyless George

1983

Steinbrenner brings back Billy Martin, who last managed the club in 1979. This is a mistake, for Steinbrenner spends most of the season baby-sitting Martin or making excuses for his antics—many of which, of course, are induced by Steinbrenner. But it's not a good year for Billy, who makes a raucous scene in the locker room in front of the local press corps, calling *New York Post* reporter Henry Hecht a "little prick" for writing a story about a closed-door team meeting in which Steinbrenner picked on various Yankees. "If that little bastard comes in here," Martin says of Hecht, "I'll put him in the fuckin' whirlpool."

This is also the year that Martin calls *New York Times* reporter Deborah Henschel a hooker, gets into a fight in an Anaheim bar, undergoes surgery for rectal hemorrhoids, and is generally sick and drunk as George scolds and the team goes nowhere.

1984

Steinbrenner fires Martin and hires Yogi Berra to manage the Yanks. They finish in third place, seventeen games behind Detroit.

1985

Steinbrenner fields another expensive squad, this time with Rickey Henderson on board, and announces that he expects a fast start. After sixteen games, he fires Berra and rehires Martin as manager. In

August, with the Yankees finally moving into high gear, he tells reporters that his second-place team is being "outplayed, outhustled, outmanaged, and out-towned." The hitting stinks: Winfield ("Mr. May") is no Jackson ("Mr. October"), whom George wouldn't mind having back. Its momentum broken, the club slumps and finishes in third place again, fifteen games behind Toronto.

But before the season ends, George endures one more of Martin's fights. This time Billy goes at it with Yankee pitcher Ed Whitson, a $4.5 million mediocrity, who pounds the manager's head into the concrete outside the Key Cross Hotel in Baltimore.

1986–87
Steinbrenner sticks with one manager for two whole seasons: Lou Piniella. But the Yanks don't win.

1988
Steinbrenner rehires Billy Martin, who is nearly killed in May in a fight at a Texas strip joint called Lace.

On June 23, Steinbrenner fires Martin and rehires Piniella. The Yankees finish in fifth place.

1989:
Steinbrenner hires Dallas Green as manager. The Yanks finish fifth again.

On Christmas Day, Billy Martin drinks all day and is killed in a car crash in upstate New York.

1990:
Steinbrenner hires someone named Stump Merrill to manage the Yankees, but isn't around to see the team finish in last place, twenty-one games behind the Red Sox. That's because . . .

. . . on July 30, after seventeen inglorious years at the helm of the Yankees, George Steinbrenner is booted out of baseball by baseball commissioner Fay Vincent. As word circulates through the crowd at Yankee Stadium, 26,000 people stand and chant, "NO MORE GEORGE! NO MORE GEORGE!"

The decision cites Steinbrenner's $40,000 payment to small-time mobster Howard Spira for delivering the good stuff on Winfield. George and Dave have been feuding for a decade. They have sued and countersued one another over the owner's contractual obligations to help support Winfield's nonprofit foundation for disadvantaged youngsters. There are rumors that the foundation's bookkeeping is . . . well, creative, and that some of Winfield's associates are not good citizens. But Steinbrenner's association with Spira clearly violates the game's ethical code, and Vincent bids him adieu: George gives up his majority ownership of the club and agrees to step aside permanently from its daily operations.

Bye-bye.

Howard Spira offered the goods on Dave Winfield to Yankee owner George Steinbrenner.

1993

Not so fast! George is back.

Vincent has been fired by the major league owners, who apparently think Steinbrenner deserves a reprieve.

Someone named Buck Showalter is now managing the ship. George promises not to interfere, and everyone guffaws. The Yanks haven't won a pennant since 1981, a World Series since 1978.

But, lo and behold, the Yankees make a run for the pennant in '93.

Bud: hold on tight. Your days may still be numbered.

George Steinbrenner is not a patient man.

Pete Rose: Modern-Day Legend

By the mid-1980s, Pete Rose was an empty man, ruled by his gambling obsession, which crowded everything else out of his life, including baseball. He hung out with the gold-chain crowd at Gold's Gym in Cincinnati, but had no real friends. He was surrounded by creeps—unemployed body builders and hustlers—who had free run of his office at Riverfront Stadium. The very week that Rose closed in on Ty Cobb's all-time record for hits in 1985, he was visited in his stadium office by a drug dealer who loaned him $17,000. Burdened by gambling debts, Rose sold the bat and ball involved in his 4,192nd hit for $129,000. He gave one of his World Series rings to a bookie to whom he owed money and was gradually stripped of sentimental possessions and awards from his long career. Rose signed thousands of autographs at baseball card shows, then stuffed his cash payments into brown lunch bags. There were reports of people showing up to collect gambling debts from Rose on the field in Florida during spring training, and at the clubhouse in Cincinnati during the regular season. Charlie Hustle was out of control.

But like anyone with an addiction, he didn't have a lot of time to ponder his spiritual decay. Rose was "attracted by criminality. Just the whiff of it made his heart beat faster," wrote Michael Y. Sokolove in *Hustle: The Myth, Life, and Lies of Pete Rose,* which gives the most complete, cogent account of Rose's downward spiral to date. Rose sold cars and jewelry to his hustler friends, who used him to launder drug money. When his friends were "flipped" by investigators as Rose headed for a crash, they recalled how Pete had expressed interest in pulling off drug deals himself. Rose loved being the bad boy. He reportedly asked a couple of thieves—friends of friends—to steal a Mercedes for him. He had bookies all over the United States and in Canada, some with mob connections. As his debts mounted, he continued to throw away $10,000 in a night, scattering bets on every imaginable sporting event, going to the track and writing checks like mad, getting high on "the action," even though he understood nothing about the science of handicapping horses. Sokolove writes that between 1984 and 1987, Rose lost as much as $1 million on wagers.

By the late 1980s, manager Rose was fat and distracted, delegating

393

Pete Rose:
Modern-Day
Legend

The end
is near.
Pete Rose
is worn out
by news coverage
of his alleged
gambling.

more and more baseball decisions to his coaches as the authorities closed in on him. In February 1989, the baseball commissioner's office retained John Dowd, a former U.S. organized crime prosecutor, to muster the case against Rose. In March, a damning story about Rose's obsessive gambling appeared in *Sports Illustrated*. Rose denied that he bet on sports with bookies, but a dozen sources told *SI* that he did. Rose vehemently denied that he bet on baseball: "I never bet baseball. I swear I never bet baseball." But nine sources told Dowd's team of lawyers and detectives that he did just that—and some said he bet as much as $2,000 a night on his own club. Rose said the whole thing was a frame-up, that his case had been prejudged by commissioner A. Bartlett Giamatti. The commissioner, Rose's nemesis, signed a letter to a federal judge in the spring that described testimony against Rose by a man named Ron Peters as "truthful." Peters, a former associate of Rose's, was about to be sentenced on drug charges. Charging that the letter showed bias against Rose, his lawyers filed a lawsuit against Giamatti, major league baseball, and the Cincinnati Reds. Rose told Dowd that he was making a big mistake in listening to the testimony of convicted felons: "Those guys could have a quintet the last three months. Because they're all singing. They're all singing a lot. They have to sing or they'll be in Sing Sing."

But Dowd's lawyers and detectives were building a convincing case against Rose. They assembled betting sheets, betting records, and day-by-day telephone records of calls made by Rose from his home, his car, and hotels and clubhouses around the country, a never-ending stream of phone calls, many to strange characters, many made in the heart of the baseball season when there wasn't much to bet on but the ol' ball game. As the evidence mounted, the baseball press corp held a death watch, traveling from city to city with the Reds, waiting for Rose to fold.

On August 23, 1989, he accepted a lifetime suspension from the game with the right to apply for reinstatement after one year. The deal was an obvious compromise: Rose avoided admitting to specific charges, but the authority of the commissioner was established, and both sides avoided a complicated, protracted court fight.

In November, Rose conceded publicly that he was a compulsive gambler. In April 1990, he pleaded guilty to a pair of felony counts for failing to report $348,720 earned at baseball card shows and memorabilia auctions between 1984 and 1987. Before going away to prison for five months, he made the talk-show rounds. He appeared on *Donahue* with his wife, bounding onto the stage to much applause, smiling, already trying to regroom his image. He had made a mistake . . . he was sorry for letting people down . . . for letting baseball down. But like so many people with addictions, he said, he was finally out of denial and getting help. Maybe it was true. Or maybe Rose was only trying to rehabilitate himself before the public so that he—"a modern-day legend," his lawyers called him in the lawsuit against Giamatti—might someday be reinstated to the game and admitted into the Hall of Fame. Admittance to the Hall was Rose's most cherished goal and his just dessert after twenty-four seasons in which he batted .303, won three batting titles, collected two hundred hits in a season ten times, and established new standards for enthusiasm and hard play. But Cooperstown was far away now, a long shot. Pete Rose had done too much hustling in his lifetime, both on the field and off.

395

Pete Rose: Modern-Day Legend

Vince Coleman: Baseball's Loving Father

In the early 1960s, the New York Mets charmed the world with their exuberance and astounding lack of skill on the diamond. Today's Mets are also an astoundingly bad ball club, but they charm no one. They are an acid crew, cursing at reporters, shoving coaches, injuring fans. Losing the way the Mets have lost in the mid-1990s, falling deep into the National League cellar under the scrutiny of the world's harshest media, has to be frustrating. But it doesn't excuse the behavior of these amazin'ly unpleasant men.

Outfielder Vince Coleman takes the cake. On July 24, 1993, he tossed an explosive device equal to a quarter-stick of dynamite into a crowd of autograph seekers at Dodgers Stadium. Does anyone have a clue as to what was on this man's mind? Coleman was being driven through the players' parking lot by Dodger Eric Davis—the Mets' Bobby Bonilla was also in Davis's Jeep—when he lit and threw the device. It injured three people, including a two-and-a-half-year-old girl named Amanda Santos who suffered second-degree facial burns and eye lacerations. Coleman and his friends didn't stick around to see the fallout of the explosion: they drove away, laughing.

Davis and Bonilla are said to have cursed at reporters who inquired about the attack. And Coleman? He said not a word for five days, then appeared at a press conference with his wife and children. There Coleman conceded that his behavior had been "inappropriate." He wished that Amanda might only get to know the real Vince Coleman: "a true friend and loving father," he called himself. Did he say he was sorry? Nope.

Coleman's attack on the fans climaxed a joyless summer for the Mets. Two weeks earlier, pitcher Bret Saberhagen threw a pack of firecrackers at a group of reporters whose backs were turned to him in the clubhouse. He didn't own up to his action for a month—not until Coleman, facing possible criminal charges in Los Angeles, came under suspicion for the earlier incident. As a topper, Saberhagen was also

*Vince Coleman,
family man,
fesses up—but
doesn't
apologize*

reprimanded by management and the press for having sprayed liquid
bleach at the backs of reporters in New York. It's a good thing they
didn't turn around while Saberhagen performed his practical joke:
bleach blinds.

Unbelievable? Sure. But are Saberhagen's dangerous actions
anything new? You will remember that Heinie Zimmerman of the
Chicago Cubs threw a bottleful of acid at the face of teammate Jimmy
Sheckard in 1908. We said it at the outset of this book and it bears
repeating: baseball, from its very beginnings, has displayed the entire
panorama of the lower end of the human experience. Alcohol. Drugs.
Wife-beating. Murder. Attempted blinding by acid. And now the
tossing of explosive devices.

A panoply of villainy!

As the 1993 season wound down, one more event stood out:
Chicago White Sox batter Robin Ventura charged the mound against
pitcher Nolan Ryan of the Texas Rangers. Ryan, the moral paragon of

modern baseball, threw an expert headlock on Ventura, immobilizing him, and then punched him six times in the head. Unbelievable? To a lot of people, yes. Anything new? You will remember that New York Giant pitcher Christy Mathewson, the Mr. Clean of an earlier era, punched a boy in the mouth for making an insulting comment while selling lemonade near the Giants' bench.

The big baseball wheel keeps turning.

Once again the public is tired of athletes who behave like criminals. Once again, the columnists tell us that it's time to banish the bums and uphold the good name of the national pastime.

"FOR THE BASEBALL GAME IS SOARING," the *Sporting News* rhapsodized long ago, even as the game was tainted by violence, greed, and corruption.

**"HIGH ABOVE IT ALL, SERENE,
UNAFFECTED BY THE ROARING—
FOR THE GRAND OLD GAME IS CLEAN!"**

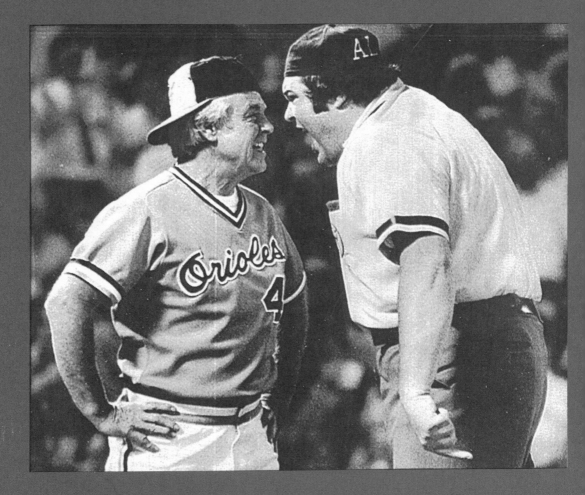

Field of Screams